Changing Patterns in State Legislative Careers

Published in conjunction with the Legislative Studies Section of the American Political Science Association

Changing Patterns in State Legislative Careers

Edited by
Gary F. Moncrief and Joel A. Thompson

Ann Arbor

THE UNIVERSITY OF MICHIGAN PRESS

Copyright © by the University of Michigan 1992
All rights reserved
Published in the United States of America by
The University of Michigan Press
Manufactured in the United States of America

1995   1994   1993   1992   4   3   2   1

Library of Congress Cataloging-in-Publication Data

Changing patterns in state legislative careers / edited by Gary F.
  Moncrief and Joel A. Thompson.
      p.   cm.
    Includes bibliographical references and index.
    ISBN 0-472-10344-X (alk. paper)
    1. Legislative bodies—United States—States.   2. Legislators—
United States—States.   I. Moncrief, Gary F.   II. Thompson, Joel
A.
  JK2488.C48   1992
  328.73—dc20   92-26575
                                                           CIP

A CIP catalogue record for this book is available from the British
Library.

To Heidi and Gloria

Acknowledgments

The project culminating in this volume began in 1988 when we organized a panel at the American Political Science Association on changing career patterns in state legislatures. In getting from that point to the publication of this book, we incurred many debts. Thanks go first to our families for their patience throughout this project. This book is dedicated to the most patient of all, our wives.

We want to express our gratitude to Glenn Parker, the editor of the Legislative Studies Section series, for his energy, optimism, and support. Colin Day, Christina Milton, and Deborah Evans, at the University of Michigan Press, have been accommodating and professional throughout. Robert Schuhmann, now a Ph.D. candidate at Virginia Polytechnic Institute, assisted in the collection of the legislators' background data we discuss in chapter 2.

Two people who deserve special recognition are Kathy Locke at Appalachian State University and Tricia Trofast at Boise State University. As departmental office coordinators, they are paragons of professionalism, always knowing when to console and when to cajole. Tricia handled the final production of the manuscript with her usual efficiency. We marvel at the level of commitment and excellence they bring to their work.

The secret to editing a book is to attract first-rate contributing authors to participate in the project. Working with people represented in this book was always a pleasure. We thank each and every one of them. Finally, we must acknowledge the contribution of Malcolm Jewell, beyond his coauthorship of two of the book's chapters. About a third of the contributing authors to this volume were trained by Mac, and he has worked with almost all the others on one or another project. He has left his mark on all of us and on the discipline he serves. May the Red Sox win the Series for you, Mac.

Contents

x   Contents

Introduction

The state legislature is the phoenix of U.S. government. By the middle of this century, the state legislature was a moribund institution, hampered by state constitutional restrictions, overshadowed by the emergent role of the federal government, and dominated by the executive branch at the state level.

But about a generation ago, state legislatures began their remarkable rebirth. First came the reapportionment revolution of the 1960s. Toward the end of that decade, groups such as the Citizens Conference on State Legislatures and the Eagleton Institute, funded by organizations such as the Carnegie Corporation and the Ford Foundation, worked to create public awareness of the woeful condition of most state legislatures. Fueled by the initiative of these and other groups (such as the National Conference of State Legislative Leaders), state legislatures underwent substantial reform.

Most of these reforms involved structural changes to the legislative institution. These changes were intended to strengthen the legislature as a policy-making body and included such reforms as longer and/or more frequent sessions, increasing the size of professional legislative staff, restructuring committee systems, the introduction of electronic technologies, and the elimination of some of the constitutional limitations on state legislative discretion (such as earmarking of funds).[1] There is little doubt that these and other such changes contributed significantly to the reemergence of state legislatures as important institutions. As Rosenthal writes in 1981, "Years ago state legislatures merited much of the criticism that is aimed at them today. Lately, however, they have proved to be more deserving; now they merit commendations rather than blame" (p. 3).

Career Patterns in Transition

In addition to the structural changes, other reforms were designed to induce capable, qualified persons to serve in the legislative institution. These changes included larger salaries and better benefit packages for legislators, the establishment of personal staff, and upgraded office facilities and resources. The

---

[1] See, for example, Rosenthal, 1972.

goal was to create an institution that would attract and retain qualified legislators. As one of the reformers writes, "Unless capable legislators opt for a legislative career, there will be no saving the institution" (Lockard 1972, 15).

One of the ironies is that twenty years ago a careerist state legislature was viewed by many as a laudable goal; today, however, the term has taken on a pejorative connotation. The majority leader of one state legislature recently commented, "The more professional, the better-paid, the better-staffed and the closer to full-time a legislature is, the more it's suspect."[2] Perhaps the best indication of the public reaction to the development of professional, careerist state legislatures is the recent movement to limit terms of office for state legislators (and other public officials). We think much of this movement is inappropriate in targeting state legislators (note: see the Appendix for a discussion of the term limit phenomenon). Nonetheless, the movement indicates a growing dissatisfaction with the legislative institution and the people who serve in it. While Rosenthal was commending state legislatures in 1981, by the end of the decade he was moved to write that "[T]here are indications that the legislature, as an institution, may be in jeopardy" (1989, 69). He attributes this problem largely to the growing careerism in state legislatures, "Contemporary trends—professionalization of careers, preoccupation with elections, and fragmentation—are taking a toll. Individualism is in the ascendancy" (1989, 97).

There appears to be, in fact, a tension between the institution and the individual in state legislatures. While there is a need for the institution to adapt to societal change, to strengthen itself vis-à-vis the other branches of government—to modernize and professionalize—such changes also encourage the individual legislator to professionalize, to begin to think in terms of a commitment to the institution as a career. This tension, and the implications for legislative reform and adaptation, are discussed in detail in the concluding chapter to this volume.

But before we get to that discussion, we must first come to understand how career patterns have changed. That, indeed, is the primary focus of this volume. Much has been written about the *institution* of the state legislature, and how it has changed over the years. Much less has been written about the *individuals* who serve in the state legislature and how they have changed over the years. Who are the state legislators of today? How are they different than those who served a generation ago? How have the avenues of entry and exit to the legislative institution changed for these individuals? How have the pat-

---

[2] Quoted in David Broder, "Legislatures Under Siege," reprinted in *State Legislatures*, July 1991, 21.

terns of influence within the institution changed? These are the questions we and the contributing authors seek to answer in this volume.

In addressing these issues, it is important to keep in mind the rich diversity in American state legislatures. It is true that the legislative institution has changed greatly in the last twenty-five years. It is also true, as various chapters of this volume demonstrate, that the state legislator has changed and that the job of state legislator has changed. But talk of career-oriented, full-time, highly professional state legislatures is only appropriate in perhaps 20 percent of the states today. At this point, most state legislatures are still part-time institutions, albeit institutions experiencing the stress of change.

The book is divided into three sections. Each section is preceded by an introduction, in which we introduce the general subject matter and specific chapter topics of the section. In the first section, we focus on the institutional reforms and the changes in the legislative personnel. The second section is devoted to issues involving elections, campaigns, and retirement. In the third section, we examine two of the most important components to the internal operation of the legislature: the committee system and the leadership structure. We conclude the section—and the book—with a framework for thinking about institutional change and individual careers.

PART 1

Changing Patterns: The Legislators

The title of this book implies that our subject matter is the individual state legislator, not the institution of the state legislature. While that is true, legislative careers are built in the institution. State legislative careers have changed precisely because the institution of the state legislature has changed. The concept of *legislative professionalism* is often used to suggest the sort of institutional changes that affect the *careerist orientation of the legislators themselves.*

In chapter 1, William Pound explores the institutional changes that have led to substantial change in the state legislative career. Pound identifies the period around the reapportionment revolution of 1962–64 as the beginning of a reform era in state legislative institutions. He notes such changes as longer legislative sessions, higher legislative salaries, more staffing, and better office facilities. All of these changes are directly related to the job quality of being a state legislator. As Pound notes, "The job of the state legislator has changed substantially as a consequence of these reforms. Virtually all state legislatures have experienced some measure of professionalization in the last quarter-century."

Pound goes on to note that these reforms created a pressure toward the creation of full-time state legislatures. He estimates that at least nine states now have full-time legislatures, based on such indicators as salary, time in session, and occupational definition of the state legislators. This last criterion is a particularly telling one. Careerism has clearly arrived when the legislators begin thinking of themselves as full-time legislators. When the position becomes a vocation rather than an avocation, then all pretense to the ideal of the "citizen legislator" is voided. As noted by Pound, over 10 percent of all state legislators now describe their primary occupation as "legislator" (only 1 percent did so a decade ago).

What is truly important about the idea of a "careerist orientation" is the understanding that legislative behavior is affected. When individuals begin to think of their legislative service as a career, goals begin to change, and actions in pursuit of those goals also begin to change. For example, legislators become more concerned about reelection. Since casework is an effective reelection tool, legislators become more interested in casework as an activity. As

5

Pound points out, the trend toward professionalization of legislators is "stimulated by the growing legislator concern with constituency service, the trend toward district offices for members, and continual fund-raising for campaign purposes."

Careerism also may affect the relationship between the rank-and-file legislator and the leadership. Again, as Pound says, "Another trend in legislatures today is the declining authority of legislative leadership."

Chapters 2, 3, and 4 examine some specifics about the legislators themselves. In chapter 2, Joel A. Thompson and Gary F. Moncrief provide a broad overview of several background characteristics, with an eye toward differences between native and nonnative legislators. The old image of "local boy makes good" may no longer be the case in state legislatures, and the authors explore this issue. They show great variation between the states in terms of the percentage of native-born state legislators and that this variation is reflected regionally. Western states (where immigration has been particularly high) tend to have low proportions of native-born legislators (17 percent in Nevada and 31 percent in Arizona). Surprisingly, the largest proportion of native legislators is found in the midwestern states (87 percent in Nebraska and 86 percent in Wisconsin). It is interesting to note that nonnatives are more likely to be members of the minority party in the state and that women represent a larger percentage of the minority party makeup. The authors suggest that recruitment patterns may differ between majority and minority parties. This could have important future implications for those states presently experiencing in-migration.

Chapter 3, by Charles S. Bullock III, examines the increase in black and Hispanic legislators and assesses the potential for continued progress in the 1990s. Since 1965, the number of blacks serving in state legislatures has quadrupled (from about ninety to four hundred). A major portion of this gain has occurred in the southern states. Bullock identifies three events as instrumental to black gains in state legislatures—especially southern state legislatures. The three events are the 1965 Voting Rights Act, the active enforcement (beginning in 1969) of the preclearance provisions of that act, and the 1982 changes in Section 2 of the Voting Rights Act. These events are all important because they bear directly on redistricting, and as Bullock points out, "the tie between redistricting and increases in black representatives is much stronger in the South than in the rest of the nation."

Bullock analyzes "cut points," the concentration of a racial or ethnic group necessary to elect a legislator of that particular racial/ethnic group. While there is variation by state here, Bullock notes that "The thresholds for electing an Hispanic are generally lower than for the election of a black." He also analyzes the impact of incumbency and finds essentially that "incumbency is color-blind." Perhaps the most important point made by Bullock is that districts that are 60 percent or more black or Hispanic almost always elect blacks or Hispanics to state legislatures and that there are a finite number of such districts that can be created. It is also worth noting that black gains in state legislatures have tended to coincide with the reapportionment cycle. In other words, minorities tend to make their largest seat gains when district lines are redrawn or when single-member districts are created out of multi-member districts.

The final chapter in this section investigates some issues concerning women in state legislatures. As Patricia Freeman and William Lyons note, the proportion of state legislators who are female has risen from 4 percent to 17 percent in the last twenty years. Freeman and Lyons provide a good overview of the recent literature on women in state legislatures. The authors then analyze some of the findings of this literature with their own data, generated from a mail questionnaire sent to four state legislatures. Their study reveals that, while women have made major inroads in attaining state legislative offices, there remain some important differences in their backgrounds, recruitment processes, and perceptions of support from their political party.

The institutional reforms identified by Pound have indeed wrought important changes in state legislatures, and they parallel other institutional and societal changes that make for a much different state legislative career pattern than existed just a generation ago. In most states, at least, the legislature is no longer the exclusive domain of the "good ol' boy."

CHAPTER 1

State Legislative Careers: Twenty-Five Years of Reform

William Pound

U.S. state legislatures have changed remarkably in recent years. It can be argued that state legislatures have experienced greater internal change in the past twenty-five years than any other of our governmental institutions and that they have changed more rapidly than during any other period in their history.

The nature of these changes is generally known, although some are more obvious than others. Legislative reform has progressed at varying rates from state to state. Most would date the legislative reform movement from the mid-1960s and, in particular, the U.S. Supreme Court decisions in *Baker v. Carr* (1962) and *Reynolds v. Sims* (1964) that launched the reapportionment revolution, although some significant reform trends were evident before then. For example, the development of staff resources in state legislatures can be traced to the early years of the twentieth century. Legislative staffing experienced a slow but steady growth in the fifteen years following World War II. This was most evident in the spread of the Legislative Council, usually accompanied by some professional research capability, and the development of independent fiscal analysis capability that began in Texas and California.

However, the pace of legislative modernization increased in the mid-1960s. The period from 1965 to the late 1970s was the peak of legislative reform, with the most recent decade being characterized more by consolidation of reforms and more gradual, somewhat less visible, but equally important changes. The job of the state legislator has changed substantially as a consequence of these reforms. Virtually all state legislatures have experienced some measure of professionalization in the last quarter-century.

Major Elements of Legislative Modernization

Court-stimulated reapportionment was a key factor in legislative reform and can be viewed as a major reform itself in many states and also as a significant causal factor in legislative modernization. The major elements of state legislative reform can be summarized as follows.

- The elimination or relaxation of many constitutional limitations on the legislatures, including session and salary limitations.
- The development and expansion of professional staff.
- The increase in time spent by legislatures in both session and session-related activity.
- The expansion and improvement of legislative facilities.
- The tremendous growth of legislative information and analysis capability, especially the utilizing of modern computer systems.
- The development of statutes on ethics, campaign finance, disclosure, and conflict of interest.

Each of these elements are discussed below.

Constitutional Limitations

The modification or elimination of constitutional restrictions included the elimination of limitations on legislative sessions or expansion of constitutional prescriptions for sessions. In 1940, only four states met in annual sessions—New York, New Jersey, Rhode Island, and South Carolina. By the early 1960s, this number had grown to nineteen. In 1975, thirty-five states met annually, and forty-three now hold annual sessions. Twelve states abolished their constitutional limits on legislative sessions. Others, such as Louisiana, South Dakota, and Washington, expanded the time available for sessions. In addition, many legislatures were given the power to convene themselves in special session, rather than remain dependent on the governor for this. Twenty-nine legislatures have this authority today. What all of this means is that the job of the state legislator is increasingly a very time-consuming one. At some point it becomes the primary occupation, rather than just an interesting part-time diversion from the legislator's "real job." As pointed out in our discussion of professionalization, a handful of states are now past that point.

Limits on legislative salary were removed from the constitution in many states and allowed to be set by law or by compensation commission recommendation. As a result legislative salaries today run from $200 a biennium in New Hampshire to $57,500 a year in New York. The majority of New York legislators also receive additional compensation, for example, for leadership and chair positions. (Legislative session provisions and salaries are identified in table 1.) Legislative salaries have increased regularly in many states in recent years, with ten to fifteen states increasing compensation each biennium. This means that it is now possible in some states to subsist exclusively on legislative pay, furthering the career orientation of legislators in those states.

TABLE 1. State Legislative Sessions: Legal Provisions

State	Year	Salary	Living Expenses during Session	Limitation on Length of Session
Alabama	Annual	$10/day	$40 per diem (vouchered). $40 1 additional day per week for committee meeting attendance + $1900/month expense allowance	30 L in 105 C
Alaska	Annual	$22,140/year	$80 per diem ($60 for Juneau legislators) (unvouchered)	120 C
Arizona	Annual	$15,000/year	$60 per diem for first 120 regular session days ($35 for Maricopa County legislators) (vouchered). After 120 session days, $20 per diem ($10 for Maricopa County members)	By legislative rule—100 session days
Arkansas	Biennial (odd year)	$7,500/year	$20 per diem (actual attendance) (unvouchered) + $350/week expense allowance	60 C
California	Annual	$37,105/year $40,816/year (as of December 1988)	$82 per diem (unvouchered). $87 per diem (as of January 1, 1988	None
Colorado	Annual	$17,500/year	$70 per diem ($35 for Denver-area legislators) for 140 days. After 140 days, $40 per diem ($20 for Denver-area legislators)	Odd—none. Even—140 C
Connecticut	Annual	$15,200/year	Senators—$4,500/year. Representatives—$3,500/year (unvouchered)	Odd—Wednesday after Monday in June. Even—Wednesday after first Monday in May
Delaware	Annual	$21,300/year	$2,500/year (unvouchered)	June 30
Florida	Annual	$19,848/year	$50 per diem (unvouchered)	60 C
Georgia	Annual	$10,125/year	$59 per diem (unvouchered) + $4,800/year vouchered expense allowance (including office expenses)	40 L

Note: Daily salaries are paid during regular session. L = legislative days; C = calendar days.

Continued on next page

Table 1—*Continued*

State	Year	Salary	Living Expenses during Session	Limitation on Length of Session
Hawaii	Annual	$15,600/year	$20 per diem ($10 for Oahu legislators) (unvouchered) + $5,000/year expense allowance	60 L (g)
Idaho	Annual	$30/day during session. $7/day outside of session	$60 per diem ($35 for Ada County legislators) (unvouchered)	None
Illinois	Annual	$35,661/year. $32,500 (holdover senators)	$72 per diem (vouchered)	None
Indiana	Annual	$11,600/year	$80 per diem (unvouchered)	Odd—61 L or April 30. Even—30 L or March 15
Iowa	Annual	$14,600/year $16,600 (1989)	$40 per diem ($25 for Polk County legislators) (unvouchered). $73 per diem (1989)	By legislative rule
Kansas	Annual	$54/day (1987). $55/day (as of January 1988)	$66 per diem (unvouchered)	Odd—none. Even—90 C
Kentucky	Biennial (even year)	$100/day	$75 per diem (unvouchered)	60 L—no later than April 15
Louisiana	Annual	$16,800/year	$75 per diem (vouchered)	60 L in 85 C
Maine	Annual	$9,000 (1987). $6,000 (1988)	$60 per diem (vouchered)	1—100 L. 2—50 L
Maryland	Annual	$22,000 (1987). $23,000 (1988). $24,000 (1989)	$78 per diem (vouchered). $81 per diem (1988)	90 C
Massachusetts	Annual	$39,040.11/year. $40,992 (as of June 26, 1988)	No per diem, but receive mileage for every session day	None
Michigan	Annual	$38,163 (1987). $39,881 (1988)	$7,700/year expenses (vouchered)	None
Minnesota		$23,244/year	$36 per diem ($23 for metropolitan legislators) (unvouchered) + $300/month housing for senators, $400/month representatives	120 L or first Monday after third Saturday in May

State	Session	Salary	Per Diem	Session Limit
Mississippi	Annual	$10,000/year	$65 per diem for actual daily attendance (none for Jackson legislators) (unvouchered). Amount based on federal rate for Jackson	125 C in first year. 90 C years two—four
Missouri	Annual	$20,851.56/year	$35 per diem (unvouchered)	Odd—June 30. Even—May 15
Montana	Biennial (odd year)	$52.12/day	$50 per diem (unvouchered)	90 L
Nebraska	Annual	$4,800/year	$64 per diem ($31.50 for legislator residing within 50 miles of Lincoln) (vouchered)	Odd—90 L. Even—60 L
Nevada	Biennial (odd year)	$130/day (no more than 60 days)	$57 per diem (vouchered)	60 C
New Hampshire	Annual	$100/year	None	45 L
New Jersey	Annual	$25,000/year	None	None
New Mexico	Annual	$75/day	None	Odd—60 C. Even—30 C
New York	Annual	$43,000/year. $57,500 (as of January 1989)	$75 per diem (vouchered)	None
North Carolina	Annual	$10,140/year. $10,644 (1989)	$79 per diem (unvouchered)	None
North Dakota	Biennial (odd year)	$90/day plus $180 each month legislator is in office	$35 per diem (unvouchered)	80 L
Ohio	Annual	$33,243 (1987). $34,905 (1988)	None	None
Oklahoma	Annual	$20,000/year	$35 per diem (unvouchered)	90 L
Oregon	Biennial (odd year)	$11,028/year	$62 per diem (unvouchered)	None
Pennsylvania	Annual	$35,000/year. $47,000 (as of December 1, 1988)	$85 per diem (vouchered) + $12,000/year unvouchered expenses + $10,000/year vouchered expenses	None

Continued on next page

Table 1—*Continued*

State	Year	Salary	Living Expenses during Session	Limitation on Length of Session
Rhode Island	Annual	$5/day	None (legislators receive mileage for each session day)	60 L
South Carolina	Annual	$10,000/year	$73 per diem (actual attendance) (unvouchered)	First Thursday in June
South Dakota	Annual	$3,200 (1987). $2,800 (1988)	$75 per diem (unvouchered)	Odd—40 L. Even—35 L
Tennessee	Annual	$12,500/year	$77 per diem (unvouchered)	90 L
Texas	Biennial (odd year)	$7,200/year	$30 per diem (unvouchered)	140 C
Utah	Annual	$65/day	$25 per diem (unvouchered) + $50/day lodging for members living outside of Davis County	45 C
Vermont	Annual	$340/week (average 18 weeks). $6,800/year	$70 per diem ($21.35/day plus mileage for legislators who commute) (unvouchered)	Odd—early May. Even—mid-April
Virginia	Annual	$11,000/year. $18,000/year (as of January 12, 1988)	$77 per diem (unvouchered)	Odd—30 C. Even—60 C
Washington	Annual	$15,500/year. $16,500 (as of July 1, 1988)	$50 per diem (vouchered)	Odd—105 C. Even—60 C
West Virginia	Annual	$6,500/year	$70 per diem (vouchered). $50 per diem for special sessions (unvouchered)	60 C
Wisconsin	Annual	$29,992/year (new members). $27,202/year (holdovers). $31,204 (as of July 1, 1989)	$55 per diem maximum (vouchered)	None
Wyoming	Annual	$75/day	$60 per diem (vouchered)	Odd—40 L. Even—20 L

Other constitutional limitations that have been modified include restrictions on legislative budget authority and on items that the legislatures may consider during the second session of the biennium. Constitutional changes have also expanded legislative authority to hold internal organizational sessions in advance of the regular session, to meet and consider gubernatorial vetoes, and to engage in legislative oversight activity. Examples of the latter are transfers of the postaudit function from the executive to the legislative branch, reversing a nineteenth-century trend, and the rapid expansion in the 1970s of legislative review of administrative rules. Two state legislatures engaged in administrative rules review in 1967; forty-two engaged in this activity to some degree in 1988.

Professional Staffing

Among the most important legislative reforms has been the growth of professional staffing, which continues today. As noted already, the reform movement accelerated an existing trend toward the development of permanent professional staff in state legislatures. This has meant an enhanced research capability in every legislature, though some still have minimal capability, and the development of fiscal staff for all legislatures.

A study conducted by the National Conference of State Legislatures (NCSL) in 1981 (Simon 1982), found that there were approximately sixteen thousand full-time, permanent staff in the fifty state legislatures and about nine thousand session-only employees (see tables 2 and 3). Current estimates are that the permanent staff level is eighteen thousand to twenty thousand persons. Staffs devoted to audit and program evaluation activity have grown, as have such functions as bill drafting and legal services, computer services, and public information and media activities. But by far the largest staff increase has occurred in leadership staff and personal staff for legislators.

The implications of the expansion of staff capacity for the legislatures are many. Foremost, it has given the legislatures independence, both from the executive branch and from those who seek to influence legislative action. Prior to this development most legislatures depended heavily on the executive or on lobbyists for information and for bill drafts. In the budget area, greater staff capacity has, in a majority of states, enhanced the legislatures' most important power, the power to tax and spend. Legislatures have become better able to develop and analyze governmental budgets and in many states are now equal, if not preeminent, partners in the budget process.

Legislative independence, however, has not been a universal consequence of the modernization movement. The governor still plays a commanding role in leadership selection and legislative control in a few states, as the organization of the Louisiana legislature in 1988 attests. Legislative budget authority remains limited constitutionally in states such as Maryland and by lack of staff resources in others, like West Virginia.

The provision of staff to each committee in a legislature, with such staff often employed or controlled by the committee chair, was a reform advocated by many. Committee staff structures have been adopted in most of the larger states, notably in California, Florida, New York, and Pennsylvania, but have not been universally adopted. Legislatures like those of Maine, Ohio, Washington, and Wisconsin provide staff to committees but retain a centralized control on staff employment and assignment.

A function of the professionalization of legislative staff is the growing attention to the development of personnel and compensation systems and professional development programs. Another aspect is national recruitment and the transfer of legislative staff between states. NCSL has experienced a considerable expansion of its training programs both for staff and legislators.

Two trends are evident in state legislative staff development in addition to

TABLE 2. Full-time Professional Staff in State Legislatures

	States			
Number of Staff	1st Quartile	2d Quartile	3d Quartile	4th Quartile
1–100	Delaware	Idaho	Iowa	Alaska
	North Dakota	Maine	Kentucky	Hawaii
	Vermont	Nevada	Mississippi	Indiana
	Wyoming	New Hampshire	Missouri	Kansas
		New Mexico	Montana	Nebraska
		North Carolina	Oklahoma	
		South Dakota	Rhode Island	
		Utah	South Carolina	
			West Virginia	
101–200	Oregon	Alabama	Arizona	Arkansas
		Colorado	Georgia	Maryland
		Connecticut	Virginia	Washington
		Tennessee		
201–300	Louisiana	Massachusetts	Minnesota	Illinois
			Wisconsin	New Jersey
301–400				
401–500	Texas			Pennsylvania
501–600	Ohio		Michigan	
601–700			Florida	
701–800	New York	California		

the continued professionalization and emphasis on specialized expertise. The first of these is a decentralization of management control within legislatures and sometimes within individual houses. The model for many years was of central service agencies working for both houses under some form of joint management control. The trend in the past decade has been toward separate house and senate staffs and the elimination or reduction in scope of joint central service agencies of the Legislative Council or Legislative Bureau. Such decentralization is far along in the large states, with the exception of Ohio, but also is evident in states as diverse as Alaska, Louisiana, Minnesota, Oklahoma, and South Carolina. Within individual houses there is evidence of further decentralization as committees are allowed to hire staff.

The second trend is in the type of staff. Staff growth is occurring significantly among personal staffs for leaders and members or committees and in partisan caucus staffs. Such staffs are hired on a decentralized basis, in some states as a result of political ties, and are usually responsible only to individual legislators. An effect of these trends is to reduce the sense of the legislature as an institution and to reduce the opportunities and the need for two houses to work jointly and cooperatively together.

TABLE 3. Sessional Staff Employment in State Legislatures

Number of Employees	States		
0–99	California	Nebraska	South Dakota
	Delaware	New Hampshire	Tennessee
	Massachusetts	New Jersey	Vermont
	Michigan	Ohio	Wyoming
	Mississippi	Pennsylvania	
100–199	Alabama	Illinois	Nevada
	Alaska	Indiana	North Dakota
	Arkansas	Louisiana	Rhode Island
	Colorado	Maine	Utah
	Connecticut	Missouri	Wisconsin
	Idaho	Montana	
200–299	Florida	Kentucky	South Carolina
	Iowa	New Mexico	Virginia
	Kansas	Oklahoma	West Virginia
300–399	Arizona	Hawaii	North Carolina
	Georgia	Maryland	
400–499	Minnesota	Oregon	
500+	New York	Texas	Washington
	(approx. 1500)	(approx. 550)	(approx. 550)

The importance of increased staff capabilities to the careers of the legislators themselves is obvious. Committee staff provide legislators with greater capability for independently gathering information. Personal staff allow individual legislators to pursue their personal policy initiatives and to conduct casework for constituents.

Legislator Professionalization

Legislative reform has created the trend toward the full-time state legislature. This trend has been resisted by many but is probably inevitable in a majority of states if the legislative branch is to be coequal and cope with the problems now facing government. The argument as to the merits of the professional versus the citizen legislator has been a recurrent one, with mixed responses among the states.

Today, at least nine state legislatures can be termed full-time, based on the criteria of salary, time spent in session, and the occupational definition of the members. These include the California, Illinois, Massachusetts, Michigan, New Jersey, New York, Ohio, Pennsylvania, and Wisconsin legislatures. A 1987 NCSL survey of legislator occupations (Bazar 1987) found that more than half of the members of the New York and Pennsylvania legislatures listed "legislator" as their occupation and that more than 10 percent of all state legislators now list the legislature as their occupation. This figure has grown from about 1 percent a decade earlier.

It is apparent that this trend toward professionalization of legislatures is growing. Many members of legislative bodies other than the nine noted earlier are full-time. Even in states with restricted sessions, such as Florida (60 days) and Texas (biennial session of 140 days), there is a discernable growth in full-time legislators. In part, this is a result of the extension of legislative committee activities to a nearly year-round schedule, even though the formal session may be limited. It is also stimulated by the growing legislator concern with constituency service, the trend toward district offices for members, and continual fund-raising for campaign purposes.

It is interesting to note a small countertrend to this growing professionalization. New session limitations have recently been adopted in several states, notably Alaska, Arizona, Colorado, and Iowa, to slow the movement to full-time legislatures. Such limits on formal sessions may have only a minor impact on the general trend. Several medium-sized states actually have spent as much time in session in recent years as have the larger, more clearly full-time legislatures. These include Arizona, Colorado, Iowa, Oklahoma, and South Carolina, as well as Alaska. Legislative reform has also brought an attempt to structure interim periods to make them more formal and effective in states like Florida, Minnesota, and Washington.

Improved Facilities and Working Conditions

The improvement of legislative facilities has both enhanced the independence of the legislatures and contributed toward the professionalism trend. At the onset of the legislative reform movement, legislators typically had only their desks in the chamber for offices, with only leaders occupying or sharing private offices. Space for committee activities was often inadequate or nearly nonexistent. Nearly all legislatures provide office space to committee chairs today and the vast majority provide private or shared space to all members. State capitol buildings have been largely taken over by the legislative branch. In states such as Connecticut, North and South Carolina, Minnesota, Ohio, and Virginia, legislative office buildings have been constructed or remodeled. Facilities for legislators and staff, leadership, and committees are greatly improved in most capitols. While this has improved the ability of legislatures to conduct business and of the public to participate in the legislative process, it has also contributed to a growing decentralization in state legislatures and a change in the institutional mores of many legislatures. Individual legislators are more isolated from each other; there is less interaction and understanding among them. The institutional "folkways" have changed from the period before legislative modernization. Many of the informal relationships and understandings that characterized state legislatures are no longer present.

Other Changes

Legislative reform brought change to the rules and procedures of every state legislature. Among the most prominent of these have been deadlines for bill introduction and committee and floor action, requirements for notice of hearings and floor action, and, in general, enhanced public information. Reforms have often been directed at making the process more streamlined and providing greater public understanding and access. Committee systems have been strengthened. States have experimented with "concept bills" rather than specific introductions (Connecticut) and with limiting bill introductions to as few as four bills per member (Colorado).

The evolution of computers and information system technology has greatly enhanced the capacity of legislatures to develop and analyze information and make it more readily available to the members. The impact of the computer on the legislative process, and on constituent work and campaign technology, has been enormous. Information now available to the legislatures, whether it be bill status, a statute data base, budget analysis, or the impact of alternative spending or taxation proposals, has made the legislative institutions and individual legislators more effective participants in the policymaking process. Information technology has led to a dispersal of power within the legislatures, to committees and to individual members, and also contributes to the power of incumbency and independence from the political party.

Finally, legislative reform brought widespread adoption of new or amended statutes regulating conflict of interest, disclosure, campaign finance, and open meetings and records. Virtually every state has enacted legislation affecting some or all of these areas. But the impact of such legislation is difficult to measure, particularly in the areas of conflict of interest, lobbying, and campaign finance. Both California and New York have typical statutes on conflict of interest but have recently been subjected to intense criticism for current practices.

Today's Trends In State Legislatures

The impact of legislative reform has clearly been to make state legislatures more independent, analytical, and capable of policy development. It has resulted in many states in a gradual decentralization of the legislatures. This can be seen in the strengthening of committees and of specialized expertise, in the greater resources provided to individual legislators and party caucuses, and in changes in legislative staffing patterns.

The growth of lobbying activity at the state level, with Political Action Committees (PACs) and independent financing of legislative campaigns, has also contributed to a fragmentation of the legislature. Developments in campaign funding present an interesting dichotomy in their impact on the legislature. On the one hand they have contributed to candidate independence and a decline of party or leadership control, yet, where some control of PAC funding and overall fund-raising can be gained by legislative leaders, they can use this to strengthen their leadership positions and develop more centralized, cohesive legislative parties. Anthony Gierzynski and Malcolm Jewell discuss this trend in chapter 7.

On the other hand, the legislatures of a number of the smallest states, while impacted by reform, have changed to a much lesser degree. States such as North Dakota, South Dakota, and Wyoming still have limited sessions, small professional staffs, relatively low legislator compensation, and less capacity for fiscal and policy analysis.

Another trend in legislatures today is the declining authority of legislative leadership. This trend is a result of many of the factors discussed above. The ability of leaders to control information, favors, and finances is no longer as great as it once was. The tenure of leaders is often short, with a turnover rate in excess of 25 percent in recent years. But some strong, long-serving leaders remain in places such as the Massachusetts and New York Senates and the House in Maine, Ohio, and Georgia. Peverill Squire explores some of these issues in chapter 10.

A trend is also evident toward increased constituency service and attention by state legislators. The professionalization of the legislatures has accelerated this development. Nine state legislatures now provide district offices for members, and expenditure allowances for district activity are growing. The advantages of this phenomenon for incumbents seeking reelection are obvious.

As a result of these trends there is an increasing level of legislative-executive conflict. This occurs with frequency over budget issues, in a growing legislative tendency to override vetoes, and as a result of legislative attempts to direct and control administration and condition executive actions on legislative approval. These tendencies are likely to become more pronounced in the next decade, particularly as state governments become the primary arenas for domestic policy activity.

On the whole, the job of the state legislator has changed remarkably in the last quarter-century. The institution of the state legislature has undergone immense reform and change. Changes in the legislative career are both causes and consequences of these institutional reforms and trends. Longer sessions, higher salaries, better physical facilities, and informational resources all professionalize the role of the state legislator.

CHAPTER 2

Nativity, Mobility, and State Legislators

Joel A. Thompson
and
Gary F. Moncrief

Many studies have documented the background characteristics of state legislators. It has been said with some certainty that state legislators reflect their
constituents in certain "birthright" characteristics such as race, religion, and
residence yet differ from them relative to other ascriptive characteristics such
as education, occupation, and income (for example, see Keefe and Ogul
1989, 115–22). This phenomenon has led to a characterization of state legislators as "local boys made good"—a reference to the fact that most are well-
to-do males who are natives and longtime residents of their districts (Dye
1981, 125).

In the opening chapter of this volume, William Pound delineates many of
the changes experienced by state legislatures in the past twenty-five years. No
one can deny that these changes have produced corresponding changes with
regard to the type of individual who now serves in the legislatures. Since
many of the research findings that were used to construct the "local boys made
good" label are almost three decades old (Wahlke et al. 1962), it may be
fruitful to reexamine this characterization, especially in regards to the residential mobility of state legislators.

The overall increase in the mobility of the American population would
suggest that constituents may no longer require that their local legislator be a
native of the state. For example, consider the following comment by one
observer of state legislative life:

> Formerly an outsider would not have had a chance of nomination or
> election. Today the mobility of Americans is high, and it is not unusual
> to find people born and raised in one state or region settling elsewhere
> and getting themselves elected. Most legislators continue to have local
> backgrounds, but many were born and brought up elsewhere. (Rosenthal
> 1981, 29).

Rosenthal supports this statement with examples from specific states but does not test it with comparative data. It is our purpose to provide some comparative data on the nativity of state legislators and to explore variations. Specifically, we investigate the variation in the percentage of legislators born outside the states they represent. We also look at native/nonnative legislators' differences in terms of their educational attainment, proportion of female legislators, and legislative leadership patterns. In conjunction with these observations, we suggest some hypotheses for future investigation.

Our data are primarily descriptive. Because of the dearth of current data on background variables, we believe that such description is worthy of consideration. We are not unmindful, however, of comments like that of Matthews: "If students of legislative recruitment and legislative careers are to progress beyond providing interesting descriptive material, they must do a better job of demonstrating how recruitment matters" (1985, 18). It is for this reason that we pose some hypotheses for future testing. Eventually we wish to know not only if there are differences between native and nonnative legislators but under what conditions such differences appear (e.g., are nonnatives more likely to be elected in certain types of districts?). Ultimately, of course, we want to find out if it matters that some states tend to elect more nonnatives. For example, Lyons and Durant (1980) demonstrate that in Tennessee, attitudes toward policies differ between native and nonnative non-elites (citizens). Does this distinction hold for native and nonnative state legislators as well? If so, the presence of a substantial number of nonnatives in the legislature may have important consequences for legislative life in the state.

The Literature

Recent studies related to state legislative careers include research on turnover rates (Rosenthal 1974b; Shin and Jackson 1979; Niemi and Winsky 1987). From these and other studies it is apparent that, while state legislative turnover varies from state to state, overall turnover rates have dropped substantially (averaging less than 30 percent in both houses in the most recent period analyzed). This suggests that individuals are staying in the legislative institution longer and that realistic opportunities for electoral success for nonincumbents are fewer than in previous eras. Research in specific states, such as Alabama (Moody 1987) and Tennessee (Hain 1985), confirms these trends.

Related to this research is a small body of work investigating the sources of career satisfaction or career change (Squire 1988a and 1988b; Calvert 1979; Hamm and Olson 1988; Francis 1985a; Francis and Baker 1986). Squire (1988a) found that legislative pay—one measure of legislative professionalism—and advancement prospects are important factors in explaining legislative membership stability. Stability, according to Squire, is not precisely the same thing as turnover rate but is clearly a related concept. Both pay and advancement prospects are related to a careerist orientation in a state legislature. This suggests that as state legislatures continue to professionalize and as more legislators develop a careerist orientation turnover rates are likely to remain low (or perhaps drop even further). At the same time, Francis (1985a) notes a countertrend: dissatisfaction with the job of state legislator is related to increased session length and is inversely related to bill passage rate. As he notes,

> Slowly but surely the transition from part-time to full-time legislatures is occurring. Whether this evolution will continue to completion is difficult to determine. It is evident now that the transition has brought with it a serious source of tension between public and private employment. (1985a, 641).

A second body of research related to legislative careers investigates the opportunities for groups that historically have encountered obstacles to electoral success, that is, blacks, Hispanics, women, and other minorities. Most of these studies investigate the trends involving female state legislators (Rule 1981; Welch 1978; Nechemias 1985; Nechemias 1987; Darcy, Welch, and Clark 1985; Blair and Henry 1981; Van Der Slik 1988; Williams 1988).

One of the more interesting findings in this body of literature is the apparent relationship between the number of women state legislators and traveling distance to the state capital (Nechemias 1985). Related to this phenomenon is the number of female state legislators in metropolitan areas. "Women's strongest showing occurs in large metropolitan areas located within striking distance—60 miles or less—of state capitals" (Nechemias 1985, 126). Similarly, Moody (1987) found that six of the seven females in the Alabama House were elected from the two largest metropolitan areas in the state. Nechemias (1987, 134) also found that women are more likely to be elected in states where the population is better educated and where income is higher. Not surprisingly, women's electoral success is also related to political culture (Nechemias 1987; Van Der Slik 1988).

A smaller body of research examines the trend in minority representation in state legislatures (Sigelman and Karnig 1976; Bullock 1987). Most of this research suggests that blacks are generally elected from urban, predominantly black districts while Hispanics have been slightly more successful in non-Hispanic districts. In general, researchers conclude that minorities "are underrepresented in all state legislatures" but have made "significant gains in recent years" (Keefe and Ogul 1989, 119).

One might predict that the electability of nonnatives might parallel that of women and minorities. For example, nonnatives may be more likely to be successful in metropolitan areas where populations are more heterogeneous and many of the voters themselves are likely to be relative newcomers. One might also anticipate that states steeped in the traditionalistic political culture, where long-standing family ties are important in the political arena, will be less open to nonnative candidates.

Aside from the types of studies discussed here, specific career profile data are relatively sparse. Wahlke and his associates (1962) report such data in their four-state study a quarter-century ago. Hjelm and Pisciotte (1968) provide a detailed account of the backgrounds of Colorado state legislators, and some data appropriate to this study can be culled from Barber's (1965) study of Connecticut. More recently, Ingram, Laney, and McCain (1980) provide relevant data in their study of representation and state legislators in the four-corner region (Utah, Colorado, New Mexico, and Arizona). With the exception of the latter, however, all of these studies were conducted more than twenty years ago, and none of the studies provide comparative data for more than a few states. We point out comparisons to these previous studies where appropriate.

Data Collection

To obtain data for individual state legislators, we utilized publications from several sources in each state, including state libraries, state archives, legislative libraries, and, occasionally, private organizations. We were able to obtain information for 4,192 state legislators from thirty states (see table 1). For most states the data are for the 1987–88 legislative years. A few states supplied data for the 1985–86 legislative sessions. These states represent a cross section of the U.S. states, varying in region, economic development, political culture, partisan alignments, and other variables.

Data were available for several state legislator variables: place of birth, party affiliation, education, gender, legislative leadership position, and, for a few states, length of residence in the state. Two observations are readily apparent from an examination of table 1: (1) a large proportion of legislators in some states are not native to the states, and (2) there is substantial variation in the number and percentage of nonnative legislators from state to state.

Results

Overall, 33.3 percent, 1,358 of the 4,082 state legislators for which we have complete data, were not born in the state they now represent. Nevada has the highest proportion of nonnative state legislators with 83 percent, followed by Alaska with 73 percent, Arizona with 69 percent, Florida with 59 percent, Oregon with 57 percent, and Washington with 51 percent. With the exception

TABLE 1.   Nonnative State Legislators, by State

State	Total Number of Legislators	Number of Nonnative Legislators	Percentage of Nonnative Legislators
Alaska	60	44	73.3
Arizona	90	62	68.8
Arkansas	133	24	18.0
California	120	41	34.1
Connecticut	154	67	43.5
Delaware	62	26	41.9
Florida	160	94	58.8
Hawaii	76	16	21.0
Illinois	177	41	23.1
Iowa	150	34	22.6
Massachusetts	198	39	19.7
Mississippi	153	23	15.0
Missouri	198	39	19.6
Montana	150	54	36.0
Nebraska	48	6	12.5
Nevada	59	49	83.0
New Hampshire	397	180	45.3
North Carolina	170	29	17.1
Oklahoma	292	34	11.6
Oregon	90	51	56.6
Rhode Island	152	41	26.9
South Carolina	167	29	17.3
South Dakota	104	16	15.4
Tennessee	131	27	20.6
Utah	104	15	14.4
Vermont	180	87	48.3
Virginia	140	54	38.5
Washington	150	77	51.3
Wisconsin	132	18	13.6
Wyoming	94	36	38.2

of Florida, all of these are western states. Other states that have a substantial proportion of nonnatives include Vermont (48 percent), New Hampshire (45 percent), Connecticut (44 percent), Delaware (42 percent), Virginia (39 percent), Wyoming (38 percent), Montana (36 percent), and California (34 percent). On the other extreme, we find states that do not elect a large number of nonnatives: Oklahoma (12 percent), Nebraska (13 percent), Wisconsin and Utah (14 percent), and Mississippi and South Dakota (15 percent).

A review of table 1 reveals a regional pattern to the election of nonnative legislators. Surprisingly, native legislators are in greater proportion not in the South, as would be predicted given the traditionalistic culture of this region, but in the Midwest, which has 80 percent native state legislators, followed by the South with 74 percent native. The East has 62 percent native, and finally the West has only 54 percent of state legislators native to the state. Because of these regional patterns, we have broken down the results for our other variables by region (see table 2). Several interesting patterns appear in this table. Nonnative legislators are more educated than their native counterparts. In all four regions there is a smaller proportion of nonnative legislators with only a high school education. In three out of four regions (South, Midwest, and East) a higher proportion of nonnatives are college graduates, and in two of the four regions (Midwest and West) there is a significant difference in the proportion of legislators with graduate or professional degrees.

A second noticeable difference between native and nonnative legislators is that women elected to the state legislature are disproportionately drawn from the ranks of nonnatives. This phenomenon is more pronounced in the South where nonnative female state legislators outnumber native female legislators by a three to one ratio. Apparently the traditional political culture of this region, where socializing agents do not emphasize participation of women, still impedes the recruitment of women to political careers. However, in two other regions (West and East), nonnative female outnumber native female legislators by a two to one ratio, and in the remaining region (Midwest) there is a substantial difference as well. Across all regions, then, there is a higher percentage of nonnative female legislators than native female legislators. What may account for this phenomenon? We may speculate that nonnative females are more educated and, hence, more active in social and political affairs.[1] Another possible explanation is that nonnatives may be recruited by the minority party and are more willing to challenge the prevailing power structures at the district level. We examine this premise later in this chapter.

Another regional difference that can be seen in table 2 is the inability of nonnative southerners to attain leadership positions in the southern legislatures. This is not surprising given the characteristics of the traditionalistic political culture. Other regional differences based on this variable are negligible. Apparently legislators in nonsouthern states are more open to "outsiders" assuming leadership positions in their chambers.

A final variable of interest in table 2 is that of party affiliation. In the South, and to a lesser extent in the East, nonnative legislators are more likely to be Republicans. In the more competitive regions of the West this difference is not as pronounced. This observation suggests that perhaps nonnatives are a pool from which the minority party may recruit potential candidates in one-party and predominately one-party states.

---

[1] This is indeed the case. More nonnative female legislators are college graduates (48.2 percent) than native female legislators (44.9 percent). Also, only 9.1 percent of nonnative female legislators has a high school education or less, compared to 12.1 percent of natives.

TABLE 2. Native and Nonnative Differences for Party Affiliation, Education, Gender, and State Legislative Position, by Region

	South Native (N = 854)	South Nonnative (N = 308)	West Native (N = 522)	West Nonnative (N = 449)	Midwest Native (N = 621)	Midwest Nonnative (N = 155)	East Native (N = 727)	East Nonnative (N = 446)
Party	(p = .000)[a]		(p = .190)		(p = .220)		(p = .000)	
Democratic	79.1[b]	59.7	53.3	48.3	52.7	58.7	59.8	44.4
Republican	20.6	40.3	46.7	56.4	47.3	41.3	39.9	55.6
Education	(p = .020)		(p = .100)		(p = .020)		(p = .050)	
High school or less	7.1	2.5	11.3	6.7	17.3	9.9	19.5	15.1
Some college	11.7	13.0	11.3	10.1	14.2	8.6	15.1	12.4
College graduate	34.8	40.0	43.2	41.4	39.9	48.0	34.4	42.5
Graduate/professional degree	46.4	44.5	34.0	41.8	28.6	33.0	31.0	30.1
Gender	(p = .000)		(p = .000)		(p = .005)		(p = .000)	
Male	94.4	82.3	88.1	75.9	85.9	76.1	85.0	6.4
Female	5.6	17.7	11.9	24.1	14.1	23.9	15.0	32.6
Legislative Position	(p = .002)		(p = .270)		(p = .840)		(p = .550)	
Majority leadership[c]	2.4	0.4	3.0	2.7	2.6	2.6	1.4	1.9
Committee chair	15.5	9.1	20.0	15.6	20.4	22.6	8.6	7.1
Rank and file	82.1	90.5	77.7	81.7	77.0	74.8	90.1	91.0

[a]Chi-square probabilities.
[b]Column percentages.
[c]Chamber Speaker or minority Speaker.

To test this hypothesis we examined a state-by-state breakdown of the fifteen states that are classified as either one-party or modified one-party states. The results are displayed in table 3. In this table we further break down the nonnatives into two groups, those born in states that are not contiguous to the state in which they now reside and those born in states that are contiguous to the state in which they now reside. In the two one-party Democratic states, Mississippi and South Carolina, a higher proportion of minority party legisla-

TABLE 3. Party Affiliation of Nonnative State Legislators (from contiguous and noncontiguous states) and Native Legislators, by State

Party System		From Contiguous States		From Noncontiguous States		Total		Native	
One-party democrat									
Mississippi	D	100.0	(9)	93.3	(14)	95.8	(23)	97.3	(144)
	R	0.0	(0)	6.7	(1)	4.2	(1)	2.7	(40)
South Carolina	D	72.2	(13)	50.0	(6)	63.3	(19)	84.5	(82)
	R	27.8	(5)	50.0	(6)	36.7	(11)	15.5	(15)
Modified one-party democrat									
Connecticut	D	23.7	(9)	48.3	(14)	34.3	(23)	47.9	(56)
	R	76.3	(29)	51.7	(15)	65.7	(44)	52.1	(61)
Florida	D	73.3	(11)	45.0	(36)	49.5	(47)	80.0	(52)
	R	26.7	(14)	55.0	(44)	50.5	(58)	20.0	(13)
Massachusetts	D	76.5	(13)	68.2	(15)	71.8	(28)	80.9	(123)
	R	23.5	(14)	31.8	(7)	28.2	(21)	18.4	(28)
Missouri	D	64.7	(11)	59.1	(13)	61.5	(24)	68.7	(101)
	R	35.3	(6)	40.9	(9)	38.5	(15)	31.3	(46)
North Carolina	D	55.6	(10)	41.7	(5)	50.0	(15)	74.5	(102)
	R	44.4	(8)	58.3	(7)	50.0	(15)	25.5	(35)
Oklahoma	D	64.7	(11)	56.3	(9)	60.6	(20)	70.5	(79)
	R	35.3	(6)	43.8	(7)	39.4	(13)	29.5	(33)
Rhode Island	D	76.5	(13)	62.5	(15)	68.3	(28)	79.3	(88)
	R	23.5	(4)	37.5	(9)	31.7	(13)	19.8	(22)
Tennessee	D	42.1	(8)	71.4	(5)	50.0	(13)	69.7	(69)
	R	57.9	(11)	28.6	(2)	50.0	(13)	30.3	(30)
Virginia	D	65.4	(16)	72.4	(21)	69.1	(37)	70.0	(56)
	R	34.6	(9)	27.6	(8)	30.9	(17)	27.5	(22)
Modified one-party republican									
Iowa	D	50.0	(6)	77.3	(17)	67.6	(23)	55.4	(62)
	R	50.0	(6)	22.7	(5)	32.4	(11)	44.6	(50)
New Hampshire	D	30.3	(33)	35.1	(27)	32.3	(60)	44.8	(86)
	R	69.7	(50)	64.9	(50)	67.7	(126)	54.7	(105)
Vermont	D	56.5	(26)	58.5	(24)	57.5	(50)	45.7	(42)
	R	43.5	(20)	41.5	(17)	42.5	(37)	54.3	(50)
Wyoming	D	12.5	(1)	28.6	(8)	25.0	(9)	38.6	(22)
	R	87.5	(7)	71.4	(20)	75.0	(27)	61.4	(35)

tors (Republicans) are nonnatives. In South Carolina only 15.5 percent of native legislators are Republicans, but 36.7 percent of nonnative legislators are Republicans. This pattern holds for Mississippi, but there are so few Republicans in the state legislature it is difficult to make any other generalizations. In the modified one-party Democratic states, nonnative Republican legislators are found in a higher proportion than native Republicans in all nine states. In most of these states the differences are quite substantial, especially in Florida, North Carolina, and Tennesssee. In the modified one-party Republican states nonnative Democrats are found in higher proportion than native Democrats in two of the four states. Only New Hampshire, where the difference is negligible, and Wyoming run counter to this trend.

However, one may argue that nonnatives "from next door" are, in reality, more like true natives in their political orientations and party affiliations, especially in one-party and modified one-party regions. In this case we would expect nonnative legislators from noncontiguous states to be members of the minority parties in higher proportions than nonnative legislators from contiguous states. In general there is support for this hypothesis. In table 3, we find that the differences in minority party affiliation between nonnatives from contiguous and noncontiguous states are quite pronounced in South Carolina, Florida, Massachusetts, North Carolina, Oklahoma, Rhode Island, Iowa, and Wyoming and are substantial in Mississippi, Missouri, New Hampshire, and, to a lesser extent, Vermont. Only Connecticut, Tennessee, and Virginia run counter to the expected trend. Connecticut may be explained by a rather large influx of Democrats from neighboring New York, the leading supplier of nonnative legislators to the state. Tennessee has a higher proportion of native Republicans than imports. This may be explained in part by its traditional mountain Republicanism (Sutton 1982).[2]

---

[2] One may be interested to know which states supply other states with nonnatives who are elected to the legislature. The top ten states are listed in the following table.

State	Number	Percentage	Rank
New York	163	12.6	1
Massachusetts	141	10.9	2
California	63	4.9	3
Pennsylvania	60	4.6	4
Illinois	53	4.1	5
Texas	45	3.5	6
New Jersey	36	2.8	7
Minnesota	35	2.7	8
Georgia	33	2.6	9
Maine	28	2.2	10 (tie)
Michigan	28	2.2	10 (tie)
Missouri	28	2.2	10 (tie)

These results support the hypothesis that nonnatives, especially nonnatives from noncontiguous states, are more likely to be members of the minority party. This finding has some important implications for legislative behavior and public policy in the states. With the high mobility of the U.S. population more and more nonnatives are likely to be elected to the legislature and to other state and local offices. These individuals may be less aware of, bound to, and constrained by the political norms and traditions of the state (Lyons and Durant 1980). They quite possibly will bring new and different attitudes to these offices. In tradition-bound bodies like the state legislature, nonnatives may serve as agents of change within the institution and offer the minority party a pool of potential recruits as they seek to attain more competitive status.

What comparisons can be drawn with previous studies that cite the proportion of nonnatives in state legislatures? Given available data, it is difficult to determine the degree of change in this phenomenon over time. Wahlke et al. (1962, 486–91) found that legislators during the 1950s in the four states in their study were, in general, natives or longtime residents of the states they represented. The proportion of native legislators varied from a low of 14 percent in California (although 42 percent had lived in the state for over thirty years) to a high of 65 percent in Ohio. Overall, 76 percent of the legislators in these states were either native to the states or had lived there for over thirty years. A profile of Colorado legislators during the 1957 to 1966 period found that 39 percent were native to the state and 84 percent had lived there for over twenty years (Hjelm and Pisciotte 1968, 704). Finally, Ingram, Laney, and McCain (1980, 55–56) found substantial variation in the residential mobility of legislators from the four corner states. Only 18 percent of legislators in Arizona were born in the state. Thirty-five percent of Colorado's legislators were native, 47 percent of New Mexico's, and 86 percent of Utah's. A majority of legislators in three states (Arizona, New Mexico, and Utah) grew up in the states, and a large majority in all four states had been residents of their districts for at least ten years.

From these earlier studies it is not possible to determine a pattern of residential or geographic mobility with any certainty. Comparing the results of these earlier studies with our findings, we find that the proportion of nonnative legislators has decreased in California from 86 percent in the Wahlke et al. study (late 1950s) to 34 percent in the late 1980s. In Tennessee the proportion of nonnative legislators increased from 14 percent to 21 percent during this

---

A regional breakdown of major suppliers reveals that New York ranks first in the South (12 percent of all nonnative legislators), second in the East (22.7 percent) and West (6 percent) and ninth in the Midwest (3.3 percent). California is the major supplier in the West (11.6 percent), Illinois in the Midwest (11.9 percent), and Massachusetts in the East (29.1 percent).

same period. And in Colorado, the proportion remained relatively stable between the 1957–66 period and the early 1980s (39 and 35 percent, respectively).

We attempted to trace change in mobility for two states for which we could obtain data—North Carolina and Wisconsin. Unfortunately, a clearer picture does not emerge. North Carolina follows a pattern that one might expect: in 1960 nonnatives made up only 3.9 percent ($N = 6$) of all legislators, and with one exception (Pennsylvania), all nonnatives were from other southern states. By 1975, the proportion of nonnatives had increased to 13 percent and, by 1987, to slightly over 17 percent, and the nonnatives were from a number of nonsouthern states. However, in Wisconsin, the proportions fluctuated over time: 17 percent in 1960, 23 percent in 1975, and 14 percent in 1987.[3] What do we make of this available evidence? One explanation may be a general increase or decrease in population immigration to the states. Some areas of the East and Midwest have a shrinking nonnative pool of potential candidates and, therefore, are electing fewer nonnatives. Also, nonnatives who immigrated to these states during the periods of industrialization generations ago have now been assimilated into the native populations. In short, there is less social flux in these states due to population change.

The alternative situation is found in the growing states of the Sunbelt. Our data support the notion that these are the states that are now experiencing the greatest social changes due to population growth and immigration, and their legislatures are beginning to reflect these changes. The irony of this explanation is that nonnatives in the legislatures are not necessarily "outsiders" but instead reflect the makeup of the states' changing populations. In these states, nonnatives function to make the legislatures more, not less, representative of the citizens of the states.[4]

---

[3] We would like to thank Ronald Hedlund for supplying the data for Wisconsin.

[4] An important variable underlying this line of study is the length of residence of nonnatives. Our basic assumption is that nonnatives are in some ways different from natives. Of course this assumption is not valid for someone who was born in one state but who has lived virtually his or her entire life in another. Obviously, the degree of difference between natives and nonnatives is in large part a function of their length of residence within the state.

Most previous studies report that nonnatives lived in their adopted state (and legislative district) for many years. We made every effort to ascertain length of residence in our data set. Unfortunately we were only able to obtain partial data ($N = 181$) on length of residence in four states: Alaska, California, Florida, and Montana. Forty-eight percent of this group had lived in their adopted state for 30 years or longer, 24.3 percent had lived there between 20 and 29 years, 25.4 percent between 10 and 19 years, and 2.2 percent between 1 and 9 years. The range for this sample was from 7 to 74 years; the average length of residence was 28.4 years.

We have no way of knowing whether or not these numbers are representative of the entire sample. If they are reasonably comparable, then about one-half of nonnative legislators would have lived approximately one-half of their lives in other states.

What factors explain variation in the proportions of nonnatives who are elected to the state legislatures? If the above explanation has any validity, we would expect that the proportion of nonnatives in a legislature would be related to the proportion of nonnatives in the state's population. Other variables that might contribute to an explanation include population mobility and change, region, political culture, and socioeconomic characteristics of the state's population. States with a greater influx of outsiders (such as the Sunbelt and West), states not bound by "good ol' boy" traditions of politics, and states where citizens are more open and tolerant of new people and ideas are more likely to elect nonnatives to represent them.

In table 4 we report the findings of our aggregate analysis. Included in this analysis are indicators of the political climate of the states (local party strength and voting turnout), legislative conditions (turnover, salaries, and staff support), political culture, and socioeconomic characteristics (income, education, urbanization, native population, migration rate, and population change). For each independent variable we conducted a simple regression with the dependent variable as the percentage of nonnatives in a state legislature. Each cell in table 4 contains the unstandardized regression coefficient and the R^2 value for that predictor for the entire sample of thirty states and for the twenty-three nonsouthern states.

TABLE 4. Predictors of State Percentage of Nonnative Legislators

Predictor	Entire Sample ($N = 30$)		Non-South ($N = 23$)	
Political variables				
Local party strength, Democrat	.11[a]	($R^2 = .11$)	1.54	($R^2 = .10$)
Local party strength, Republican	1.43	($R^2 = .21$)	2.55	($R^2 = .47$)
Voting turnout, 1984	−.014	($R^2 = .0$)	−1.79	($R^2 = .24$)
Legislative variables				
Turnover	−.28	($R^2 = .07$)	−.31	($R^2 = .04$)
Salary	.001	($R^2 = .01$)	.00	($R^2 = .0$)
Support	.001	($R^2 = .07$)	.00	($R^2 = .0$)
Political culture				
Moralistic	.07	($R^2 = .01$)	−1.81	($R^2 = .04$)
Individualistic	1.00	($R^2 = .06$)	2.73	($R^2 = .08$)
Traditionalistic	−.70	($R^2 = .04$)	−5.49	($R^2 = .03$)
Socioeconomic variables				
Income	.02	($R^2 = .01$)	.02	($R^2 = .06$)
Education	19.0	($R^2 = .10$)	50.4	($R^2 = .09$)
Urbanization	1.94	($R^2 = .05$)	4.37	($R^2 = .09$)
Percent native	−.89	($R^2 = .59$)	−1.20	($R^2 = .82$)
Migration rate 1960–1980	669.8	($R^2 = .44$)	674.5	($R^2 = .74$)
Population change 1960–1980	227.3	($R^2 = .15$)	449.0	($R^2 = .58$)

[a]Unstandardized regression coefficients

Political variables, especially local Republican party strength, are associated with higher percentages of nonnative state legislators. The positive association between nonnative legislators and Republican party strength is consistent with our previous findings and speculation concerning recruitment of minority party candidates. However, unlike Nechemias's finding in regards to women legislators (1987, 133–34), we do not find that local Democratic party strength serves as a barrier to outsiders being elected to the legislature. Outside the South, voting turnout is inversely related to the proportion of nonnatives serving in the legislature. This result may be confounded by the presence of other factors, especially the political culture and participatory behavior of the Rocky Mountain and western states.

Legislative conditions are not strong predictors of the proportion of nonnatives serving in the legislature. As expected, turnover is inversely related to nonnative representation, and staff support is positively, but very weakly, related. None of the legislative variables are significant in a stepwise regression analysis. However, when Alaska and Florida, two states that skew the population growth variable, are removed from the sample, the staff support variable is one of three variables that enter into the regression equation, along with percentage of native population and local Republican party strength.[5]

Surprisingly perhaps, political culture is only moderately related to the proportion of nonnative legislators. The traditionalistic political culture is the greatest barrier to the election of outsiders, a finding that is consistent with expectations. However, outside the South, the moralistic culture also has a deleterious effect on the presence of nonnatives in the legislature. The individualistic culture operates consistently to facilitate the election of nonnatives.

The socioeconomic environment has a significant impact on the proportion of nonnatives elected to the legislature. The usual measures of economic development—income, education, and urbanization—are moderate predictors of the dependent variable. However, the highest R^2 values are found for three indicators that reflect social change within the state: population change, migration rate, and percentage of population native to the state. As one would expect, population change and migration rate are positively associated with the dependent variable, while native population is inversely related. The R^2 values for these variables are quite large, indicating that they are good predictors of the dependent variable.

The indicators of social change and other variables included in the aggregate analysis are not independent of each other. In an attempt to sort out the

---

[5] Alaska and Florida were removed in an exploratory analysis because these states experienced very large increases in growth and migration rates between 1960 and 1980 relative to the other states in the sample.

interrelationships between these indicators and develop an explanation of the differences among the states, a series of stepwise regression analyses were conducted on the data. Variables that were highly related to each other such as migration rates and population change were entered into separate equations. We also conducted the analyses for the entire sample and for nonsouthern states separately. In all cases the results were equivalent. The percentage of the state's population that is native to the state consistently was found to be the single most important determinant of the dependent variable. This variable explains 59 percent of the variance in the proportion of nonnatives in the legislature (82 percent for nonsouthern states). No other variables added significantly to the explanation.

These results indicate that legislatures are responsive to changing social currents. States that have experienced, and are experiencing, significant population changes, especially due to emigration from other states, reflect that phenomenon in the composition of their legislative bodies. At least in this respect, state legislatures are representative of their constituents.

Summary and Conclusions

This research has investigated the residential mobility of state legislators from thirty states. Our analysis yielded some interesting findings and suggests several avenues for future research. Among our findings are these:

1. A significant proportion of state legislators (approximately one-third) are not native to the state they represent. It appears that this proportion may be increasing in states of the Sunbelt and decreasing in states of the Rust Belt.
2. The proportion of nonnative legislators varies significantly from state to state. A larger percentage of nonnative legislators is associated with state population growth and change. In this respect, outsiders in the state legislature function to make the legislature more representative of the changing composition of the state's population.
3. There are significant regional variations in the proportion of nonnatives in the legislature. Nonnatives are found in a higher proportion in the East and West and are less prevalent in the Midwest and South.
4. Nonnative legislators are more educated than their native counterparts. This is probably due to the interrelationship between residential mobility and nonlegislative career opportunities.
5. A higher proportion of female legislators is drawn from the nonnative ranks than native ranks. This finding offers several interesting avenues for further exploration. To what extent is this phenomenon a function

of the career mobility of married female legislators' husbands? Is this finding a result of the higher educational attainment of nonnative females? Has residential mobility created a greater interest and involvement in politics among these women? Are nonnative women recruited more heavily by minority party officials? Finally, does an explanation of this phenomenon evolve from a combination of these and other variables?

6. Nonnative southerners are very unlikely to achieve positions of leadership in the southern legislatures. Legislatures in other regions are not as parochial in the selection of leaders.

7. Nonnatives are more likely to be members of the minority parties in one-party and modified one-party states. Apparently, nonnatives, especially those who emigrate from two-party regions, are less hesitant to run against candidates from the dominant party. In this regard, nonnatives may serve as an important resource for the minority party as it attempts to reach a competitive position vis-à-vis the majority party.

Besides offering interesting fodder for discussion and speculation, our findings suggest a number of hypotheses for future research. Drawing parallels from the literature on female legislators (for example, see Darcy, Welch, and Clark 1987), we would hypothesize that (1) nonnative state legislators are more likely to be elected from metropolitan areas of a state than rural areas and (2) nonnative state legislators are more likely to be elected from multimember districts than single-member districts. These hypotheses are supported in a preliminary test (Moncrief and Thompson 1989).

Other questions need to be addressed by subsequent research. For example, is there a difference in the rate of turnover of native and nonnative legislators? Are nonnatives more politically motivated to run for office or are they more heavily recruited, especially by the minority party? Finally, the most important question for this line of research is does it matter whether a legislator is a native of the state or not? Again, drawing from the literature on female state legislators, we know that men and women differ in terms of attitudes and behavior (Werner 1968; Kirkpatrick 1974; Diamond 1977; Thomas and Welch 1989). Some available but very limited research suggests that nonnatives may hold different perceptions of political objects (Lyons and Durant 1980). Our premise throughout this research has been that nonnatives, especially recent emigrants from noncontiguous states, are likely to have a set of political attitudes that may vary from those held by natives. These individuals may exhibit behavior patterns that are not indigenous to the native legislative chamber. Their attachment and loyalty to political traditions and legislative norms may not be as strong as those of native legislators. They may bring to the chamber new ideas and different perceptions or points of view on salient issues facing the state. To the extent that these speculations are true, nonnative legislators may be an important source of institutional change and a group worthy of subsequent study.

CHAPTER 3
Minorities in State Legislatures

Charles S. Bullock III

Among the many changes that have occurred in state legislatures since the mid-1960s, increased racial diversity is one of the more pronounced. While regular tabulations of the numbers of black legislatures goes back only to 1969 when the Joint Center for Political Studies began publishing its *National Rosters of Black Elected Officials*, we know that the first black elected to a southern legislature in recent years was Leroy Johnson, elected to the Georgia Senate in 1962. At that time there were but a handful of black nonsouthern legislators. By 1987, there were twenty-eight blacks in the Georgia General Assembly and four hundred black state legislators nationwide.

Data on blacks are more plentiful, but some attention in this chapter is given to the country's second largest minority—Hispanics. Most of the information on Hispanics comes from Florida and Texas, but it is augmented by recent data from California, New Jersey, and New York. When possible, the presentation on Hispanics parallels the materials on blacks.

This chapter traces the growth in the number of black legislators and explores some potential correlates of increases in black legislative membership. Particular attention is given to the relationship between the racial composition of districts, redistricting, and incumbency and the election of black members. Also of interest is the alliance of blacks and Republicans that operated in many states during the post-1980 census redistricting and is showing signs of a decennial reemergence.

To understand the increase in minority legislators during the last quarter-century, it is necessary to review key elements of federal requirements concerning population equality and minority vote denial and dilution. A brief review of these provisions appears in the following section.

The Federal Role in Increasing Minority Legislators

The Voting Rights Act initially passed in 1965 and subsequently renewed and modified three times has been central to the growth in the number of minority group legislators. In much of the South, the 1965 Voting Rights Act removed obstacles to black political participation by eliminating literacy and good character tests and by greatly circumscribing the ability of local registrars to intimidate blacks or to reject their registration applications for trivial errors (see Rodgers and Bullock 1972, chap. 2). Between 1960 and 1966, black registrants increased from fewer than 1.5 million to almost 2.7 million.

This increase would have resulted in the elections of black legislators, but the types of constituencies from which blacks were elected had been predetermined by a series of cases that first reached the Supreme Court in 1962. In *Baker v. Carr* (1962) and *Reynolds v. Sims* (1964), the high court held that legislative districts must have equal populations, which in the South transferred many seats from the rural, Black Belt counties to central cities and suburbs. But for *Baker* and *Sims*, many blacks from the rural South would ultimately have been sent to state legislative chambers that guaranteed at least one seat to every county. Implementation of equipopulous requirements reallocated some seats to increasingly black central cities.

The third factor contributing to heightened numbers of minority members was the active enforcement, beginning in 1969, of the preclearance provision of the 1965 Voting Rights Act. The five deep South states plus Virginia and about half of North Carolina were required to submit changes in their electoral laws or practices to the federal government before implementing them. Once redistricting was found to be within the purview of preclearance, the Justice Department and federal judges began rejecting plans that had multimember districts where one or more single-member districts could be created having black majorities. This impacted most deep South states as they redistricted after the 1970 census and spread to the remaining legislative chambers a decade later. In addition to requiring the subdivision of many multimember districts, preclearance allowed Justice Department personnel to reject plans that were unlikely to create districts favorable to the candidacies of blacks. The 1975 renewal of the Voting Rights Act extended coverage to linguistic minorities, such as Hispanics, which made all of Texas and portions of other states subject to preclearance.

The fourth aspect of federal law promoting the election of minority legislators is the version of Section 2 incorporated into the Voting Rights Act as renewed in 1982. This legislation provided a cause of action for minority groups when election procedures diluted their political influence. Thus while the 1965 legislation was directed at eliminating obstacles that prevented minorities from participating, Sec. 2 was intended to attack procedures, which made it harder for minorities to win office, even after obstacles to participation had been removed. Sec. 2 has been used to challenge plans that have been precleared by the Justice Department or in jurisdictions that are not subject to preclearance. With this provision, districting decisions have been challenged when they did not create as many heavily minority districts as could have been designed under an alternative format, and multimember districts have been attacked.

Numbers of Minority Legislators

In tables 1 and 2 the numbers of black state representatives and senators are shown, respectively, from 1969 through 1987. Membership in lower chambers has more than doubled from 140 to 311 while presence in the smaller upper chambers has almost tripled from 32 to 89. As of 1987, eight states had no black legislators, thirty-six states had at least 1 black senator, and all but nine states had at least 1 black house member. Illinois had the greatest number of black senators with 7, and Georgia and Maryland had 6 each. Georgia led

TABLE 1. Black State House Members, 1969–87

State	1969	1971	1973	1975	1977	1979	1981	1983	1985	1987
Alabama	0	2	3	13	13	13	13	13	19	19
Arkansas	0	0	3	3	3	3	4	4	4	4
California	5	5	6	5	6	6	6	6	6	6
Connecticut	4	5	5	4	5	5	6	7	7	7
Florida	1	2	3	3	3	4	4	10	10	10
Georgia	12	13	14	19	21	21	21	21	21	22
Illinois	12	15	14	14	14	15	15	14	14	14
Indiana	4	2	6	5	4	5	5	6	6	6
Louisiana	1	1	8	8	9	9	10	11	14	14
Maryland	9	14	15	14	14	14	14	19	19	21
Massachusetts	2	3	5	7	8	5	5	5	4	6
Michigan	10	13	11	11	13	12	12	14	14	13
Mississippi	1	1	1	1	4	5	15	18	18	18
Missouri	13	13	13	13	13	13	16	11	12	12
New Jersey	5	4	6	6	4	4	4	6	6	6
New York	10	9	11	10	10	12	11	15	16	16
North Carolina	1	2	3	4	4	3	2	11	13	13
Ohio	10	10	9	9	10	10	10	10	10	11
Pennsylvania	9	9	11	11	12	13	14	15	15	15
Rhode Island	1	1	1	1	1	1	2	3	3	5
South Carolina	0	3	3	13	13	13	15	20	16	16
Tennessee	6	6	7	9	9	9	9	10	10	10
Texas	2	2	8	9	13	14	13	12	13	13
Virginia	1	2	1	1	1	4	4	5	5	7
Other states	21	25	29	29	31	24	27	25	27	27
Total	140	162	196	222	238	237	257	291	302	311

Source: Compiled from appropriate volumes of *Black Elected Officials: A National Roster.*

TABLE 2. Black State Senators, 1969–87

State	1969	1971	1973	1975	1977	1979	1981	1983	1985	1987
Alabama	0	0	0	2	2	3	3	3	5	5
Arkansas	0	0	1	1	1	1	1	1	1	1
California	1	1	1	2	2	2	2	2	2	2
Connecticut	1	1	1	1	1	1	4	3	3	3
Florida	0	0	0	0	0	0	0	2	2	2
Georgia	2	2	2	2	2	2	2	4	6	6
Illinois	4	5	5	5	6	6	6	6	6	7
Indiana	1	0	1	1	2	2	2	2	2	2
Louisiana	0	0	0	1	1	1	2	2	4	5
Maryland	2	4	4	5	5	6	6	5	5	6
Michigan	3	3	2	4	4	3	3	3	3	3
Mississippi	0	0	0	0	0	1	2	2	2	2
Missouri	2	2	2	2	2	2	2	3	3	3
New Jersey	0	0	1	1	1	1	1	1	1	2
New York	3	3	3	4	4	4	4	4	4	4
North Carolina	0	0	0	2	2	1	1	1	3	3
Ohio	3	2	2	2	2	2	2	2	2	2
Oklahoma	1	1	1	1	1	1	1	2	2	2
Pennsylvania	1	2	2	3	3	3	2	3	3	3
South Carolina	0	0	0	0	0	0	0	1	4	4
Tennessee	2	2	2	2	2	3	4	3	3	3
Texas	1	1	0	0	0	0	0	1	1	2
Virginia	0	1	1	1	1	1	1	2	2	2
Other states	5	6	9	11	12	11	10	13	13	15
Total	32	36	40	53	56	57	61	71	82	89

Source: Compiled from appropriate volumes of *Black Elected Officials: A National Roster.*

the nation with 22 black house members while Maryland had 21. Fourteen other states had between 10 and 19 blacks in their lower chambers.

Black mobilization coupled with the shift to single-member districting is responsible for increases in black membership in southern state legislatures.[1] In Alabama, the number of black House members has risen from 0 to 19, in Mississippi it went from 1 to 18, and in Texas the increase was from 2 to 13. Since 1969, there has never been a single decline in the number of black House members in six of the southern states. In the eleven-state South, of ninety-nine comparisons of one year with the subsequent biennium, there have been only six occasions in which there was a decline in black seats. The

[1] In this chapter, the South designates the eleven states of the Confederacy—Alabama, Arkansas, Florida, Georgia, Louisiana, Mississippi, North Carolina, South Carolina, Tennessee, Texas, and Virginia.

largest drop occurred in 1985 in South Carolina when the number of blacks fell from 20 to 16.

Outside the South, Maryland experienced the largest increase in black House members, going from nine to twenty-one. In the more populous states, where the creation of new legislative seats in heavily black districts has been infrequent, the increases have been modest. Net gains since 1969 have been one each in California, New Jersey, and Ohio, two in Illinois, three in Michigan, and six each in New York and Pennsylvania. In 20 of the 117 biennial, nonsouthern comparisons possible in table 1 there were declines, with the largest being in Missouri when the number of blacks fell from sixteen to eleven after the latest redistricting. Pennsylvania and Rhode Island are the only nonsouthern states with sizable black House contingents in which black membership has not dropped at least once since 1969.

While the general trend has been upward, the number of black legislators frequently holds constant from one term to the next. In almost half of the southern interterm comparisons, the number of black house members did not change. Constancy was the pattern in fifty-five of the interterm comparisons in the non-South, a rate very similar to that in the South.

Declines in black membership are rarer in the senates than lower chambers. Only three times (North Carolina in 1979, Tennessee in 1983, and Texas in 1973) has the number of black senators in a southern state been reduced.[2] Drops in black senators are more common outside the South, having occurred seven times. All declines in both regions have been by a single seat.

Summing up, in the South the number of blacks generally holds constant or increases while outside the South there is more fluctuation when deviations from constancy take place. There are fewer and smaller changes in the senates than in the houses, in keeping with the slower growth in the number of black members in upper chambers.

Blacks

While the number of southern black legislators has increased, the bulk of the increases in southern lower chambers has been concentrated in a few elections per state. Matching times of nonincremental increases with dates of redistricting reveals that major reallocations of districts are necessary but not sufficient for marked growth in the numbers of black legislators. There tends to be one point in each decade when black house membership increases by more than

---

[2] The elimination of the one black senate seat in Texas in 1973 was reportedly done with the concurrence of its incumbent, Barbara Jordan, in return for the creation of the black congressional district in Houston, which she won in 1972.

one or two members. The time of these increases varies among states because of differences in their electoral cycles or because more than one reapportionment was necessary before the demands of the Justice Department or federal judges were met. In a few instances (e.g., Mississippi after the 1970 census) most of the decade was consumed in protracted litigation. As a result, in table 1 between 1971 and 1981 Mississippi twice increased by more than two members. Of twenty-one increases of more than two black members reported in table 1, all but three came following a redistricting.

The growth in black Alabama legislators illustrates the tendency for additional black members to be elected following redistricting. The first effort to adjust district lines to accommodate population shifts of the 1960s did little to increase black membership, with one additional black elected in the house while the senate remained all white. When the Justice Department rejected the first proposal, a second one was implemented prior to the 1975 session, and it brought ten more black representatives and the first two black senators. Redistricting after the 1980 census (as a decade earlier, the first plan was rejected) produced six more black representatives and two new black senators. Of Alabama's nineteen black representatives, only the first two, who took office in 1971, did not join the body following a redistricting. Of the five senators, only the one elected in 1979 did not come into office in the immediate wake of redistricting.

The tie between redistricting and increases in black representatives is much stronger in the South than in the rest of the nation. In Alabama, Arkansas, Florida, Louisiana, Mississippi, North Carolina, and South Carolina, at least half of the black House seats were first won in a postredistricting election. Indiana is the only nonsouthern state in which the bulk of the black increase followed redistricting, and there a relapse occurred after the initial gains. In the senates, most of the black gains followed redistricting in Alabama, Arkansas, Florida, Louisiana, North Carolina, and South Carolina, again demonstrating a stronger linkage in the South.

Georgia was the first southern state to experience a growth in black legislators resulting from redistricting. The post-1980 trends for Georgia, along with two states having much smaller black populations, Arkansas and Tennessee, show similarities with the non-South. That is, in these three states, like most of the rest of the nation, blacks had few postredistricting gains. The implication is that there is a finite number of districts blacks are likely to win, and once these have been created, additional gains are infrequent. The paucity of additional black-held seats after the initial postredistricting gains shows that the speculation raised in some quarters (see Brace, Grofman, and Handley 1987) that blacks will win additional seats during a decade is infrequently supported.

TABLE 3. Hispanic State Legislators for Selected States, 1971–87

State Legislature	1971	1973	1975	1977	1979	1981	1983	1985	1987
California									
House	n.a.	n.a.	n.a.	n.a.	n.a.	6	6	6	5
Senate	n.a.	n.a.	n.a.	n.a.	n.a.	n.a.	4	4	4
Florida									
House	2	0	0	0	1	1	4	7	7
Senate	0	0	0	0	0	0	0	0	1
New York									
House	n.a.	n.a.	n.a.	n.a.	n.a.	4	5	5	5
Texas									
House	9	8	11	14	14	15	19	18	19
Senate	1	3	3	4	4	4	3	4	5
Total	n.a.	n.a.	n.a.	n.a.	n.a.	n.a.	n.a.	n.a.	123

Hispanics

Data on legislators with Hispanic surnames are not as readily available as the lists of black legislators published regularly by the Joint Center for Political Studies.[3] For this chapter, recent lists of legislators in four states were inspected; from these, figures on the racial composition of districts were obtained. Hispanic legislators are defined as those whose surnames appear on the U.S. Bureau of the Census's list of Hispanic surnames.

In table 3 an important difference between the figures on Hispanic legislators and those of black legislators is shown. Generally, redistricting was followed by a smaller increase in Hispanic than black legislators. In the Texas and Florida Houses in 1983, there were sizable jumps in Hispanic membership in a redistricting year. However, in none of these examples was a majority of all Hispanic seats added in one redistricting. In the Florida House, the 1973 redistricting had just the opposite effect with the two Hispanic legislators dropping out of the chamber. The 1980 redistrictings in California and New York did little to increase the presence of Hispanics.

Lenz and Pritchard (1989) discount the creation of single-member districts in place of the multimember districts that were common in the Florida legislature prior to 1983 as a factor in the rise of Hispanic members during the 1980s. They attribute the election of additional Hispanic members to population shifts that occurred after redistricting (p. 15). While these districts may

---

[3] There is a *National Roster of Hispanic Elected Officials*, but in 1987, it was only in its fourth edition, thus providing less of a historical record than *Black Elected Officials: A National Roster*.

have become more heavily Hispanic after being drawn, the 1980 census shows each of them to have had a Hispanic majority.

Minority Members and the Racial and Ethnic Composition of Their Districts

Blacks

Research on blacks' (Engstrom and McDonald 1982; Bullock and MacManus 1987; MacManus and Bullock 1987) and Hispanics' (MacManus and Bullock 1987; Bullock and MacManus 1989) presence on city councils has shown a strong relationship between the percentage of seats held by minorities and the racial makeup of the city. This pattern occurs nationwide.

Logically the relationship between racial composition of the electorate and the presence of minority legislators has to be anchored at zero and one hundred. In an all-white district, minority legislators will not be elected since they would not be residents, and in an all-minority district there would be no white residents and thus no white legislators. The thresholds at which minorities first win office and the highest percentage of blacks, or Hispanics, in districts that whites can still win can be determined empirically.

Some courts (*Ketchum v. Byrne* 1985) and the Justice Department, at times, have required that districts be at least 65 percent black, on the assumption that because of racial differences in age, registration, and turnout extraordinary concentrations of blacks are needed if black political influence is not to be diluted. Scholars contend that the 65 percent should not be treated as a magic figure (Hedges and Getis 1983; Brace et al. 1985), and indeed, federal authorities have begun accepting districting plans in which blacks or Hispanics constitute less than 65 percent of the total population. Courts have held that considerations of differential black and white participation rates are inappropriate in deciding whether or not blacks are entitled to relief in the form of single-member districts (*Solomon v. Liberty County* 1988; *McDaniels v. Mehfoud* 1988). Racial minority plaintiffs must show, however, that they would constitute a majority of the voting age population in at least one district before they can successfully challenge an at-large or multimember electoral format (*Thornburg v. Gingles* 1986; *McNeil v. Springfield Park District* 1988). Since the black population is typically younger than the white population, districts must usually have a black population somewhat in excess of 50 percent.[4] Hedges and Getis argue that in areas of New York districts need

---

[4] Plaintiffs must demonstrate that a compact, contiguous district in which minorities would constitute a majority of the voting age population can be fashioned if the plantiffs are to successfully challenge at-large elections, but courts have accepted districting plans in which blacks

TABLE 4. Share of Seats Held by Blacks in State Houses by Percentage of Blacks in their Districts' Populations, 1983–88

State	< 10	10–19.9	20–29.9	30–39.9	40–49.9	50–59.9	60–69.9	> 70
Alabama	0	0	0	0	0	100	100	100
Arkansas	0	0	0	0	0	0	100	100
California	0	17	0	100	100	100	—	—
Florida	0	0	0	50	0	100	100	100
Georgia	0	0	0	0	3	11	75	100
Illinois[a]	0	7	0	0	100	—	100	88
Louisiana	0	0	0	0	0	25	75	100
Mississippi	0	0	0	0	0	0	63	81
Missouri	1	0	0	0	0	—	0	100
New Jersey	0	0	8	50	0	50	—	100
New York	0	0	25	0	100	78	50	88
North Carolina	0	0	5	2	55	100	95	—
South Carolina	0	0	0	0	0	41	88	100
Tennessee	0	0	0	20	0	—	100	100
Texas	0	2	0	42	100	83	100	—
Virginia	0	0	0	0	0	17	100	100

[a]Data are for voting age population.

an 80 to 90 percent minority population for a minority member to win (1983, 17).

In table 4 it is shown that blacks hold very few of the seats in state houses in districts in which the 1980 population was less than 30 percent black. Figures for state senates, as reported in table 5, show that blacks hold virtually none of the seats in districts less than 40 percent black. In contrast, all but one senator representing districts more than 70 percent black were black. In the lower chambers, at least 80 percent of the seats in districts that were 70 percent or more black were filled by blacks. Except for the Mississippi Senate and the Missouri and South Carolina Houses, at least half the districts with populations between 60 and 70 percent black in both chambers were represented by blacks.[5] Greater interstate variety exists for districts between 50 and 60 percent black. In the Alabama, California, Florida, and North Carolina Houses and in the Missouri, New York, and Texas Senates, all seats in this range of black population were filled by black legislators. At the other extreme, in none of twenty-four House or twenty-one Senate elections in 50 to

constitute a majority of the total population but not of the voting age population as an adequate remedy to an admittedly discriminatory at-large system (*James v. City of Sarasota* 1985).

[5] It should be kept in mind that some categories have few cases and at times a cell has a single district. Thus there is only one South Carolina senate district that is 60.7 percent black, and it elected a white in 1984.

60 percent black districts in Mississippi has a black won. Blacks also have occupied less than half of the seats in this category in the Alabama, Arkansas, Georgia, New Jersey, South Carolina, and Tennessee Houses and in the Senates of Arkansas, Georgia, Louisiana, South Carolina, and Virginia. Thus while there are differences among states, a relationship between racial composition of districts and the incidence of black members is readily apparent in upper and lower chambers.

A rough idea is given in tables 4 and 5 of the "tipping point" beyond which districts almost always elect blacks. Again there are differences across states and between the chambers within a state. For example, no white represents a majority black Alabama House district or a Senate district that is at least 60 percent black. In the California House the tipping point is 30 percent black, while in the Florida Senate it is 40 percent black.

Despite the variations noted here, there are several patterns discernible in tables 4 and 5. First, the incidence of black seat holding increases with the proportion black in the district. Second, the thresholds at which blacks begin to get elected tend to be lower in houses than in senates. Third, the percentage of blacks at which districts tip, that is, the point at which districts usually elect blacks, is higher, particularly for lower chambers, in those states initially covered in toto by the Voting Rights Act.

TABLE 5. Share of Seats Held by Blacks in State Senates by Percentage of Blacks in their Districts' Populations, 1983–88

State	< 10	10–19.9	20–29.9	30–39.9	40–49.9	50–59.9	60–69.9	> 70
Alabama	0	0	0	0	0	0	100	100
Arkansas	0	0	0	0	0	0	100	—
California	3	0	0	—	50	—	—	—
Florida	0	0	0	—	100	—	100	—
Georgia	0	0	0	0	11	17	67	100
Illinois[a]	0	0	50	0	—	—	78	100
Louisiana	0	0	0	0	0	75	100	100
Mississippi	0	0	0	0	0	0	0	100
Missouri	0	0	—	—	0	100	100	100
New Jersey	0	0	0	0	0	0	—	100
New York	0	0	0	0	100	100	50	50
North Carolina	0	0	0	0	0	75	100	—
South Carolina	0	0	0	3	0	44	0	—
Tennessee	0	0	0	0	—	0	100	100
Texas	0	0	0	—	33	100	—	—
Virginia	0	0	0	25	0	—	100	—

[a]Data are for voting age population.

In table 6 another view is presented of cut points between the kinds of districts that elect whites and blacks. In this table, the figures are provided on the highest percentage of blacks in the districts electing whites and the smallest percentage of blacks in districts electing blacks. From this we can determine whether or not there is a clear demarcation between districts represented by whites and those that elect blacks, as in the Florida Senate, where the most heavily black district represented by a white was 27.6 percent black while the two districts that were more heavily black elected blacks. Alternatively, we see that in the Florida House the cut points overlap so that the most heavily black district that has elected a white (43.3 percent black) has more blacks than the least black district in which a black has won (32.5 percent black).

The pattern for figures for the lower chambers is for the two thresholds to overlap while in upper chambers there is frequently a clear break between the percentage of blacks in districts electing blacks and the racial composition of districts that elect whites. Within these general patterns are regional differences. Florida is the only southern state that has consistently had thresholds for electing blacks in districts below 50 percent black. Outside the South, the

TABLE 6.   Thresholds of Black and White State Legislative Presence

State Legislature		Smallest Percentage of Blacks Electing a Black	Largest Percentage of Blacks Electing a White
Alabama			
Senate	(1983)	65.2	58.5
	(1984–88)	64.8	54.2
House	(1983)	61.7	69.9
	(1984–88)	51.3	49.3
Arkansas			
Senate	(1983–88)	60.5	50.8
House	(1983–88)	60.5	52.0
California			
Senate	(1983–88)	46.9	29.1
House	(1983–88)	15.2	27.7
Florida			
Senate	(1983–88)	48.8	27.6
House	(1983–88)	32.5	43.3
Georgia			
Senate	(1983–84)	68.4	65.3
	(1985–88)	44.6	65.3
House	(1983–86)	59.3	63.0
	(1987–88)	43.4	63.0

Continued on next page

Table 6—*Continued*

State Legislature		Smallest Percentage of Blacks Electing a Black	Largest Percentage of Blacks Electing a White
Illinois[a]			
Senate	(1983–86)	29.8	62.7
	(1987–88)	29.8	33.9
House	(1983–88)	18.0	74.3
Louisiana			
Senate	(1985)	57.8	53.8
	(1986–88)	53.8	48.5
House	(1985–88)	52.7	62.6
Mississippi			
Senate	(1983–84)	65.4	66.3
	(1985–88)	71.1	67.6
House	(1983–88)	60.4	71.5
Missouri			
Senate	(1983–88)	55.7	45.7
House	(1983–88)	1.3	60.4
New Jersey			
Senate	(1983–86)	70.1	51.4
	(1987–88)	41.0	51.4
House	(1983–88)	28.4	41.0
New York			
Senate	(1983–88)	46.9	74.1
House	(1983–88)	29.2	66.9
North Carolina			
Senate	(1983–84)	54.9	55.1
	(1985–88)	54.9	45.6
House	(1983–84)	21.8	46.4
	(1985–88)	29.8	48.3
South Carolina			
Senate	(1983–84)	39.9	47.3
	(1985–88)	50.2	63.2
House	(1983–84)	51.2	58.1
	(1985–88)	51.2	60.0
Tennessee			
Senate	(1983–88)	63.1	50.6
House	(1983–88)	31.7	46.0
Texas			
Senate	(1983–86)	54.9	49.9
	(1987–88)	49.9	28.5
House	(1983–84)	33.0	37.5
	(1985–86)	14.1	37.5
	(1987–88)	14.1	65.3
Virginia			
Senate	(1983–88)	32.7	48.7
House	(1983–84)	60.1	55.7
	(1985–86)	56.6	60.6
	(1987–88)	56.6	55.7

[a]Data are for voting age population.

only instances of thresholds for electing blacks that were greater than 50 percent black were in the New Jersey Senate (1983–86) and the Missouri Senate (1983–88). The threshold beyond which only blacks are elected is not as clearly distinguishable along regional lines. While the break point is below 30 percent black for both chambers of the California legislature, whites were still elected in heavily black districts in the New York legislature (74.1 percent black in the Senate and 66.9 percent black in the House), and a white represented a 74.3 percent black Illinois House district. By 1988, no white represented a majority black lower House district in Alabama, Florida, North Carolina, Tennessee, or New Jersey.

While there are clean breaks between the highest percentage black district electing a white and the least heavily black district electing a black in many chambers, the more common pattern is for the two thresholds to overlap. Overlapping is more common in both the South and the non-South. Clear breaks are the trend in senates, occurring in almost two-thirds of the years from 1983 to 1988. In the houses, overlaps in the thresholds are the pattern, occurring 78 percent of the time. The smaller numbers of senate districts may help explain why overlaps occur less there than in lower chambers.

As was to be expected, since in many states the numbers of black legislators did not change between 1983 and 1988, the thresholds usually have been the same throughout the period covered in table 6. When thresholds have varied during the six-year period, the threshold at which blacks are elected declined in nine chambers while increasing in three. The threshold beyond which whites are not elected fell in six chambers and rose in five. To illustrate, following the redistricting necessary before the 1984 Alabama legislative session, the threshold at which blacks are elected dropped from 61.7 to 51.3 percent black in the house, and the most heavily black district from which a white came declined from 69.9 to 49.3 percent black. South Carolina provides one of the few examples in which thresholds rose, and the cause for this atypical pattern is the shift from multimember to single-member districts in the Senate. Prior to 1985, most South Carolina senators came from multimember districts, with no district having a black majority. Adoption of single-member districts created several having black majorities, including one that returned the lone black incumbent. However, a number of other districts with black majorities were won by white incumbents.

Regardless of the longitudinal trend in thresholds or whether or not the thresholds overlap, by 1988 only in the Mississippi Senate did black officeholding begin when a district was more than 65 percent black. Generally the onset of blacks elected as legislators occurred in districts less than 55 percent black. In only seven of thirty-two chambers were whites serving in districts more than 65 percent black as of 1988. Results reported in tables 4 to

6 underscore that cut points for the elections of blacks and whites vary and that districts 65 percent black now have higher percentages than are usually necessary for blacks to have a fair opportunity to be elected. Moreover, the trend is toward lower cut points with New York (see Hedges and Getis 1983; Brace et al. 1985) and Mississippi being notable exceptions.

Hispanics

There are five states for which we have a percentage of Hispanic-surnamed residents in each district. These results are reported in table 7. Save for a few districts, most of which are in Texas, Hispanics are not elected in districts in which the Hispanic-surnamed make up less than 50 percent of the population. Most but not all districts that have Hispanic-surnamed majorities are represented by legislators who have Hispanic surnames. Doubtless some of the representatives of heavily Hispanic districts who have non-Hispanic names are nonetheless Hispanic. For example, if surnames are used to identify Hispanics, Luis Morse, who was elected in a 82 percent Hispanic Florida House district, does not qualify as Hispanic although that is his ancestry and he considers himself to be Hispanic (Vargas 1988). At the same time some of the Hispanics elected from overwhelmingly Anglo districts may have little in common with the representatives from predominantly Hispanic districts, and at least some of these anglicized Hispanics do not participate in Hispanic caucuses (Vargas 1988).[6]

Reported in table 8 are the thresholds of the districts with the smallest percentage of Hispanics that elect a Hispanic-surnamed legislator and the highest percentage of Hispanics from which a non-Hispanic—surnamed legislator comes. Generally the thresholds overlap, and in the Florida House and the Texas Senate, the magnitude of the overlap has widened since 1983. The thresholds for electing a Hispanic are generally lower than for the election of a black, probably because it is easier for class and interests to override ethnic backgrounds than to obliterate racial differences.

There is a wide range in the points beyond which those lacking Hispanic names are not elected. For California and New Jersey, the low figures in the right-hand column of table 8 are, in part, a product of few heavily Hispanic districts. In the Florida and Texas lower chambers where the thresholds are high, there are at least two possible explanations. One is that the standard used (i.e., the last name of the incumbent) is a less precise criterion for

---

[6] In the U.S. Bureau of the Census's list of Hispanic surnames, Florida's Elvin Martinez is classified as a Hispanic although he does not consider himself to be one (Vargas 1988). It is expected that reliance on Hispanic surnames results in canceling out legislators, as in Florida. Both Martinez and Morse are included in the *National Roster of Hispanic Elected Officials* (1987).

TABLE 7. Share of Hispanic-surnamed State Legislators by Percentage of Hispanics in Their Districts' Populations, 1983–88

State Legislature	< 10	10–19.9	20–29.9	30–39.9	40–49.9	50–59.9	60–69.9	> 70
California								
Senate	0	0	14	0	—	100	—	100
House	6	0	15	0	0	50	100	100
Florida								
Senate	0	0	—	0	0	0	33	—
House	0	0	33	0	—	100	100	67
New Jersey								
Senate	0	0	0	—	0	—	—	—
House	0	0	0	—	50	—	—	—
New York								
House	0	0	0	0	20	75	100	—
Texas								
Senate	0	7	0	0	33	33	100	100
House	2	3	0	22	0	100	75	72

TABLE 8. Thresholds of Hispanic and Anglo State Legislative Presence

State Legislature		Smallest Percentage of Hispanics Electing a Hispanic	Largest Percentage of Hispanics Electing a Non-Hispanic
California			
Senate	(1983–88)	23.0	39.1
House	(1983–88)	7.2	53.9
Florida			
Senate	(1983–86)	0.0	60.8
	(1987–88)	60.8	55.5
House	(1983–84)	27.5	36.3
	(1985–88)	27.5	82.7
New Jersey			
Senate	(1987–88)	0.0	48.4
House	(1987–88)	48.4	48.4
New York			
House	(1983–88)	46.0	50.4
Texas			
Senate	(1983–84)	55.1	57.0
	(1985–88)	18.4	57.0
House	(1983–84)	5.4	91.5
	(1985–86)	3.6	91.5
	(1987–88)	3.6	76.0

Note: Hispanic legislators are identified as those having one of the Hispanic surnames listed by the U.S. Bureau of the Census.

determining ethnicity than race is for identifying black legislators. The second factor may be low levels of political participation among Hispanics generally, especially in communities in which there are large numbers of aliens. Some of the districts with Hispanic majorities in their populations may have Anglo majorities among the registered electorate or those who actually turn out.

Impact of Incumbency

The advantages of incumbency are manifold. Officeholding provides access to the media, which can be exploited to develop name recognition. It also creates opportunities to curry public support by providing services and taking popular issue stands. All of these factors, plus the expectation that incumbents are odds-on favorites for reelection, enable them to raise large campaign war chests. The benefits of incumbency are so widely recognized that even the politically ambitious often wait patiently until an open seat is available rather than try to unseat an officeholder.

If a district has a sufficiently large black population, it will elect a black; however, the percentage of blacks will have to be greater if the district has a white incumbent. Redistricting or going from multimember to single-member districts can facilitate the election of additional blacks, not just by increasing the percentage of blacks in some districts' populations but by creating open seats or by disrupting the relationships between incumbents and their constituencies by putting new voters in the districts. The power of incumbency is apparent in a review of fifty-seven instances in which the necessary electoral data are available; the review shows that in only eight did the additional black legislator (that is, the new black did not replace another black) defeat a white incumbent.[7]

The power of incumbency for white legislators in the face of a black majority can be demonstrated by the South Carolina Senate. When the multi-member districts in the South Carolina Senate were eliminated prior to the 1984 election, ten majority black districts were created. The three new black senators elected that year were the only ones running in districts without incumbents. White incumbents withstood black challenges in six districts that had black majorities, including one in which blacks constituted 63 percent of the population.

As reported in table 9, the unsuccessful blacks, with one exception, lost even though more blacks than whites went to the polls. Blacks lost because

---

[7] One instance each involved an Alabama and a Florida senator, two instances involved Mississippi House members, three involved Georgia senators, and the last case involved a Georgia representative.

the share of blacks who crossed over and supported white candidates exceeded the proportion of whites who voted for black candidates. Except in District 45, where blacks and whites crossed over at about the same rate, the successful candidates were the ones who drew a larger share of the racial crossover vote. Winners did a better job of both holding on to the support of voters of their race and of attracting support from members of the other race. The pattern of crossover voting, except for District 45, is what one would expect if retention of a legislator's own race's support and attraction of another race's support is keyed to visibility and campaign experience associated with previous officeholding.

Past service in the South Carolina House also paid dividends akin to those reaped by Senate incumbents. The three newly elected blacks had served in South Carolina's lower House and triumphed over whites who lacked that experience. House experience also paid off for two of the unsuccessful black challengers who pushed white senate incumbents into runoffs where one black lost by less than 1 percentage point and the other fell 2.4 percentage points short.

Previous political experience also contributed to the successes of several of the eight blacks who defeated white incumbents in other states. In two instances, a black house member beat an incumbent white senator, and another black succeeded in returning to the Mississippi House after a one-term absence. Three Georgians who lost to white incumbents in their first attempt

TABLE 9. Conditions Associated with 1984 South Carolina Senate Elections in Majority Black Districts

District Number	White Incumbent	Percentage of Blacks			Percentage of Crossover Voting		Race of Winner
		1980 Population	1984 Registration	1984 Turnout	By Whites	By Blacks	
7	No	50	46	68	56	0	Black
19	No[a]	59	55	51	16	1	Black
21	Yes	51	44	56	20	38	White
30	Yes	59	42	59[b]	2	12	White
32	Yes	58	53	52	6	47	White
36	Yes	63	57	53	0	22	White
39	No	59	55	53[b]	21	0	Black
40	Yes	51	49	50	6	19	White
42	No	59	59	55	23	1	Black
45	Yes	55	53	48[b]	7	6	White

[a]District 19 had a black incumbent.
[b]South Carolina provides a single turnout figure when there has been a primary and a runoff, and it is this figure that is reported. Except for Districts 30, 39, and 45, we are sure that the turnout figure is for the determinative election.

continued running until they won. Only two of the blacks who defeated white incumbents did not have previous experience as legislators or legislative candidates.

Jacobson and Kernell's work (1983) on strategic politicians suggests that the better quality black officeholders will hesitate to challenge white incumbents since current officeholders are reluctant to risk their positions even to seek higher office. In 1984, four of South Carolina's unsuccessful black Senate candidates were members of the House. Three of these challengers were so risk-averse that they hedged their bets by acting as Lyndon Johnson did in 1960 and Lloyd Bentsen did in 1988, winning reelection to their house seats even as they were thwarted in their bids for the senate.

The persistence with which blacks once elected hold on to their offices suggests that incumbency is color-blind (Bullock 1984a). Indeed once a black wins a post, even though the district's population divides about evenly between the races, white challengers are weak or nonexistent. Potentially strong white challengers seem to accept that a district has become a black district and whites need not compete. In time some of these black districts, like "unbeatable incumbents," could be upset by aggressive campaigns. In other contexts it has sometimes been observed that black turnout peaks at the election in which the first black to hold a particular position is chosen. Black turnout subsides in subsequent elections, and the black incumbent is defeated (Bullock 1984b; Button 1989).

Redistricting after the 1990 Census

As pointed out, the recruitment of minority legislators is related to the racial or ethnic compositions of legislative districts. Districts that are more than 60 percent black or Hispanic almost always elect members of those groups while heavily Anglo districts infrequently elect non-Anglos. The ability of blacks to win predominantly black districts can be impeded by white incumbents. What do these findings portend for the 1990s following the next round of redistricting?

The reallocation of legislative seats from rural areas to single-member districts—proportionally distributed to central cities and their adjacent suburbs—which began in the 1960s was completed by the mid-1980s. As this transformation took place in a state, particularly in the South, there was a rapid increase in the number of black legislators in the lower house. The slower growth in minority legislators once the major adjustment was implemented suggests that the early 1990s will not witness large numbers of additional black or Hispanic legislators. If the minority population has grown in a city or has become more concentrated, then a few more minority legislators may be elected. Or if the shifting of district lines sufficiently alters the districts of some whites who now represent predominantly minority districts, the incumbents may choose to retire and be replaced by members of the districts' dominant racial or ethnic groups. The prospect for additional blacks under that scenario is greater in the deep South—particularly Mississippi—and greater in the upper than the lower chambers.

Because the Anglo population grew at a more rapid rate than the minority population during the 1980s, the number of heavily minority districts could decline, or they could decline if the minority population became more dispersed. The possibility of decline is small, however, because of the non-retrogression standard under which the Justice Department will reject plans from states subject to the preclearance requirement if they reduce the percentage of minorities in districts having concentrations of minorities. Elsewhere, reducing minority populations in districts represented by minorities would probably set off private litigation under Sec. 2 of the Voting Rights Act. Nonetheless it may be impossible to maintain all of the current black and Hispanic districts in some states, which could result in decreases in black legislators as was registered in the Missouri House in 1983.

In the post-1980 redistricting battles, Republicans and blacks united to devise alternatives to the plans of the white Democrats who dominated the legislatures (Bullock 1987; Cain 1984). Each partner scored successes, with black Republicans picking up more seats in southern senates than did white Republicans while white Republicans gained more seats in southern lower chambers than did black Republicans (Bullock 1987, 66). In the South Carolina Senate, plans that created more black seats invariably helped the GOP (Brace, Grofman, and Handley 1987). If these unions of convenience emerge in the early 1990s, as seems likely, Republicans should be the major beneficiaries. The greatest increases in black legislators in the 1980s came in the wake of dismantling multimember districts in the South Carolina Senate and the North Carolina House. A similar impetus will be missing in 1991.

In some southern states, such as Florida and Tennessee, a GOP-black coalition may come close to holding a majority of the seats in one or both chambers. And depending on the outcome of the 1990 gubernatorial elections, Republican chief executives may be in a position to veto Democratic gerrymanders and have these vetoes upheld by the black-GOP coalition. The coalition may be able to squeeze out a few more majority black districts, and if these can be drawn to exclude white incumbents, blacks may be elected. Potential gains for Republicans should be greater since the coalition can prevent the cracking and packing that has advantaged Democrats in the past. Moving a few thousand voters can potentially convert a safe Democratic district into a competitive one. Or the coalition can put the homes of two white Democratic incumbents into a single district, creating an open district more friendly to a Republican candidate.

If minority group demands are met, the plans should survive Justice Department reviews in preclearance areas and escape Sec. 2 litigation. If the population variations are kept small enough—and with the computer software available there is no excuse for not minimizing population variations even as party henchmen go about their tasks—then Republican handiwork should survive challenges like those that overturned Republican efforts in some states in the early 1980s.

In Florida, Hispanic legislators are generally Republicans, so they stand to be aided if the GOP acquires additional seats. In other states most Hispanic legislators are Democrats, and they may get caught in the black-GOP pincher along with Anglo Democrats.

For neither blacks nor Hispanics is it necessary that their minority group constitute 65 percent of the population in order to win. On the other hand, even some districts more than 65 percent black or Hispanic continue electing Anglos. More complex models may need to be developed to anticipate the outcome of districts with varying racial compositions.

CHAPTER 4

Female Legislators: Is There a New Type of Woman in Office?

Patricia Freeman
and
William Lyons

Since 1969 the number of women in state legislatures has quadrupled, increasing from 301 (4 percent) to more than 1,300 (about 18 percent). Do the explanations previously given for female underrepresentation remain valid given this increase? To what degree do the women elected to the legislature today differ from female legislators serving twenty-five years ago?

Currently, a great deal of uncertainty exists about the relationship between gender and political recruitment in the United States. Researchers are not certain how to interpret the increasing percentage of female legislators. There was speculation during the 1960s that the trend toward a more professionalized state legislature would reduce the number of women in office: increases in salary and other changes associated with professionalization would lead more men to seek state office, and they would replace many women in the legislature (Diamond 1977). However, the projected shift in male/female ratios in state houses has not occurred. Perhaps the expectation that increased professionalization would lead to fewer female lawmakers was not particularly well-founded. Indeed, many of the explanations traditionally given for female underrepresentation are disputed by recent empirical research (Darcy, Welch, and Clark 1987; Nechemias 1985). This theoretical ambiguity makes any prediction regarding women's future recruitment patterns uncertain. In addition, one would have difficulty in assessing the degree to which women serving in contemporary state legislatures differ from those who have served in the past.

In order to examine the recruitment experiences of female state legislators, we used survey data collected from all members of the houses (men and women) in four states. Legislators were queried about the resources available for their campaigns and elections, family responsibilities, and background characteristics such as education and occupation. Those doing earlier research found that women in the state legislature differed significantly from men in terms of background characteristics and motivations for legislative service. We sought to ascertain whether these differences remain or, as many have suggested, there is a new type of female political activist.

Women and the State Legislature

Until recently, there was general agreement concerning the factors that kept women out of political office: lack of support to run for office, family obligations, little political experience, and professional backgrounds that did not put them in the pool of eligibles from which legislative candidates are typically drawn.

Family Obligations

Most discussions of female underrepresentation have begun with the observation that women's traditional role in the family makes officeholding very difficult. Previous research found that female political elites were more likely than male elites to be widowed, divorced, or never to have been married in the first place (Sapiro and Farah 1980, 13). First-term female state legislators were at least four years older than their male counterparts. This age difference, it is argued, reflects the fact that women wait until their children are older before embarking on a political career (Carroll 1982; Kirkpatrick 1974, 221). Other research found that having young children virtually excluded women, but not men, from holding public office (Center for the American Woman and Politics 1982, 32; Stoper 1977). A survey of party activists done fifteen years ago shows that women were much more apt to give up political ambition for family responsibilities than were men. Although both men and women perceived conflict between political and family demands, women were the ones to give up on politics (Sapiro 1982).

Family roles have changed in the past decade. Consequently, we may no longer find a significant gender difference in how family responsibilities affect political activism. Men play a more active role in the family, and large numbers of women are juggling motherhood and a career. Today, over half of all women with children under the age of three are in the labor force, up from 16 percent in 1960 (Women's Research and Education Institute 1988, 375). These changes may lead more women to seek election to the state legislature and to seek election at a younger age.

Support and Resources

It has long been assumed that women have a much more difficult time getting elected to public office. In fact, gender no longer has a significant impact on elections. Public opinion about women in politics has shifted, and women now get as much voter support as men (Darcy, Welch, and Clark 1987, 54–57; Hedlund et al. 1979).

Of course, voter choice in an election is only the last stage in a process that ends with the nomination of a candidate. Women have long complained that they get little assistance from key influential people when they run for political office. These influential people, usually men, affect elections because of their positions in the community, influence within the political party, or ability to give or to solicit financial contributions (Tolchin and Tolchin 1973). Male/female comparisons of campaign financing is problematic because it is difficult to get these data. Two studies compared the campaign funds raised and spent by male and female candidates. In two states (Oklahoma and Pennsylvania), no gender differences were found (Darcy, Welch, and Clark 1987, 61; O'Connor 1985).

The one area of assistance that does seem to have changed for women is the amount of support given to them from the Democratic party. Researchers argue that Democrats have not been as supportive of female political candidates as the Republican party. This assessment is based primarily on the fact that during the previous two decades female legislators were more likely to be Republican than Democrat. Some argue that members of the Democratic party actively discouraged women from running for office (Rule 1981, 64; Constantinia and Craik 1977, 225; Porter, Matasar, and Matasar 1974). More recent evidence suggests that the relatively small number of Democratic lawmakers is a product of the southern traditional political subculture where many Democratic strongholds are located. This subculture is not conducive to female political candidacies (Nechemias 1987, 134).

Background Characteristics

Background characteristics have also been found to affect political recruitment. Most state legislators are of middle or upper-class socioeconomic status and are in professional or business occupations (Jewell and Patterson 1986, 50). According to one explanation, because relatively few women held professional positions and their average income and educational level fell below men's, their entry into the legislature was limited.

Women are increasingly entering professional and business positions. The percentage of female lawyers, the most common occupation in the legislature (Jewell and Patterson 1986, 50), increased significantly in the past decade. In 1985–86, women earned 31 percent of all MBA degrees and 39 percent of all law degrees, compared to 6.6 percent of the MBA and 11.4 percent of the law degrees in 1973–74. Female education and income levels have also risen (Women's Research and Education Institute 1988, 361–63). These changes led to speculation that more women would enter the legislature because their representation in the eligible pool—the business and professional occupations from which most public officials are recruited—has increased (Welch 1978).

Prior Political Experience

Local officeholding is commonly a starting point for recruitment to the state legislature (Rosenthal 1981). Political party activism may also facilitate recruitment, at least in states where political parties are strong (Jewell and Patterson 1986, 28). Women have traditionally held few local offices. A 1974–75 study shows that females constituted less than 3 percent of all county governing bodies and about 5 percent of all mayors and members of municipal or township councils. Even on school boards women held only 13 percent of the positions (Center for the American Woman and Politics 1976, xi, xxi). Women believed that many men in party organizations tried to keep women out of leadership roles (Darcy, Welch, and Clark 1987, 57–59).

The number of women who hold local public offices has increased substantially since the mid-1970s. Female members of local councils have more than doubled and the number of females serving in county offices has tripled (Women's Research and Education Institute 1988, xix). Data are lacking on the number of women holding leadership positions in their political party. In the mid-1970s relatively few female state legislators reported experience in local political offices (16 percent had served in elected positions and 12 percent in appointed positions). About a third of the legislators had played leadership roles in their political party. If more women in the legislature today have experience in local offices or in political party positions, there is evidence that women's increased involvement in these areas has contributed to their recruitment to the state legislature.

Thus data suggest that a number of the explanations for female underrepresentation in political office are no longer valid or at least have declined in significance. What variables affect the electability of women? The political subculture or region receives more empirical support than any other variable (Hill 1981; Werner 1968). The highest percentage of females serve in states with moralistic subcultures. Most adverse to electing women is the traditional subculture, which dominates in southern states. Moreover, according to a recent longitudinal analysis by Nechemias (1987), the political subculture was a more important determinant of women's recruitment in the 1980s than it was during the 1960s or 1970s.

The mobility a state demands of its legislators is also a factor in female recruitment to the legislature. States where the capital is located a long distance from most residences have fewer women representatives. As a result, the highest number of female legislators comes from metropolitan areas located within sixty miles of the capital (Nechemias 1985).

Data Sources

To gather information regarding the characteristics of female legislators today and how they differ from their male counterparts, we used a mail questionnaire. A survey was sent to all members of the Houses in four states: Tennessee, Pennsylvania, Vermont, and Washington. The states were selected because they vary in geographical region, political subculture, and the number of the women serving in the state legislature. Vermont and Washington rank among the top five states nationwide in the number of females serving in the legislature, with 24 percent and 25 percent respectively. Tennessee and Pennsylvania fall within the ten states electing the fewest female lawmakers. The House in Tennessee is 10 percent women while in Pennsylvania only 8 percent of the representatives are women.

The four states represent the three dominant political subcultures described by Elazar (1972). Tennessee has predominantly a traditional political subculture, while Pennsylvania has an individualistic subculture. In Vermont a moralistic subculture prevails. Washington is described as having both moralistic and individualistic subcultures. None of the sample states rank very high or very low on a legislative professionalism scale, using legislative salary as the measure of professionalism.

The overall response rate for the four states was 59 percent, and approximately the same percentage of legislators returned the questionnaires from each state. A higher percentage of women than men returned the survey; the average response rate for females was 68 percent compared to 53 percent for the men. As expected, states with a high percentage of female legislators (Vermont and Washington) had significantly more women return the questionnaire. The female respondents in these states did not differ significantly from the female respondents in the other sample states. Thus, there is no reason to believe the data is skewed by the respondents of any one state. Of the respondents, 50 percent of the women and 30 percent of the men were in their first or second term.

Findings

According to one explanation of female underrepresentation in the United States, few women were recruited to the state legislature because they lacked the characteristics of suitable candidates (education, income, and occupation levels). One way to test whether or not this explanation is correct is to determine if most of the female legislators today fall within the eligible pool from which legislators have been traditionally recruited—candidates that are middle or upper-class, are attorneys or have other professional occupations, and are well educated. Our data, presented in tables 1, 2, and 3, show that significant gender differences between male and female legislators remain.

TABLE 1. Education by Gender

Education	Men (N = 256)	Women (N = 64)
High school degree	16%	6%
	(40)	(4)
Some college	22%	24%
	(56)	(15)
College degree	25%	42%
	(65)	(27)
Graduate school	37%	28%
	(95)	(18)

Notes: Total $N = 320$. $p < .05$.

The smallest gap is in educational level. Although relatively few women have graduate degrees, most do have some college education (table 1). In fact, a higher percentage of women than men have at least college degrees. The differences between men and women in occupations remain significant, as seen in table 2. A large number of female legislators do not work outside the home—the largest occupational category for women is homemaker. Although

TABLE 2. Occupation by Gender

Occupation	Men (N = 224)	Women (N = 61)
Business	26%	16%
	(58)	(10)
Education	11%	15%
	(24)	(9)
Law	10%	8%
	(23)	(5)
Professional	25%	22%
	(56)	(13)
Blue collar	14%	3%
	(32)	(2)
Clerical	2%	3%
	(4)	(2)
Homemaker	0	26%
		(16)
Student	1%	2%
	(3)	(1)
Farmer	11%	5%
	(24)	(3)

Notes: Total $N = 285$. $p < .05$.

a sizable number of female respondents are in business (16 percent) or in professional careers (22 percent), men are recruited from more prestigious jobs than are women. Finally, women report less income than men (see table 3). From these data we conclude that the education, income, and occupation of male and female legislators remain distinct.

Male and female legislators do not differ significantly, however, in political experience prior to their election to the state legislature. A large number of both men and women held elected political positions (49 percent of the men and 41 percent of the women). The elected offices were very likely at the local level for both sexes (less than 1 percent held national offices, and less than 4 percent held state offices).

Slightly more women than men served in appointed political offices before election to the legislature. Again, this prior experience was in local offices for most of the men and women. Of the women, 34 percent had been in appointed political positions (23 percent at the local level and 11 percent at the state level) compared to 30 percent of the men (24 percent at the local, 5 percent at the state, and 1 percent at the national level). Female legislators are more likely than men to have held offices in their political party prior to their election to the legislature. Of the female respondents, 48 percent held political party offices compared to 39 percent of the male respondents. According to these data, female state legislators have considerably more local political experience than did female legislators in the mid-1970s. More women lawmakers have occupied elected and appointed positions today, and more report leadership in a political party.

TABLE 3. Income by Gender

Income	Men (N = 196)	Women (N = 60)
Under $25,000	16%	37%
	(30)	(22)
$25,000–$34,999	18%	25%
	(36)	(15)
$35,000–$44,999	34%	27%
	(67)	(16)
$45,000–$54,999	18%	3%
	(36)	(2)
$55,000–$65,000	3%	0
	(6)	
Over $65,000	11%	8%
	(21)	(5)

Notes: Total N = 256. $p < .05$.

Support and Resources

We asked the legislators what types of assistance they received the first time that they ran for the legislature. They were to indicate whether or not leaders from their political party, business leaders, community leaders, friends, the press, and family provided the following kinds of support: financial assistance, campaign assistance, or moral support.

Male and female respondents do not differ in their perceptions of support from business or community leaders, friends, or family. However, there are significant differences in perceptions of support from the party. A higher percentage of Republican women than Republican men feel that they received financial help (69 percent versus 42 percent). There are no significant differences in perceptions of financial support among the Democrats. A statistically significant difference is found between Democratic men and women in perceptions of moral support from party leaders. While 65 percent of the men feel they received moral support the first time they ran for office, only 45 percent of the women report moral support. There are no significant gender differences among the Republicans in perceptions of moral support. These data thus provide some indication that the Republicans are slightly more supportive of female candidates than are the Democrats.

Women generally describe the press as less supportive of their candidacies the first time they ran for the state legislature than do men. As shown in table 4, while 22 percent of the female respondents describe the press as not supportive, only 9 percent of the men feel that way. However, women report significantly more support from family and friends (campaign, moral, and financial support). Moreover, more women than men perceive high levels of spouse support for their political activity. While 74 percent of the women report that their spouses are "very much in favor" of their political activity, only 51 percent of the men make this claim (see table 5). Whether or not

TABLE 4.   Perceptions of Press Support
by Gender

Perception of Press Support	Men ($N = 203$)	Women ($N = 58$)
Very supportive	39%	21%
	(80)	(12)
Somewhat supportive	52%	57%
	(105)	(33)
Not supportive	9%	22%
	(18)	(13)

Notes: Total $N = 261$. $p < .05$.

TABLE 5. Spouse Support for Political Activity by Gender

Support from Spouse	Men (N = 193)	Women (N = 50)
Very much opposed	4%	2%
	(6)	(1)
Somewhat opposed	7%	0
	(14)	
Somewhat in favor	38%	24%
	(74)	(12)
Very much in favor	51%	74%
	(99)	(37)

Notes: Total *N* = 243. *p* < .05.

women actually receive greater support from friends and family than men we cannot determine from these data. Female legislators believe, however, that greater support exists.

Just as Nechemias (1985) had demonstrated, we found that female representatives live closer to the capitol than men (see table 6). We believe that this pattern occurs because it is easier for women to maintain family responsibilities if their homes are not too distant from the statehouse. More women enter the legislature when the commuting distance is relatively short.

Family Obligations

Most of the female legislators disagree with the statement "it is almost impossible to be a good wife and mother and hold political office too" (67 percent disagree, and 33 percent agree). Indeed, women report less conflict between

TABLE 6. Commuting Distance by Gender

Commuting Distance (One-Way)	Men (N = 251)	Women (N = 64)
Under 50 miles	23%	44%
	(58)	(28)
50–100 miles	32%	29%
	(80)	(19)
101–300 miles	41%	25%
	(103)	(16)
Over 300 miles	4%	2%
	(10)	(1)

Notes: Total *N* = 315. *p* < .05.

political life and family obligations than men. In response to the question "to be really active in politics, men have to neglect their wives and children" 58 percent of the males agree while 42 percent disagree. Despite the fact that male and female legislators state similar beliefs about how their political activism affects their family lives, the career paths of men and women in the legislature still differ a great deal. It appears as if women's career paths continue to revolve around their family responsibilities. As shown in table 7, women are still older than men when first elected to the state legislature.

Women are also more apt to be single—either through divorce (15 percent of the women and 8 percent of men) or from the death of their spouses (7 percent of the female legislators have deceased spouses compared to 1 percent of the males). The male and female legislators also differ significantly in the ages of their children. Most women have grown children (aged nineteen years or older); of the legislators with children, 85 percent of the women have children over nineteen compared to only 56 percent of the men. While almost a third of the males (30 percent) have children aged 6 to 18 years, only 5 percent of the females have school-aged children. The percentages of male and female legislators with preschoolers are similar (11 percent of the men and 9 percent of the women).

Summary and Conclusions

A number of the explanations traditionally given for the relatively small number of women in elected political positions in the United States have been called into question by recent empirical studies and demographic trends. Political scientists confront two central questions about the election of women to political office. First, what accounts for the fact that the United States still lags behind other nations in female representation? Does the fact that repre-

TABLE 7.   Age When First Elected to the State Legislature by Gender

Age	Men ($N = 215$)	Women ($N = 61$)
25–35	30%	11%
	(65)	(7)
36–45	29%	33%
	(63)	(20)
46–55	22%	31%
	(47)	(19)
Over 55	19%	25%
	(40)	(15)

Notes: Total $N = 276$. $p < .05$.

sentation has increased mean that some explanations are no longer valid? We cannot yet determine with certainty what factors continue to inhibit women from obtaining political office and those that were once important but no longer are. Secondly, if certain barriers to political recruitment have changed, does the type of woman recruited into office differ from female legislators of the past?

Our findings suggest that some of the reasons other researchers have discounted may still be significant in explaining female underrepresentation in state legislatures. We studied four states with nonprofessional state legislatures, so generalizations must be confined to the states without professionalized legislatures. We uncovered slight evidence that the amount and kinds of support given to women by the two political parties differ. There are significant gender differences in perceptions of financial assistance from the Republican party; women feel as if they receive more assistance than men. In terms of moral support, female Democrats report less party support than male Democrats. Thus, this research shows differences between the political parties in support given to female candidates or, at least, that females in the Republican party perceive more support than female Democrats. In recent studies, authors have argued that the Democratic party is at least as supportive of female candidates as the Republican party. The fact that areas controlled by the Democrats elect fewer women than Republican-dominated areas has been attributed to the political subculture rather than to any actions on the part of the Democratic party. These data, however, indicate that there may still be genuine differences between the parties in the support given to women.

Men and women in the legislature continue to differ markedly in background. As in the past, women are more apt to be single, to be the parents of grown children, and to be older when first elected to the house. They have less education and hold jobs with less status. Women who serve in the legislature live closer to the capitol than their male counterparts. A high percentage of the female legislators did not work outside the home prior to their election to the legislature. More women than men report high levels of support from their spouses for their political activity.

In this analysis of members from nonprofessionalized state legislatures we find that the female elected to the state legislature today does not differ a great deal from the female legislator serving twenty-five years ago in terms of background factors and the central role that family obligations play in career decisions. We do not find evidence of a new type of female activist today, at least in terms of background. Female legislators still differ significantly from men in background and in their political career paths. Of course, women who are more like men in terms of background may be increasingly recruited in the future and present in small numbers now. The number of female legislators in this sample was too small to permit extensive analysis of subgroups.

Are the women recruited to professional legislatures today different from those recruited a decade ago? Perhaps they are. Professional legislatures recruit members with higher levels of education and occupational status than nonprofessional legislatures do. Women have less representation in professional legislatures, likely because of the importance given in these states to the education and occupations of the candidates (Darcy, Welch, and Clark 1987, 104–5). Thus, the women currently serving in a professional legislature may be quite distinct from the female state legislators twenty years ago.

A number of questions remain to be addressed: five important issues concern the impact of a political subculture, the affect of higher levels of education and occupational status among women, why more women do not run for office, whether or not a woman's experience in the state legislature differs from a man's, and, finally, the policy impact of female legislators.

To use political subcultures as an explanation for differences in the number of women elected to the state legislature provides little insight into what factors set some states apart from others. Do cultural differences result from differences in attitudes? If so, who believes that women should be restricted? The regional patterns may be a reflection of some other difference, such as the number of women holding professional positions. The concept of political subculture is of limited use unless the particular components producing the differences can be identified.

Many feel that the number of female legislators will increase as the number of women holding professional positions increase. One could examine how the election experiences of female legislators without professional careers differ from those of their professional counterparts. Darcy, Welch, and Clark (1987, 105) have shown that low educational level and occupational status are handicaps only in states with legislatures ranking high in professionalism.

We know virtually nothing about how women's experiences as legislators differ from men's. Do they experience similar levels of job satisfaction? In Tennessee, female representatives of both parties recently complained about their inability to get positions of power. Finally, and most importantly, we do not know whether or not female legislators behave differently than males while in office. The Center for the American Woman and Politics (1976, 1982) surveyed men and women in elected offices and found women's views to be more liberal and more feminist than men's on a variety of policy issues. A gender gap emerged on issues like the ratification of the Equal Rights Amendment, how well the private sector could do solving the nation's economic problems, and the death penalty. The election of more women to the state legislature may have significant policy consequences, especially on issues of particular interest to women (such as comparable worth, the rights of divorced women, and domestic violence).

PART 2

Changing Patterns in the Electoral Connection

For most, the legislative career officially begins when the election is won. For years political scientists in the United States have studied the electoral connection to the national legislature, the U.S. Congress. Until recently, however, there was very little written about state legislative elections. Some of the people who have been at the forefront of recent interest in this topic are included as authors in this section.

Largely at the initiative of Malcolm Jewell, state legislative election data are now available for most states. Several of the chapters in this section are based on data made available through the State Legislative Elections project. One of those chapters is "Winning Big: The Incumbency Advantage in State Legislative Races," by David Breaux and Malcolm Jewell. They note that there are some important differences between congressional and state legislative elections (the latter elections generally involve less support from the political parties, require fewer financial resources, and represent smaller, more homogeneous districts), but there are also some growing similarities. First, the chapters by Breaux and Jewell and by Harvey J. Tucker and Ronald E. Weber demonstrate that electoral stability appears to have arrived in state legislatures. Tucker and Weber note that comparative state politics scholars have tended to think in terms of "systemic" (or macrolevel) competition (i.e., the frequency with which partisan control of the state legislature and the governor's office changes). Hidden beneath the notion of systemic competition, however, is that of "district" (or microlevel) competition. Tucker and Weber demonstrate that control of the legislative chambers may be very competitive but that overall district competition is dropping. In other words, there is an increase in the proportion of "safe seats," probably for each party. Control of the chamber then comes down to who wins in the remaining few truly competitive districts. This argument is certainly corroborated by Breaux and Jewell. Breaux and Jewell note that the number of state legislators seeking reelection, and the percentage of those incumbents who win reelection, did not change very much during the time period studied (1968–86). What *did* change was the nature of the incumbents' electoral victories. As the authors demonstrate, the average *margin of victory* has grown in state legislative races, just as it has in congressional elections. This is largely accounted for by a rise in the proportion of uncontested legislative races. The reasons for the apparent increase in uncontested elections is that, like their congressional counterparts, incumbent state legislators increasingly seem to be able to discourage qualified opposition. The advantages of incumbency may not be as great as in a congressional election, but they are nevertheless imposing. As state legislatures professionalize, office perquisites increase (personal staff to perform casework, travel funds to return to the district, an allotment for a district office, etc.). Moreover, incumbents are far more likely to be able to generate campaign contributions, especially from Political Action Committees (PACs), as the cost of financing campaigns escalates. As Anthony Gierzynski and Jewell note in chapter 7, "As the costs of getting elected to the legislature rise, the advantages enjoyed by incumbents over challengers almost inevitably rise. The incumbency advantage of the state legislator, in financial terms, begins to resemble that of the member of Congress."

An interesting countertrend to this development is the growth in the campaign finance arms of the state legislative party. Gierzynski and Jewell look at this recent phenomenon. They relate that by the mid-1980s legislative party campaign committees accounted for more than 20 percent of the total campaign funds in some states (e.g., California and Illinois). While the practice was recently curtailed in California with the passage of an initiative, it is likely to continue to grow in many states. What are the effects of these legislative party campaign committees? Gierzynski and Jewell show that in most cases a greater proportion of these funds are being funneled to *nonincumbents* than to incumbents. They also find that the funds are distributed more strategically than is the case for PAC funds (i.e., the money is more likely to be targeted to close races). The authors also speculate on the future implications of this phenomenon, if it continues to grow.

The chapters thus far focus on the legislative career, and one of the general themes of this book is that as the state legislature professionalizes the state legislator is likely to become more career-oriented. In chapter 6 Breaux and Jewell provide evidence that many state legislatures have reached what appears to be a set point of membership continuity, a figure around 75–80 percent in most states analyzed. We know that most who do leave do so at the end of their terms.

But what about those individuals who exit in midterm? If state legislators are indeed professionalizing and becoming more career-minded, we would not expect many to voluntarily leave in midsession. The final chapter in this section analyzes the extent of, and reasons for, midsession vacancies in state legislatures. Based on a unique data set derived from a questionnaire they sent to house and senate clerks in all fifty states, Keith Hamm and David M. Olson uncover some interesting evidence. On average, only about 3 percent of state legislators exit in midsession in any given year, and 30 percent of those individuals exit involuntarily (i.e., they die, are recalled, or must resign due to criminal proceedings). One of the most important findings by Hamm and Olson is that most of those who leave voluntarily do so because they sought other elective offices or were appointed to other public offices. In other words, when state legislators exit the institution voluntarily, it is usually to further their political careers. As we might expect, this is especially true in the more professionalized state legislatures. As Hamm and Olson observe, "The greatest number of voluntary midsession vacancies occurs in larger chambers and in those in which 'full-time' legislators predominate."

Hamm and Olson provide a useful summary of the legal provisions in each state for filling midsession vacancies. They find that variations exist between the states and that the method used (appointment or special election) is important in the success or failure of these legislators in the subsequent election to retain their new seats.

Elections obviously are a very critical part to the building of the legislative career. We have seen abundant research on many facets of the campaign procedures and electoral mechanisms at work at the congressional level. As state legislative careers become more professional, and as the full array of data from the State Legislative Elections project is disseminated, we will surely see this underresearched area attract greater and greater attention.

CHAPTER 5

Electoral Change in U.S. States:
System Versus Constituency Competition

Harvey J. Tucker
and
Ronald E. Weber

Partisan competition is an important theoretical concept and empirical variable in research on U.S. states. Quantity and quality of competition are key elements of a state's political environment. There are reasons to expect that partisan competition interacts with and affects other elements of a state's political environment, including state policy decisions and political career opportunity structures.

As Patterson and Caldeira note, partisan competition has come to stand for a number of rather different political phenomena:

> In the American context, scholars have commonly assessed competition in terms of closeness of the two major parties: the proportion of close outcomes over a span of elections, the average electoral margins for selected offices, the evenness of party contingents in the legislature, the division of party control between the executive and the legislature, or margins between parties in registration, partisan identification, or participation in primaries. (1984, 692)

With the exception of partisan identification, all of the above have been used to measure partisan competition in the states.

Scholars have long recognized, in principle, the complexity of partisan competition in the states (Weber and Parent 1985). Intraparty competition has been distinguished from interparty competition (Key 1949; Uslaner 1978), competitiveness and control have been identified as separate dimensions (Schlesinger 1955), and closeness of two-party competition has been shown to inhibit party control (Dawson and Robinson 1963). State partisan competition has been shown to vary across the states at any given time and over time for any given state (Gray 1976; Tucker 1982a; Barrilleaux 1986). Partisan competition is different for primary and general elections (Jewell and Olson 1982) and for various elective offices (Bean 1948; Hofferbert 1964; Pfeiffer 1967). We know that partisan competition is a complex, multidimensional phenomenon. Nevertheless, a single approach to partisan competition has dominated the state politics and policy-making literature for nearly thirty years. That approach focuses on the state as a whole and combines measures of the division of legislative seats, the division of the gubernatorial vote, and the division of control over the legislative houses and the governorship. An index developed by Ranney has become the most popular measure of state interparty competition (Ranney and Kendall 1954; Ranney 1965, 1971, 1976; Crittenden 1967; Sharkansky 1968; Cnudde and McCrone 1969; Carmines 1974; LeLoup 1978; Tucker 1982a, 1982b, 1984; Bibby et al. 1983; Patterson and Caldeira 1984; Barrilleaux 1986; Bibby et al. 1990).

In this chapter we explore the differences between the conventional, state (or macrolevel) approach to partisan competition and an alternative, constituency (or microlevel) approach to partisan competition. We are not the first to identify these differences (Ray and Havick 1981; Ray 1982; Tidmarch 1982; Weber and Parent 1985). However, the literature contains no systematic consideration of the conceptual and empirical differences between the two approaches to partisan competition. We demonstrate that macro and microlevel definitions are conceptually distinct and tend to be empirically independent. Microlevel competition is different from macrolevel competition. Yet it is by no means clear whether hypotheses linking differences in partisan competition with other interstate differences require microlevel competition, macrolevel competition, or both.

Partisan Competition: System Versus Constituency Approaches

What we call the macrolevel approach to state partisan competition focuses on the state as a whole. The leading macrolevel measure of partisan competition in state legislatures is the division of legislative seats among the two parties. What we call the microlevel approach focuses on individual election districts and constituencies. The leading microlevel measure of partisan competition in state legislatures is the proportion of legislative districts in which elections are competitive, or marginal.

The two approaches are conceptually distinct. It is possible for a legislature to be perfectly competitive for one and perfectly uncompetitive for the other. For example, there could be an even division of legislative seats (perfect macrolevel competition) with all elections uncontested (no microlevel competition). Conversely, all election contests could be extremely close, and one party could win all contests. As Schlesinger (1966) argues: "under the cover of a competitive statewide situation, it is possible for relations between two parties to vary considerably in the subconstituencies" (p. 133).

Macro and microlevel measures of competition are independent concepts. Are they linked empirically? Several previous studies can shed some light on this question. Schlesinger (1966, 133–35) found, using a standard measure of macrolevel competition, that in two states—Indiana and Michigan—where the parties were very competitive, the parties at the microlevel were competitive in Indiana and uncompetitive in Michigan. Jewell (1982) reports data on microlevel competition for legislative seats during the 1970s in eight states under varying conditions of macrolevel competition. His data suggest that microlevel competition is more prevalent in the macrolevel competitive states (California, Colorado, Indiana, and Ohio) than in the states (Kentucky, North Carolina, Tennessee, and Texas) that are least competitive at the macrolevel (p. 44). On the other hand, Ray and Havick (1981), employing micro and macrolevel level data for eight states between 1958 and 1972, indicate that there is no relationship between micro and macrolevel competition and some evidence that the relationship may be negative. Tidmarch (1982), using data from only the 1978 election year for forty-seven states, reports that there is a strong correlation between macro and microlevel competition for the lower houses of state legislatures. From this limited empirical evidence it is unclear whether macro and microlevel partisan competition are cross-sectionally or longitudinally independent for state legislative elections.

It is noteworthy that the macrolevel approach to partisan competition dominates the study of state legislatures while the microlevel approach is most prevalent in studies of the U.S. Congress. Why is this the case? We suggest that an answer may be found in the different conceptual views of partisan competition that were employed when major conceptual contributions were made in each field. The state politics and policy-making field is dominated by the work (real and imagined) of V. O. Key, Jr. Key's major publications on state parties appeared in the 1940s and 1950s. He studied state parties during a period when the discipline and state politics scholars in particular were concerned with responsible party government and the idea of party cohesion. On the other hand, the contemporary literature on the Congress and congressional elections stresses the decline of party unity and the rise of individualism in congressional election contests and in the behavior of members of Congress.

The macrolevel approach to partisan competition was developed for the study of competition in state legislatures in an era when competition existed at the macrolevel. The microlevel approach dominates the study of partisan competition in Congress in an era in which competition exists at the microlevel. Given increasing evidence that electoral and legislative party cohesion are declining in states, it is reasonable to speculate that the macrolevel approach to competition in state legislatures may be less appropriate now than in the past.

Finally, a case can be made that each approach to partisan competition is more appropriate than the other. The traditional notion that competition makes legislators more likely to keep their promises and the somewhat controversial relationship between competition and welfare policies favoring the disadvantaged is linked to macrolevel competition when parties are cohesive contesters of elections and makers of policy. When party cohesion breaks down, models of microlevel competition may be drawn by analogy from microeconomics (see Downs 1957). Weissberg's (1978) notion of collective representation may bridge the gap between micro and macrolevel approaches. If we stress the policy-making element of the competition-policy model in the state literature, then a case can be made for macrolevel definitions of competition. If we stress the individual constituency level of competition and how competition should breed electoral accountability, then a stronger case can be made for microlevel approaches to competition. These issues did not arise during the responsibility party period of the 1940s and 1950s when Key was developing his ideas and pursuing his state parties research.

Methods and Data

The principal question addressed in this chapter is whether macro and microlevel indicators of state legislative partisan competition are independent empirically. We examine this question using a longitudinal design and correlate indicators of both forms of competition across time within each state selected for this study. In addition to this principal question, we describe the overall degree of partisan competition for state legislative seats in selected states and examine the question of whether or not partisan competition for legislative seats is changing over time.

District-level election returns for lower house legislative elections in eighteen selected states between 1950 and 1986 are employed in totality or in part in this analysis of micro and macrolevel partisan competition. The eighteen states are

California	Colorado
Connecticut	Iowa
Kansas	Massachusetts
Michigan	Missouri
New Jersey	New York
Ohio	Oregon
Pennsylvania	Tennessee
Washington	West Virginia
Wisconsin	Wyoming

These eighteen states were selected on the basis of several criteria. First, the data for the full time period had to be readily available in our files or be easily obtainable from state election officials. Second, the states had to display some variability on previous macrolevel measures of partisan competition but not include states where macrolevel competition is unknown. Such one-party states do not experience much constituency-level competition in general elections; instead, the competition usually occurs in the primary election (see Jewell 1967, 1982; Grau 1981a for discussions of microlevel competition in one-party states). All of these eighteen states except Massachusetts are found in the top three categories of macrolevel competition reported in Patterson and Caldeira (1984). Third, the states had to come from several regions of the country, display some variability in terms of factors like political culture and the socioeconomic environment, and elect their legislators using either single-member districts or a combination of both single-member and multimember districts. In addition to data from these eighteen states, we also employ some data for general elections to the U.S. House of Representatives between 1950 and 1986. These data are used for making some basic comparisons between legislative competition in the state legislatures and in the U.S. Congress.

In this chapter we employ two measures of microlevel partisan competition: (1) the proportion of seats that were marginal in the legislative general election and (2) the proportion of seats that were contested by Democratic and Republican candidates in the legislative general election.

Marginality is a well-known phenomenon in legislative elections in the United States. While most scholars will agree that the marginality of a legislative district is a good measure of microlevel competition, there is widespread disagreement on how to measure marginality. In the state legislative election literature the operational definition varies from one study to another. Ray and Havick (1981), Tidmarch (1982), and Tidmarch, Lonergan, and Sciortino (1986) define as marginal or competitive those seats where the winning candidates poll about 55 percent or less of the major party vote, whereas Jewell (1982) prefers a measure that defines competition as elections where the winners receive 60 percent or less of the major party vote.

More consensus on how to measure marginality is present in the literature on congressional elections. For example, leading studies like those of Mayhew (1974b), Cover and Mayhew (1981), and Gross and Garand (1984) all employ a cutoff of 60 percent of the two-party vote to differentiate between competitive and safe congressional seats. A recent article by Jacobson (1987) on congressional elections calls into question the use of both the 55 and 60 percent definitions of marginality. He indicates that the cut point between safe and marginal congressional seats may need to be expanded upward in light of evidence that a 60 percent win in the previous election does not guarantee that a seat will be retained by the party's candidate in the next election. Since no work comparable to that of Jacobson (1987) has been done on state legislative elections until the recent study by Garand (1991), we decided to employ the cutoff point of 60 percent of the two-party vote to differentiate between competitive and safe legislative seats. Seats where the winning candidates won 60 percent or more of the two-party vote were classified as safe, and those where the winning totals were below 60 percent were classified as competitive.

The procedure for multimember districts was somewhat different. In those situations, we used the same procedure as that employed by Jewell (1982, 193) in his study of legislative elections. In this procedure, the votes for all the candidates running within a multimember constituency are aggregated to achieve a total vote for the constituency. Then each candidate's vote is divided by that total to achieve a percentage that is then multiplied by the number of seats allotted to the constituency. This procedure produces a figure for each candidate that is roughly equivalent to the percentage figures for single-member constituencies. Then the same 60 percent cutoff point was used to determine if the seat was competitive or safe. In these situations, we compared each winner's vote total with the total of the loser who received the greatest number of votes. In the cases where the margin of difference was greater than 20 percent we declared the seat safe, while where the margin of difference was less than 20 percent we determined the seat to be competitive.

Contesting is our second indicator of microlevel partisan competition for state legislatures and is measured as the proportion of seats that both the Democratic and Republican party contested in the legislative general election. Contesting has been a widely used indicator of microlevel competition for state legislative seats. Key (1956), Standing and Robinson (1958), Jewell (1967), Wiggins and Petty (1979), Grau (1981b), Tidmarch (1982), and Tidmarch, Lonergan, and Sciortino (1986) all employ some operationalization of contesting in their studies of state legislative electoral competition. The Tidmarch, Lonergan, and Sciortino (1986) study of general election competition in forty-eight states during the 1970s reports widespread variation across those states in general election contesting, with the least amount of contesting going on in states that are usually classified as one-party or modified one-party on macrolevel indicators of competition and with the greatest amount of contesting occurring in states classified as two-party.

Our indicator of system or macrolevel partisan competition for state legislatures is the one employed by Dye (1966) in his comprehensive study of state politics and policy outcomes. The specific measure is calculated as one minus the percentage of seats in the lower house of the state legislature held by the majority party. Scores on this indicator can range from zero to a maximum of fifty in a case where the two parties are evenly divided in their control of legislative seats.

Findings

Our first concern is with describing the overall degree of micro and macrolevel partisan competition for legislative seats for the eighteen selected states during the 1950–86 time period. This we do by reporting mean levels of competition for the marginality and contesting microlevel indicators and the macrolevel indicator of one minus the percentage of seats held by the majority party (see table 1). The data on marginality reveal that in only seven states— Colorado, Connecticut, Iowa, New Jersey, Oregon, West Virginia, and Wyoming—were more than 50 percent of the lower House seats competitive during the 1950–86 period. The other eleven states have more safe seats than competitive seats, with the proportions of safe seats being the greatest in Massachusetts and Tennessee—two states that generally are classified as modified one-party on leading indicators of overall systemwide partisan competition. Bibby et al. (1983) classify these two states in their middle category of systemwide competition, while Patterson and Caldeira (1984) report that Massachusetts is low on their measure of systemwide competition and that Tennessee is leaning toward two-party competition. For purposes of comparison, the average proportion of competitive or marginal seats in the U.S.

TABLE 1. Average Level of Constituency and System-Level Partisan Competition for the Lower House in Eighteen Selected State Legislatures, 1950–86

State	Percentage of Marginal Seats	Percentage of Contested Seats	Percentage of System Competition
California	32.1	86.1	40.0
Colorado	55.2	83.3	39.0
Connecticut	50.3	96.0	35.5
Iowa	56.4	87.7	32.3
Kansas	42.7	72.3	35.4
Massachusetts	26.5	67.6	32.4
Michigan	32.1	89.8	43.0
Missouri	32.9	68.6	34.5
New Jersey	55.2	99.7	36.4
New York	30.7	97.9	41.1
Ohio	43.3	91.0	37.5
Oregon	52.8	90.7	41.2
Pennsylvania	43.8	94.1	46.5
Tennessee	21.6	44.7	32.3
Washington	48.1	90.5	42.9
West Virginia	50.5	83.2	25.2
Wisconsin	38.6	88.4	39.6
Wyoming	56.6	82.4	36.6

House of Representatives was 35.5 percent for the 1950–86 period. The average levels of contesting in legislative general elections are strong in most of the eighteen states, with only the states of Kansas, Massachusetts, Missouri, and Tennessee showing levels of contesting below 75 percent. Even in the absence of competitive district circumstances, most of the districts in these states except for Tennessee will find minority party candidates contesting the lower house election races.

The data on average levels of system-level, or macrolevel, partisan competition for state legislative seats in these eighteen states indicate that competition between the two parties for lower House control was close in only six states—California, Michigan, New York, Oregon, Pennsylvania, and Washington—where the systemwide measures are 40 percent or higher. In only one of these states—Oregon—were more than 50 percent of the seats considered competitive at the microlevel based on the marginality indicator. The remaining twelve states have system-level competition scores that suggest that on the average the majority party has had solid control of the lower house and that even in some cases it was in a position to have the two-thirds level of support frequently necessary to override gubernatorial vetoes when the other party controlled the governorship. For comparison purposes, the average level of macrolevel competition for U.S. House seats was 40.8 percent for the same time period. Finally, five of the seven states that had a majority of legislative seats competitive on the marginality indicator are found among the ten with the lowest levels of macrolevel competition. This seems to suggest that in a cross-sectional comparison there is an inverse relationship between micro and macrolevel legislative seat competition for these eighteen states, a finding that is consistent with the previous findings of Ray and Havick (1981).

Now that we have presented data on the overall levels of micro and macrolevel competition for state legislative seats in our eighteen selected states, we turn to an examination of the question of whether or not partisan competition for lower house seats is changing over time. Here we are interested in the vanishing marginals hypothesis that has been the subject of much study by congressional election scholars. In order to determine if partisan competition for legislative seats is increasing, remaining stable over time, or decreasing, we correlated the three indicators of partisan competition with the dates of the elections. If competitiveness at either the micro or macrolevel were increasing with time, we would expect the correlation coefficients to be positive. On the other hand, if competitiveness is decreasing, we would expect the correlation coefficients to be negative. If competitiveness is stable, we would expect the correlation coefficients to be small in magnitude irrespective of direction.

The results of this analysis are reported in table 2. All but one of the correlation coefficients for the marginal seats indicator are negative, indicating that competitiveness in terms of marginality is decreasing. The relationship is strongly negative in eight states—Colorado, Massachusetts, Michigan, Missouri, Ohio, Oregon, Pennsylvania, and Washington. In no state except Tennessee is competitiveness in terms of marginality on the increase over the 3 1/2 decades of the 1950s, 1960s, 1970s, and 1980s. The data in table 2 also suggest that contesting appears to be on the decrease in most of the eighteen selected states. The proportion of general election contests has been declining particularly in Colorado, Connecticut, Massachusetts, Missouri, New York, Pennsylvania, Washington, and Wyoming and to a lesser extent in Iowa, Oregon, and Wisconsin. Only in California and Tennessee has contesting been on the increase, and the California finding is largely a consequence of California's decision to ban cross-filing in both party primaries during the middle 1950s. General election contesting jumped dramatically in California with the abandonment of the cross-filing system. Across these eighteen states the picture is one of decreasing microlevel competition for state legislative seats, with marginal districts vanishing in eight of them.

The pattern of change for system-level partisan competition is less clear, with there being more evidence for increasing than decreasing competition.

TABLE 2. Simple Correlation of Indicators of Constituency and System-Level Partisan Competition for the Lower House in Eighteen Selected State Legislatures with Time, 1950–86

State	Percentage of Marginal Seats	Percentage of Contested Seats	Percentage of System Competition
California	−.292	.638**	−.048
Colorado	−.890**	−.806**	.150
Connecticut	−.354	−.633**	.420*
Iowa	−.483*	−.431*	.743**
Kansas	−.494*	−.247	.732**
Massachusetts	−.963**	−.906**	−.977**
Michigan	−.671**	.084	.059
Missouri	−.884**	−.632**	−.568*
New Jersey	−.388*	−.345	.381*
New York	−.462*	−.723**	.044
Ohio	−.913**	.038	.529*
Oregon	−.793**	−.399*	.392*
Pennsylvania	−.942**	−.762**	.371
Tennessee	.206	.469*	.735**
Washington	−.663**	−.191	−.042
West Virginia	−.536*	−.698**	−.212
Wisconsin	−.461*	−.464*	.411*
Wyoming	−.428*	−.600**	−.010

*Significant at the .05 level.   **Significant at the .01 level.

Only in Massachusetts and Missouri does macrolevel competition show a strong decrease over time, while in Iowa, Kansas, and Tennessee the trend is toward increasing macrolevel competition. At the same time that microlevel partisan competition appears to be decreasing in some states, macrolevel competition is increasing. This suggests that micro and macrolevel competition for lower house legislative seats may be empirically independent in a number of these selected states.

Finally we turn to the analysis of the question of whether or not over time in each state the micro and macrolevel indicators of general partisan competition for state legislative seats are empirically independent of each other. This question is examined by correlating the two microlevel indicators with the macrolevel measure of competition. In addition we report the interrelationship between the two microlevel indicators of competition to see the extent to which marginality and contesting are empirically similar. The results for these analyses are reported in table 3.

Marginality of seats is statistically independent of system-level competition over time in eleven of the eighteen states. In only Connecticut, Massachusetts, Missouri, Pennsylvania, Tennessee, West Virginia, and Wyoming are there statistically significant relationships between the proportion of lower

TABLE 3.   Simple Correlation among Three Indicators of Constituency and System-Level Partisan Competition for the Lower House in Eighteen Selected State Legislatures, 1950–86

State	Marginal Seats with System-Level Competition	Contested Seats with System-Level Competition	Marginal Seats with Contested Seats
California	.112	.157	.389*
Colorado	.035	.121	.858**
Connecticut	.469*	−.234	.535*
Iowa	.001	−.032	.749**
Kansas	.067	.211	.851**
Massachusetts	.926**	.925**	.864**
Michigan	.140	−.175	−.051
Missouri	.572*	.212	.814**
New Jersey	.083	−.282	.408*
New York	.371	.201	.649**
Ohio	−.358	.149	.235
Oregon	−.085	.010	.584*
Pennsylvania	−.412*	−.315	.825**
Tennessee	.628**	.822**	.827**
Washington	.149	.047	.646**
West Virginia	.718**	.390*	.604**
Wisconsin	.222	−.052	.613**
Wyoming	.342	.266	.269*

*Significant at the .05 level.   **Significant at the .01 level.

house seats that were marginal and the level of macrolevel competition for those seats. In five of these six states the relationships are positive (i.e., the higher the proportion of marginal seats, the higher the level of system-level competition for lower house legislative seats). Only in Pennsylvania is the relationship negative (i.e., the higher the proportion of marginal seats, the lower the level of system-level competition for lower House legislative seats). For comparison purposes, micro and macrolevel competition for U.S. House seats is also independent for the same time period, with the correlation being −.079. Contesting for seats is also statistically independent of system-level competition in fifteen of the eighteen states, with only Massachusetts, Tennessee, and West Virginia showing significant statistical relationships between the micro and macrolevel indicators of competition. Lastly, it can be inferred from table 3 that marginality and contesting are statistically independent indicators of microlevel competition in only three of the selected states. Depending on the state being studied, marginality and contesting may be good alternative indicators of constituency-level competition.

The results presented in table 3 clearly indicate that using a system-level, or macrolevel, indicator to describe the degree of partisan competition for lower house legislative seats is a flawed approach. By only employing the macrolevel approach to measure state legislative partisan competition, state politics and policy-making scholars end up with an incomplete understanding of competition in the states. To fully understand legislative partisan competition one should use both the macro and microlevel approaches. Marginality and contesting can be measured employing state legislative election returns as has already been demonstrated by Tidmarch, Lonergan, and Sciortino (1986) with data from forty-eight of the fifty states. To create average indicators for use in cross-sectional research, the data are now available for every state legislative chamber except Vermont from about 1968 onward.

Conclusion

We demonstrate, employing data from eighteen selected states, that system and constituency-based indicators of general election partisan competition for lower house legislative seats are for the most part statistically independent. Furthermore, we show that the levels of microlevel competition vary across states that are usually classified as two-party competitive in leading studies of system-level competition in the states. Finally, we present evidence that microlevel competition is declining over time in most of the eighteen states included in the study. Just as there is evidence that marginal congressional districts are vanishing, we find that a similar phenomenon is occurring in the states for lower house legislative districts.

Our work should be of particular interest to those scholars who employ party competition in cross-sectional or longitudinal studies of state policy-making. These studies often hypothesize that partisan competition will lead to certain policy consequences or facilitate a linkage between constituents and the policy-makers. Since these studies typically rely only on party competition indicators developed under the macrolevel approach, their findings about the impact of party competition upon policy-making are bound to be incomplete. In a political environment where state legislators as particular actors in the state policy process are district-oriented, competition at the macrolevel of the legislative chamber may be largely irrelevant. What really counts is whether or not the constituency is electorally secure for the incumbent or the incumbent's party when the seat becomes vacant. Our data suggest rather clearly that the macrolevel approach to partisan competition tells us very little about what is going on electorally in the constituencies. Both macro and microlevel competition for state legislative seats may have policy consequences, but the nature of those consequences may differ depending on what type of partisan competition is present.

This study should also be of some interest to election scholars. Although we present evidence on how microlevel competition varies for these selected states and on how constituency-level competition for state lower house legislative seats appears to be on the decline during the 1950s, 1960s, 1970s, and early 1980s, we make no attempt to account for the occurrence of these phenomena. To what extent do other microlevel factors such as incumbency and campaign financing help explain the variation in and the decline of microlevel competition? And is the level of microlevel competition impacted by macrolevel factors like the timing of legislative elections and legislative redistricting? A good data base of microlevel information on state legislative districts and elections should enable election scholars to further examine these and similar questions.

Finally, our study should be of interest to students of political careerism in state legislatures. Our evidence of declining microlevel competition for lower house legislative offices suggests that turnover in state legislative seats due to electoral defeat should also be declining with the result that the average length of legislative careers is probably increasing. This should be particularly true in the states where we found sharp decreases in electoral competition at the constituency level during the almost forty-year time span of this study. When we link our findings with those of David Breaux and Malcolm Jewell (chap. 6) on the impact of incumbency in state legislative elections and those of Weber, Tucker, and Brace (1991) on the influence of institutional resources on state legislative electoral competition, it is clear that the political opportunity structures for state legislative office have also been declining. Political careers in the state legislature are now likely to be longer on the average and aspiring young politicos must wait longer to have the opportunity to run for open state legislative seats.

CHAPTER 6

Winning Big: The Incumbency Advantage in State Legislative Races

David Breaux
and
Malcolm Jewell

It is widely agreed that U.S. state legislatures have become more professional in the last thirty years and that in many respects the gaps between the most and the least professional legislatures have narrowed. Professionalism is defined in a number of ways, including definitions based on length of sessions, adequacy of staffing, and salaries. But its definition usually includes changes in two characteristics of individual members: the proportion of those who devote all or most of their time to their legislative jobs and the proportion who serve long-term careers in the legislature.

The stereotype of the amateur legislator is one who enters the legislature with no intention of making a career of it and retires from the legislature, or perhaps is defeated, after two or three terms. The stereotype of the career legislator is one who enters the legislature—often relatively early in life— with the intention of serving a long term, who continues to win at the polls, and who serves many terms in the legislature. When career legislators decide to leave after only a few terms, we would expect them (more often than amateurs) to seek higher elective offices.

Data on turnover show that there has been a steady decline in turnover and thus an increase in the proportion of members returning to the legislature from the 1930s to the present. The proportion of members returning to the lower house, averaged for all states, has grown from 41 percent in the 1930s to 55 percent in the 1950s to 72 percent in the first three elections of the 1980s. (A similar change has occurred in state senates.) Most of this increased stability has occurred in the states that had the highest turnover in the early decades.

In order to understand what changes have been occurring in legislative

Much of the research found in this chapter previously appeared in Jewell and Breaux 1988.

career patterns, we need to know more than turnover rates. We would like to have data on the average length of service for members; it would be even better to know how many terms each member had served when he or she left the legislature. Such data have not been collected longitudinally for the fifty states.

We would also like to know the conditions under which members leave the legislature, whether or not these conditions have changed over time, and whether or not they vary among the states. Except for members who die in office, there are four major reasons for leaving office. Members may retire because of age or poor health; they may leave in order to return—or devote all their time—to other careers; they may run, successfully or not, for other elective offices; or they may be defeated in primaries or general elections. If members are becoming more career-oriented, a smaller proportion of those who leave voluntarily should be doing so to pursue nonpolitical careers and a larger proportion should be running for political offices. In other words, a growing number of members may be oriented to careers in politics but not necessarily careers in the legislature. Finally, we would expect a declining proportion of members to be defeated for renomination or reelection. As members serve longer terms (and as they gain more staff help and more visibility in the districts), they should be less vulnerable to defeat at the polls.

No comprehensive, long-term data are available on legislators who retire because of age or illness, who change careers, or who seek other elective offices. We do have data over a twenty-year period (1968–86) on the proportion of members who seek reelection and of those who win, as well as on their margins of victory. In this chapter we make use of those data for eighteen states, selected because they employed single-member districts during all or most of the twenty-year period. (Data are included only for the years in which all legislators were elected in single-member district elections.)

A study of elections is important to studying legislative careers for several reasons. The larger the number of members who can get reelected, and the larger their margins, the greater will be the opportunities for members to have long tenures in the legislature. Moreover, we would expect that, as members serve longer terms, they would gain the experience and develop the political bases that would make them less vulnerable to defeat. In other words, we would expect legislative incumbents to gain many of the advantages that have been enjoyed by congressional incumbents in recent years.

Longitudinal analyses of congressional elections document that, since the mid-1960s, incumbents have sought reelection at higher rates and the electoral benefits derived from incumbency have increased (Erikson 1971; Tufte 1973; Mayhew 1974b; Burnham 1975; Nelson 1978–79; Ferejohn 1977; Cover 1977; Born 1979; Parker 1980; Alford and Hibbing 1981). In other words, not only have congressional incumbents been running for and winning reelection more frequently but they have been winning by larger margins of victory as well. Furthermore, the increasing margins of victory enjoyed by incumbents have often been linked to the decreasing rate of electoral turnover in Congress. Thus, decreasing turnover is seen as a function of district marginality, which in turn is a function of incumbency.

During the last decade we have learned much from voting survey data about the advantage enjoyed by congressional incumbents. The increased visibility of members of Congress, through constituency service, polling, advertising, and credit claiming, have been found to afford them an overwhelming advantage over challengers in the amount of information that voters possess about the candidates. Constituents know much more about incumbents and tend to view them in a favorable light, particularly incumbents' roles in the constituencies. Large numbers of voters cross party lines in order to vote for incumbents (Hinckley 1981; Jacobson 1983; Jacobson and Kernell 1983).

Not all of the questions about the incumbency advantage have been answered, of course. Long-term data on congressional elections raise some doubts about the recent surge in incumbents' success (Garand and Gross 1984). And the relationship between increased margins of victory and the decline in electoral turnover has been seriously questioned (Collie 1981; Jacobson 1987).

Despite some obvious similarities between state legislative and congressional incumbents, we believe that state legislative elections differ in certain important respects from congressional elections. Most legislators campaign on their own with little support from their party organizations. Most legislators do not have the resources necessary for frequent communications with their constituents. Although incumbents probably enjoy an advantage over challengers in raising money, the relatively low cost of most legislative campaigns reduces the importance of this advantage. In the absence of survey data at the state level, we cannot tell whether or not state legislators enjoy advantages over challengers in name recognition, visibility, and contact that are comparable to those enjoyed by members of Congress.

One other important difference is that almost all legislative districts are smaller and more homogeneous than congressional districts. As a consequence, it appears likely (though systematic data are lacking) that a larger proportion of state legislative districts are safely controlled by one party. This has great significance for our study of incumbency advantages in legislative elections.

If we find that more incumbents are running for reelection or that they are winning by bigger margins in some states than in others, this may mean that incumbency has greater political advantages in some states, or it may mean that some states have a larger proportion of districts dominated by one party. If in some states there are greater increases in the rate of incumbency reelection and/or the winning margins of incumbents, it may mean that in these states the incumbency advantage is growing faster or that there has been a decrease in the proportion of seats that are marginal in terms of party allegiance. In our analysis, we make an effort to separate out the effects of incumbency from such partisan factors.

Data Sources

Until recently it has been impossible to carry out comprehensive, systematic analyses of state legislative elections because data have not been available in a computer-readable form. The State Legislative Elections project of the Inter-university Consortium for Political and Social Research (ICPSR) is designed to solve that problem by collecting and compiling computer files on legislative elections in the fifty states for the period beginning in 1968.

The analysis in this chapter is based on data for the upper and lower chambers in eighteen states for the 1968–86 elections. This includes fifteen states that used single-member districts in both chambers throughout the period and three other states that used single-member districts except for the first one or two elections in this time period. Tennessee and Oregon began using single-member districts in both chambers in 1972. Kansas used single-member districts in the lower chamber from the beginning of the period but only since 1972 in the upper chamber. (Oklahoma, which used single-member districts throughout the period, is omitted because the election returns did not include uncontested elections.) By analyzing returns only from single-member districts, we can control for the effects that varied patterns of districting might have on the impact of incumbency.

More specifically, this chapter is based on the candidate-constituency files in the data set. These files provide information on each candidate, including incumbency status, party membership, and the votes cast for that candidate; they also provide data on the district race, such as the total vote, votes for other candidates, and incumbency status of other candidates.

Before moving to the analysis, we must note that the data set provides information on general elections only. It does not provide information on primary elections. This shortcoming in the data is not neutral; it holds important implications for the analysis. For example, when the percentage of incumbents running for reelection is reported, it is actually the percentage who survived the primary and then ran in the general election. The same holds true for the percentage of incumbents winning reelection: it is actually the incumbents who won in the primary and were successful in the general election. In general, the absence of primary data should have a relatively negligible effect on the ensuing analysis, missing those few incumbents beaten in the

primary. However, for the three border or southern states in the analysis—
Missouri, Kentucky, and Tennessee—the implications may be less benign.
For in these states competition is likely to be stiffest in the primary rather than
in the general election. Therefore, for Missouri, Kentucky, and Tennessee the
analysis may mask the true level of incumbency success.

Findings

Have state legislators been running for and winning reelection with greater
frequency and by larger margins of the vote over the last twenty years? Trends
in the electoral success of legislators are addressed in the following analysis.

Incumbents Seeking and Winning Reelection

Has there been an increase, over the last twenty years, in the tendency for
state legislators to seek reelection? An answer to this question requires one to
track changes over time in the proportion of legislators seeking reelection.
This was accomplished for each chamber by dividing the number of legislators seeking reelection, in each election cycle, by the total number of legislators in the chamber. If there has been an increase in the tendency for state
legislators to seek reelection, the quotient obtained from the computation
should increase over the time period. (Since there are fewer senate elections
because of the relative size of the chambers and because in most states senate
elections are staggered, this and other parts of the analysis will give greater
weight to trends in the state houses.)

In the first two columns of table 1 the percentage of legislators seeking
reelection is reported for each of two time periods, 1968–76 and 1978–86.
The data suggest that in most states there has not been an increase in the

**TABLE 1. Percentage of Incumbents Running for and Winning
Reelection, 1968–86**

State Legislature	Running		Winning	
	1968–76	1978–86	1968–76	1978–86
Connecticut				
Senate	76	82	81	78
House	71	80	82	87
Rhode Island				
Senate	76	74	95	93
House	75	78	92	96

Continued on next page

Table 1—*Continued*

State Legislature	Running 1968–76	Running 1978–86	Winning 1968–76	Winning 1978–86
Delaware				
Senate	73	84	92	94
House	62	83	93	89
New York				
Senate	82	88	97	98
House	79	85	90	95
Pennsylvania				
Senate	79	74	89	94
House	81	84	93	97
Michigan				
Senate	74	64	89	99
House	82	79	96	95
Ohio				
Senate	73	81	82	83
House	81	83	94	96
Wisconsin				
Senate	67	75	87	92
House	81	82	90	93
Iowa				
Senate	66	69	77	89
House	67	79	89	92
Kansas				
Senate	74	84	84	86
House	78	82	93	95
Missouri				
Senate	67	84	89	99
House	69	84	93	98
Kentucky				
Senate	55	70	79	96
House	67	80	92	96
Tennessee				
Senate	70	58	95	95
House	69	77	90	98
Colorado				
Senate	60	57	87	96
House	70	70	91	89
New Mexico				
Senate	69	65	88	90
House	77	79	91	94
Utah				
Senate	70	74	90	81
House	73	72	85	84
Oregon				
Senate	73	69	79	88
House	75	73	83	94
California				
Senate	86	81	93	93
House	84	81	95	97

tendency for legislators to run for reelection over the last twenty years. Rather, many of the states began the period with such a relatively high proportion of legislators running for reelection that there was virtually no room for any increase over time. For example, ten of the eighteen states in 1968 (or in the first year of the time period) had at least one chamber in which at least 80 percent of its members sought reelection, and in two of them the entire membership ran for reelection.

The lowest percentages of incumbents running for reelection in the first half of the time period are found in the Delaware, Iowa, Kentucky, Missouri, Tennessee, and Colorado legislatures. During the second time period the percentages of incumbents seeking reelection increased in all of these states except Colorado. Moreover, changes in the data for Kentucky, Missouri, and Tennessee might appear greater if primary elections were considered. However, as mentioned before, incumbents defeated in primaries are not coded as seeking reelection within the data.

The lack of a longitudinal trend in the data was confirmed by a regression of the proportion of legislators seeking reelection in the election year, run separately on each state. The analyses failed to yield any statistically significant slope coefficients (i.e., .05). Moreover, the signs of the coefficients varied across the states, some indicating a slight increase in the proportion of legislators running for reelection, others indicating a marginal decrease over time. Therefore, for the states and time periods employed in this analysis, the claim that there has been an increase in the tendency for state legislators to seek reelection over the last twenty years must be considered a tenuous one at best.

Running for reelection with greater frequency, however, is only a prerequisite for reelectoral success. Has the tendency for state legislators to win reelection increased in the last twenty years? To answer this question, the success rate of legislative incumbents was traced over time. This was accomplished for each chamber by dividing the number of legislators winning reelection, in each election cycle, by the total number of legislators running for reelection. An increase over time in the quotient obtained from the calculation would signal an increase in the tendency for legislators to win reelection. The percentage of incumbents who ran and won reelection over the two time periods is shown in the third and fourth columns of table 1.

The most striking feature of the figures on reelection is their stability over time. The percentage of legislators able to win reelection, in most states, in 1986 is approximately equivalent to the percentage who were able to do so twenty years earlier. Once again, the lack of a trend in the data may be due, in large part, to the extremely high success rates enjoyed by legislators, in most of the states, at the beginning of the period. Fourteen of the eighteen states at the start of the time period, for example, had at least one chamber in which the success rate was 90 percent or better, and five of the chambers began the period with a 100 percent success rate. With such extraordinarily high success rates at the beginning of the period, virtually no room for improvement existed. Once again, a regression of the proportion of legislators winning reelection in the election year for each state confirmed the lack of any statistically significant trend over time in the data.

If the proportion of incumbents winning has remained quite stable over twenty years and the proportion running has increased in only a few states during this time period, would we find greater changes over a longer period of time? Although we lack earlier data on incumbents running and winning, we do have data on turnover rates in each state for earlier periods. Shown in table 2 is the proportion of members of the lower house who returned to the house for each of four time periods from the 1950 through the 1986 elections. Data for the 1950–68 periods come from the analysis of Shin and Jackson (1979); data for the 1968–86 periods are calculated by multiplying the percentage of incumbents running by the percentage winning. (There is an overlap for the 1968 election.) Only the lower house is included because the use of staggered terms in many senates makes precise comparisons difficult.

It is possible to determine from table 2 how much change there has been

TABLE 2.   Percentage of Continuity of Membership in Lower House of State Legislature, 1950–86 Elections

State	1950–58	1960–68	1968–76	1978–86
Connecticut	51	58	58	70
Rhode Island	71	67	69	75
Delaware	29	47	58	74
New York	79	72	71	80
Pennsylvania	70	71	75	81
Michigan	74	71	79	75
Ohio	65	65	76	80
Wisconsin	67	69	73	76
Iowa	57	49	60	73
Kansas	61	60	73	78
Missouri	62	66	64	82
Kentucky	39	49	62	77
Tennessee	34	45	62	75
Colorado	52	54	64	62
New Mexico	34	53	70	74
Utah	45	46	62	60
Oregon	50	66	62	69
California	75	75	80	79

Source: Data for the 1950–58 and 1960–68 periods were taken from Shin and Jackson 1979, 95–104.

in continuity of membership over almost four decades and in which time periods increases occurred. It is not possible to tell, during the first twenty years, how much of the change resulted from greater electoral success and how much from decreased voluntary retirement. But because electoral success rates are so stable in the last twenty years, we believe that most of the change in continuity in the first twenty years is due to decreased voluntary turnover.

There are five states in which a high proportion of legislators were retained throughout the four decades: Rhode Island, New York, Pennsylvania, Michigan, and California. In each of these the retention rate was at least 70 percent in the 1950s.

There has been a noticeable increase in retention in each of the other fourteen states. Wisconsin has had a modest, gradual increase throughout the period. The increase in Oregon occurred after the 1950s. In Connecticut there was an increase in the 1960s and another in the last period. The retention rate was substantially higher in the 1970s and 1980s than in the earlier period in Ohio, Iowa, Kansas, and Utah. In Colorado there was a modest increase starting in the 1970s, but the retention rate remained comparatively low. A substantial increase in Missouri did not occur until the last time period.

The most dramatic examples of increases in legislators' retention are found in four states: Delaware, Kentucky, Tennessee, and New Mexico. In each the retention rate climbed from less than 40 percent to at least 74 percent over the four decades. In three of the four there was a substantial increase in retention in each time period; in New Mexico the rate leveled off during the last period. In these states during the last twenty years the increase has resulted almost exclusively from less retirement—except in Tennessee where there has also been a growth in reelection rates.

The Margin of Victory

Have legislators been able to increase their margins of victory over the last twenty years? To answer this question, the average winning incumbent vote, in each chamber for each election cycle, was calculated. The average winning votes for legislators over the time period are presented in table 3. (Note that New York is excluded from the remainder of the analysis because the candidates in that state are permitted to run on more than one party's ticket in a given election.)

Though we found little evidence of a trend in running for or winning reelection over twenty years, a clear trend in the size of electoral margins over the same period can be inferred from the figures in table 3. The average winning votes for legislative incumbents, in most states, in 1986 were greater than their average winning votes twenty years earlier.

Furthermore, the increases over time in the average winning incumbent

TABLE 3. Percentage of Votes for Winning Incumbents, 1968–86

State Legislature	1968	1970	1972	1974	1976	1978	1980	1982	1984	1986
Connecticut										
Senate	60.1	59.2	59.9	64.0	59.9	64.4	59.6	61.5	63.4	68.8
House	62.0	62.1	62.1	66.3	62.9	65.1	67.9	66.4	63.4	71.6
Rhode Island										
Senate	64.7	65.4	65.0	78.8	75.1	83.2	74.9	68.9	72.8	72.8
House	64.7	65.3	66.8	77.9	76.5	83.2	79.7	83.5	76.2	77.4
Delaware										
Senate	63.5	66.6	66.5	73.0	60.9	73.8	74.0	75.2	80.2	85.6
House	62.1	60.8	64.1	68.8	70.0	72.9	75.7	78.3	80.7	81.4
Pennsylvania										
Senate	63.9	60.8	65.9	65.6	64.4	62.2	69.2	70.7	74.4	78.8
House	63.8	62.8	65.4	66.0	68.5	67.7	73.1	72.4	74.9	81.1
Michigan[a]										
Senate	—	67.2	—	70.1	—	75.3	—	72.6	—	70.3
House	68.5	70.1	70.3	72.5	70.5	75.0	74.8	75.7	70.0	73.1
Ohio										
Senate	69.4	63.4	65.3	68.2	60.7	71.7	65.2	63.9	63.0	72.6
House	71.2	66.3	66.7	68.2	69.2	68.3	72.9	66.6	69.0	71.6
Wisconsin										
Senate	72.3	60.9	61.7	72.0	67.3	72.0	73.8	68.5	70.0	68.3
House	66.8	65.9	67.9	72.0	70.9	72.8	74.6	70.1	71.0	74.2
Iowa										
Senate	67.3	59.9	61.2	64.2	65.3	66.9	63.0	65.9	76.7	85.2
House	65.3	62.5	63.0	65.3	65.0	73.7	65.8	70.2	72.9	77.0
Kansas										
Senate	—	—	69.2	—	78.1	—	70.8	—	71.1	—
House	67.0	76.1	75.2	75.4	76.8	73.7	80.7	78.5	80.0	83.8
Missouri										
Senate	74.2	68.4	88.0	87.0	78.8	71.6	78.9	74.9	86.6	81.9
House	67.0	75.3	73.9	81.5	85.0	77.9	83.7	84.4	89.7	84.9
Kentucky[b]										
Senate	80.7	80.3	85.2	80.8	88.0	83.4	84.3	85.2	—	90.4
House	76.7	80.4	85.1	82.5	84.7	86.4	85.2	—	83.8	88.4
Tennessee										
Senate	—	—	86.2	84.3	80.0	87.5	69.0	89.1	91.5	84.3
House	—	—	78.9	83.2	87.4	84.5	80.4	91.1	88.4	89.0
Colorado										
Senate	68.6	69.5	69.3	64.7	70.3	86.2	73.0	91.0	83.8	81.2
House	66.9	68.2	67.3	68.7	70.4	75.7	75.5	74.7	81.0	78.1
New Mexico										
Senate	—	71.4	75.3	69.0	80.5	73.1	82.7	—	75.1	—
House	64.4	72.3	73.3	75.1	79.2	80.7	77.8	77.0	79.7	80.5
Utah										
Senate	70.3	63.8	67.6	65.3	68.0	71.1	77.0	67.5	77.0	78.6
House	62.6	67.8	69.1	63.6	65.4	69.3	66.7	73.6	74.2	70.5

Table 3—*Continued*

State Legislature	1968	1970	1972	1974	1976	1978	1980	1982	1984	1986
Oregon										
Senate	—	—	64.8	65.3	75.4	71.8	80.2	58.0	66.5	64.8
House	—	—	62.0	66.4	68.2	70.1	70.6	66.4	70.1	66.3
California										
Senate	67.2	65.8	66.4	69.4	65.5	67.4	68.4	70.6	70.4	69.2
House	66.0	66.7	68.3	64.8	67.7	68.8	68.6	71.9	72.0	70.7

ᵃTerms of office for the Michigan Senate, unlike those of all the other states, are four years rather than two.
ᵇDue to the fact that Kentucky scheduled legislative elections in odd years until 1984, the figures for 1968 to 1982 are in fact for elections held from 1969 to 1983.

votes appear to be greater within the less-professionalized states. Compare, for example, the increase in the average incumbent winning vote in a less professionalized state such as Delaware to that in a state such as California. The average winning vote in the Delaware House increased from 62.1 percent in 1968 to 81.4 percent in 1986, while the average winning vote in the California Assembly increased from 66 percent to 70.7 percent over the time period. Evidence of a more dramatic increase among the less professionalized states is expected due to their greater potential for change. It would appear, therefore, that legislators in these states have been able to increase their margins of victory over the last twenty years in much the same way congressional incumbents have. (In two less-professionalized border states, Kentucky and Tennessee, the increases in margins were relatively modest, presumably because most seats have been consistently safe; at the start of the time period, the incumbents' margins were higher in these states than in any others.)

There would appear to be two potential explanations for the observed increase in the average winning votes of incumbent legislators. On one hand, the trend could reflect an increase in the number of electorally safe districts over the time period. Such an increase could have perhaps resulted from bipartisan gerrymandering. Alternatively, it could reflect the growing electoral strength of incumbents. If the increase in the average winning votes for incumbent legislators is due to the growth in the number of electorally safe districts, the connection between incumbency and greater electoral safety may simply be spurious. Therefore, it is extremely important to distinguish between these two competing explanations.

In order to distinguish between these two explanations for growing electoral margins, the average votes of winning incumbents are compared to the average winning votes in open seat contests. If the increase in average winning margins is due to an increase in the number of electorally safe districts, then the same trend over time should be found in contests for open seats, as well as in those involving incumbents. In other words, not only incumbents but all winners should have been able to benefit from an increase in the number of electorally safe districts. The average winning votes in open seat contests are presented in table 4.

When the average winning votes in open seat contests are traced over the last twenty years, any evidence of a trend over time simply disappears. Although the number of open seat contests in some states is extremely small, making trends more difficult to witness, the average winning votes in contests for open seats in 1986 appear to be approximately equal to the average winning votes in similar contests twenty years earlier. Since the average winning votes only appear to increase when incumbents are involved, the trend over time may be attributed to the growing electoral strength of legislative incumbents, rather than an increase in the number of electorally safe districts.

In order to arrive at a more empirically precise answer to the question, a regression analysis of the average winning votes for each state was undertaken. The analysis was run with two separate dependent variables, first using the average votes for winning incumbents and again using the average votes for winners in open seat contests. The results are presented in table 5.

Note that the signs for all of the slope coefficients for the equations including the average votes for winning incumbents are positive. This confirms an increase over time in legislators' winning margins. In addition, the difference in the magnitude of the trend between more and less professionalized states is demonstrated by the differences in the size of their slope coefficients. Once again, consider the difference in the magnitude of the increase in Delaware as compared to that in California. The slope coefficient for Delaware is 1.15, while for California it is .27. Clearly the trend toward a greater average winning incumbent vote was of greater magnitude in the less-professionalized state legislature. There are a few states where this generalization does not hold up. Pennsylvania, which is quite professionalized, has a slope coefficient of .84; Oregon, much less professionalized, has a slope coefficient of only .02. The modest slope coefficients in Kentucky (.46) and in Tennessee (.4) can be explained by the large percentage of safe seats throughout the time period.

The independent impact of incumbency is once again substantiated by the failure of the analysis of the average winning votes for winners in open seat contests to produce any statistically significant findings, with the exception of Kansas. All of the other states failed to demonstrate any significant increase over time in the average winning votes in open seat contests.

As political scientists began to more closely examine the incumbency advantage within the context of congressional elections, it became clear that the growing strength of incumbents was due, in part, to a growing lack of competition. Congressional incumbents have become adept at discouraging "competitive" challengers, leaving incumbents uncontested or opposed by

TABLE 4. Percentage of Votes in Open Seat Contests, 1968–86

State Legislature	1968	1970	1972	1974	1976	1978	1980	1982	1984	1986
Connecticut
Senate	59.3	59.2	59.5	61.1	58.1	59.0	64.7	63.2	57.7	58.1
House	61.9	60.3	60.6	60.8	61.8	61.4	61.9	62.0	61.0	61.0
Rhode Island
Senate	68.4	61.6	57.2	71.2	75.7	76.7	69.4	58.6	66.1	69.0
House	63.5	61.3	60.8	70.8	70.2	84.8	71.5	65.1	77.6	72.2
Delaware
Senate	61.8	—	63.4	78.2	66.4	63.4	68.6	66.3	51.3	50.4
House	60.2	60.1	59.4	69.5	64.5	67.5	60.8	58.6	74.6	55.4
Pennsylvania
Senate	61.9	57.3	59.8	64.6	78.2	60.4	62.7	61.6	65.1	63.1
House	62.6	62.0	61.8	63.9	65.6	64.2	63.6	65.6	65.8	66.9
Michigan[a]
Senate	68.6	64.0	—	64.3	—	66.2	—	58.5	—	59.9
House	64.8	63.2	61.8	67.0	64.9	70.5	66.0	65.8	63.0	59.2
Ohio
Senate	69.3	60.2	56.6	56.2	61.2	59.2	53.0	56.8	61.7	57.8
House	61.8	67.0	58.6	58.3	24.5	59.4	67.7	60.2	62.7	66.7
Wisconsin
Senate	60.4	60.6	58.3	73.7	75.7	67.2	81.2	73.4	68.8	59.4
House	67.7	59.6	63.6	67.2	73.6	67.8	77.2	63.5	68.5	71.1
Iowa
Senate	56.6	57.3	58.5	55.2	55.5	58.4	60.2	64.8	54.9	57.5
House	58.5	60.7	58.5	58.2	63.4	57.9	69.2	61.8	56.9	64.8
Kansas
Senate	—	—	59.0	—	65.4	—	68.0	—	70.1	—
House	60.4	64.0	63.2	59.1	63.4	64.7	64.8	61.1	66.4	64.6
Missouri
Senate	—	70.0	82.4	66.1	78.4	64.6	85.9	67.5	65.7	60.6
House	74.1	73.0	67.3	75.6	74.0	78.3	67.6	66.3	75.0	71.6
Kentucky[b]
Senate	90.1	72.4	91.0	84.1	80.7	78.3	67.2	70.6	—	78.8
House	71.5	70.6	79.2	77.4	81.1	86.1	82.6	—	77.1	80.2
Tennessee
Senate	—	—	72.3	59.0	85.2	86.8	63.3	81.1	83.4	63.7
House	—	—	72.8	75.6	75.7	73.6	73.1	79.2	84.1	74.0
Colorado
Senate	63.9	64.9	71.5	64.5	61.3	68.4	74.0	65.9	78.6	59.1
House	62.6	58.1	60.8	58.4	61.3	64.9	64.3	70.2	66.7	62.8
New Mexico
Senate	—	62.8	59.3	69.7	72.4	61.7	61.3	—	63.5	63.4
House	61.9	63.6	68.7	66.8	68.4	61.2	70.1	72.3	59.3	77.6
Utah
Senate	56.3	59.1	57.8	63.5	67.8	60.2	50.7	66.2	91.7	61.5
House	62.5	58.5	66.5	57.8	57.6	61.8	64.5	62.3	63.9	72.5

Continued on next page

Table 4—Continued

State Legislature	1968	1970	1972	1974	1976	1978	1980	1982	1984	1986
Oregon										
Senate	—	—	65.8	71.2	78.1	72.5	63.6	64.4	79.8	69.4
House	—	—	58.0	61.2	61.0	56.5	61.1	58.5	64.6	58.8
California										
Senate	—	51.7	50.3	66.2	59.4	60.9	57.0	62.2	62.9	49.4
House	63.7	58.5	57.3	61.0	59.9	64.4	55.7	60.8	61.3	59.0

[a]Terms of office for the Michigan Senate, unlike those of all the other states, are four years rather than two.

[b]Due to the fact that Kentucky scheduled legislative elections in odd years until 1984, the figures for 1968 to 1982 are in fact for elections held from 1969 to 1983.

political unknowns who are unable to raise the campaign funds required to make a respectable showing in congressional races (Jacobson and Kernell 1983).

It is possible that challengers have vanished at the state level as well, resulting in a growing number of incumbents winning with little or no opposition. Therefore, it is important to determine the extent to which the increase in incumbents' winning margins is due to a decrease in competition.

Although the data set does not permit us to identify weak challengers because it does not include information on their experiences, we can arrive at an estimate of competition in state legislative races by tracing the proportion of uncontested races over time. The average proportion of races won by incumbents that were contested over two time periods is shown in the first two columns in table 6. Two different patterns emerge from the data. In four states, Connecticut, Michigan, Ohio, and California, most of the incumbents' victories were contested throughout the periods. For the remainder of the states there appears to have been a decrease in the proportion of contested races. In Rhode Island, Delaware, Pennsylvania, Iowa, and Colorado, and in the Missouri House, there has been a relatively substantial decrease; in Wisconsin, Kansas, Kentucky, Tennessee, New Mexico, Utah, and Oregon, the decrease appears to have been more moderate.

In order to arrive at a clear picture of the competition in legislative elections, the proportion of contested races with incumbents is compared with the proportion of contested open seat races (as shown in table 6). (Once again, greater weight is given to trends in state houses because of the smaller numbers of senate races, particularly ones with open seats.)

In Connecticut, Michigan, Ohio, and California, it appears that nearly all elections were contested, regardless of whether there were incumbents seeking reelection or not. Connecticut, Michigan, and Ohio are states with relatively strong party organizations that are active in the recruitment and nominations process. Party organizations in these states, therefore, may make a concerted effort to recruit candidates to run against incumbents, while the other states may have to rely more on the ambitions of self-starters. As for California, its extraordinarily large legislative districts may serve to generate greater levels of competition.

TABLE 5.   Regression of Election Year on Average Votes

State	B	Incumbents Beta	B	Open Seats Beta
Connecticut	.40**	.66	.02	.08
	(.10)		(.07)	
Rhode Island	.62**	.58	.38	.33
	(.21)		(.26)	
Delaware	1.15**	.92	−.28	−.23
	(.12)		(.28)	
Pennsylvania	.84**	.88	.20	.29
	(.11)		(.16)	
Michigan	.22	.51	−.23	−.44
	(.11)		(.13)	
Ohio	.08	.15	−.09	−.12
	(.13)		(.17)	
Wisconsin	.29**	.46	.38	.35
	(.13)		(.24)	
Iowa	.79**	.74	.17	.28
	(.17)		(.14)	
Kansas	.67**	.65	.41*	.52
	(.22)		(.18)	
Missouri	.63*	.56	−.33	−.29
	(.22)		(.27)	
Kentucky	.46**	.76	−.13	−.08
	(.10)		(.39)	
Tennessee	.40	.34	.26	.15
	(.30)		(.45)	
Colorado	.93**	.76	.29	.32
	(.19)		(.20)	
New Mexico	.61**	.69	.20	.22
	(.17)		(.22)	
Utah	.54**	.69	.61	.44
	(.14)		(.30)	
Oregon	.02	.02	.11	.07
	(.29)		(.40)	
California	.27**	.76	.01	.02
	(.05)		(.20)	

Notes: B = unstandardized coefficient, beta = standardized coefficient. Standard error is in parentheses.

   *.05 level of significance.   **.01 level of significance.

TABLE 6. Percentage of Contested Races (controlling for incumbency) and Margins in Contested Races

| | Percentage of Races Contested | | | | Average Percentage for Winning Incumbents in Contested Races | |
| | With Winning Incumbents | | With Open Seats | | | |
State Legislature	1968–76	1978–86	1968–76	1978–86	1968–76	1978–86
Connecticut						
Senate	100	97	100	98	60.62	62.50
House	97	90	100	96	62.18	63.35
Rhode Island						
Senate	86	74	93	84	65.32	65.74
House	85	60	93	70	65.13	65.66
Delaware						
Senate	94	55	78	95	63.93	60.75
House	90	63	92	89	61.18	65.06
Pennsylvania						
Senate	97	85	90	100	62.89	66.31
House	94	80	98	92	63.21	67.53
Michigan						
Senate	96	86	100	96	67.22	68.33
House	89	87	93	94	66.90	69.06
Ohio						
Senate	97	93	100	100	64.30	64.86
House	89	89	95	95	64.36	66.82
Wisconsin						
Senate	86	78	88	87	61.64	62.11
House	90	79	89	81	65.28	65.30
Iowa						
Senate	89	69	100	96	58.99	59.05
House	90	72	95	89	60.47	60.92
Kansas						
Senate	66	76	94	90	59.90	61.65
House	65	57	92	87	59.98	64.08
Missouri						
Senate	56	62	67	96	63.26	65.84
House	66	48	73	73	64.67	66.33
Kentucky						
Senate	45	40	43	70	62.37	65.18
House	50	40	62	50	64.30	64.95
Tennessee						
Senate	50	42	62	58	66.90	63.72
House	48	37	67	64	65.16	64.96
Colorado						
Senate	79	49	89	77	59.76	65.70
House	81	63	96	87	60.92	63.54
New Mexico						
Senate	64	60	91	93	60.00	61.67
House	71	55	85	77	61.86	61.90

Table 6—*Continued*

	Percentage of Races Contested				Average Percentage for Winning Incumbents in Contested Races	
	With Winning Incumbents		With Open Seats			
State Legislature	1968–76	1978–86	1968–76	1978–86	1968–76	1978–86
Utah						
Senate	85	74	97	93	61.23	65.34
House	87	80	94	90	60.69	64.78
Oregon						
Senate	79	83	81	77	60.30	61.10
House	88	84	97	95	61.10	62.88
California						
Senate	96	95	100	100	65.33	67.68
House	97	90	99	100	65.49	67.14

The seven states having only a modest decrease in contested races with incumbents running also had a small or negligible decrease in contests with open seat races. It does not appear that the decline in contests in these states can be attributed to the growing political strength of incumbents. In all of these states except Wisconsin, however, the proportion of contests was higher in races with no incumbent running. It should be remembered that the Kentucky and Tennessee data do not include primaries in which the stiffest competition occurs. Rhode Island had a sharp drop in contested races with or without incumbents. In the five other states having a sharp drop in contests with incumbents running—Delaware, Pennsylvania, Iowa, Missouri, and Colorado—the proportion of contests in open seat races dropped only slightly or remained virtually unchanged. In these five states, at least, the decline in contested races appears to be directly linked to the strength of incumbents.

If the decline in races with incumbents that are contested is primarily responsible in many states for the increase in the average winning margins of incumbents, then there should be little change in the incumbents' margins once competition is controlled for. As a means of controlling for competition the average winning margins for incumbents in contested races only were calculated. In the last two columns in table 6, the average winning margins are shown for contested incumbents in two time periods.

In most states there was only a slight increase in the average winning margins of contested incumbents. In eight states—Connecticut, Rhode Island, Wisconsin, Iowa, Kentucky, Tennessee, New Mexico, and Oregon—there was virtually no change between the two time periods while in the remaining states the increase was just a few percentage points. We conclude that, in states where the average winning percentage of incumbent candidates has grown, it has largely been a consequence of a larger proportion of uncontested races.

Conclusions

The findings of the analysis may be summarized as follows. There does not appear to have been an increase in either the proportion of legislators running for or winning reelection in the last twenty years. Rather, most states began the period with legislators running for and winning reelection at such relatively high rates that virtually no room for improvement over the time period existed. However, the decline in turnover rates documented by previous research (Rosenthal 1974b; Shin and Jackson 1979; Calvert 1979; Jewell 1982) calls attention to a limitation of the data employed in the present analysis. Analysis of turnover and retention data for the 1950–68 period shows that in many of the states retention rates increased substantially, and it seems plausible that most of this resulted from the drop in the proportion of members leaving voluntarily.

The data do document, however, that legislators have been able to capitalize on the electoral benefits of incumbency by increasing their margins of victory over the last twenty years. That is, the average winning incumbents' votes in 1986 were significantly greater, in most states, than they were twenty years earlier. Moreover, the trend toward larger margins of victory was not found in open seat races. It is the winning margins for incumbents (not simply all winners) that have increased over the time period. Therefore, increasing margins may be directly attributed to the electoral benefits of incumbency, rather than an increase in the number of electorally safe districts.

In most of the states in the analysis, increases in the winning margins of incumbents appear to be largely accounted for by decreases in competition. More and more incumbents have been winning reelection without opposition. And for the most part, decreases in competition in races involving incumbents were not paralleled in open seat contests. Those states where incumbents appear to consistently face opposition are those with state party organizations active in the recruitment and nominations process.

These findings suggest several topics that need to be explored in future research. The growth in margins appears to be largely attributable to the growing political strength of incumbents, but we need to collect more evidence on possible changes in the "normal party votes" in legislative districts. This can be estimated, using the county-level files for legislative voting, by comparing the partisan votes in legislative races with those for other offices.

We need to learn more about the reasons for the decline in the proportion of contested races, particularly in cases where incumbents are running. This results in part from the political strength of incumbents. When an incumbent becomes well entrenched and apparently unbeatable, there is less and less incentive for a challenger to run, even in districts where the incumbents' parties do not have large partisan advantages.

The reduction in contested races may also result from the declining effectiveness of party organizations in recruiting challengers. We need to learn more about how candidates are recruited and what efforts the state and local parties make to recruit and support candidates to challenge the incumbents. Is recruiting done by local parties or by the state party organization, and has there been any trend in the priorities or strategies of recruiting? It is possible that in some states a decline in the number of contested races may be a sign not of weak party organizations but of more careful targeting by the party organizations. In other words, political parties may spend more effort and resources recruiting and supporting challengers in districts where the parties have realistic chances of defeating the incumbents and may ignore districts they are sure cannot be won.

We also need to learn more about the reasons why members leave the legislature voluntarily. There is evidence that the number running for reelection declines after a redistricting, presumably because members perceive it will be more difficult to win in the new districts (Jewell and Breaux 1988). How often does a member retire following a decline in his or her electoral margins in the district? Data must be gathered on the number of members who leave in order to run for other political offices—including particularly members of the lower house who run for the senate. Data are also lacking on the number of members who leave the legislature because they are defeated for reelection or lose a race for another office and subsequently are elected for another term in the legislature.

In addition to such electoral data, we need more interview data with members on their career plans. How well-defined are these plans when candidates are first elected to the legislature? How do their plans and preferences change over time? To what extent is the decision to stay in the legislature or run for another office affected by their success in winning leadership positions or committee chairs in the legislature? And to what extent is it affected by political opportunity—the chance to run for an open seat in the upper house, Congress, or a statewide or major local office? Finally we should recognize that personal as well as political motives affect career decisions, including financial pressures, the time pressures the part-time legislators face in their other occupations, and family considerations.

CHAPTER 7

Legislative Caucus and Leadership Campaign Committees

Anthony Gierzynski
and
Malcolm Jewell

Conventional wisdom suggests that, except in the larger states, the cost of campaigns for state legislative seats has been low enough so that most members have been able to finance the campaigns from their own resources and by soliciting modest amounts from their friends. There is evidence that in recent years, however, the cost of legislative campaigning has grown much more rapidly than the rate of inflation and in some urban districts in the larger states has approached the cost of U.S. House races (Jewell and Olson 1988; Jones 1984; Sorauf 1988).

Conventional wisdom suggests that most legislative candidates must organize their own fund-raising campaigns for both general and primary elections. State party organizations concentrate fund-raising efforts on statewide and occasionally congressional districts. Local organizations may assist in races for mayor or for county offices. But state legislators, whose districts do not usually coincide with county boundaries and who have little patronage to distribute, are on their own.

Because incumbent legislators have experience in fund-raising and because they are usually perceived as more likely to win reelection, they have obvious advantages over challengers in raising funds. As the costs of getting elected to the legislature rise, the advantages enjoyed by incumbents over challengers almost inevitably rise. The incumbency advantage of the state legislator, in financial terms, begins to resemble that of the members of Congress (see chapter 6 for evidence on incumbency success rates at the state level).

As the cost of campaigning rises, fund-raising becomes a serious and often a burdensome problem for legislative candidates. As the legislature grows more important and more professional in many states, interest groups devote more attention to legislators. Taken together, these trends lead to increasing involvement by political action committees (PACs) in legislative races. There are data from some states indicating that a larger proportion of funding for legislative than for gubernatorial campaigns comes from PACs. These trends raise the possibility that legislators may become more heavily indebted and committed to interest groups that have supported their campaigns financially.

There is another trend that has been occurring and that until recently has attracted little attention from political scientists. Over the last decade (or in some states more) legislative party leaders and party caucuses have begun to raise money for legislative races, usually in the general election. Sometimes this fund-raising has been initiated by legislative leaders, who may operate largely on their own. In other cases this has been raised by party caucus operations. In some legislatures fund-raising has been undertaken only by one party, but usually the other party has found it necessary to follow this lead.

In some state legislatures party fund-raising began on a very modest scale, and small sums of money were distributed evenly to incumbent members. But the process has grown more sophisticated, with the parties concentrating their resources on marginal seats and also extending assistance to challengers who are perceived to have a chance of winning.

This trend is important for several reasons. Because much of the money is apparently from PACs, it is possible that the legislative party can serve as a buffer between legislators and PACs. But at the same time, the party leadership may become more heavily committed to those interests whose PACs provide funds. Because the leadership usually determines, directly or indirectly, how the funds are distributed, this new technique could theoretically strengthen the power of legislative leaders.

Because these funds raised by legislative leaders and caucuses are usually distributed to marginal races, this practice might make the two legislative parties more competitive. If these funds are distributed to serious challengers as well as incumbents, this practice could reduce the financial advantages of incumbency. It is also very possible that this trend will increase the disparities in spending among races, with much more being spent on races perceived to be marginal and relatively less spent on all other races—very much like the pattern that has developed in congressional races.

These speculations and hypotheses are derived from our knowledge of congressional campaign funding and from scattered bits of evidence reported in a few states. To understand what trends are occurring, and to find out whether legislative caucuses are actually behaving as these theories suggest they do, we need a more systematic comparative analysis of data. That is the purpose of this chapter.

Literature

Research on the campaign activity of legislative parties has focused on the congressional campaign committees at the national level, or it has consisted of studies of individual states. Comparative research, examining the differing practices between states and types of committees, has yet to be done.

Legislative party campaign finance at the national level has been investigated by Adamany (1984), Herrnson (1986, 1988), Jacobson (1985), and Jacobson and Kernell (1983). In a series of interviews with executive members of the Democratic Congressional Campaign Committee (DCCC) and Republican National Congressional Committee (RNCC), and in a survey of 385 U.S. House candidates, along with an analysis of actual campaign finance data, Herrnson (1986, 1988) found high levels of activity on the part of both committees in assisting selected candidates—particularly those involved in close races. In addition to direct campaign contributions, assistance from the DCCC and RNCC included media help, such as providing media facilities and experts to produce campaign advertisements; campaign consultants, sometimes bought en bloc by the committees and sold at a discount to candidates; polling; and direct mail specialists (Herrnson 1986). Similar findings were reported by Jacobson (1985) and Sorauf (1988).

Research on legislative party campaign committees at the state level consists mostly of case studies. One exception is a study by Jewell (1986). Jewell surveyed political scientists in each of the fifty states, asking questions regarding the existence of legislative party campaign committees and the extent of their activities. He found "fragmentary" evidence of legislative party campaign committees in at least thirty-two states. In twelve of the states the legislative party campaign committees were providing levels of support high enough to have a significant impact on state legislative elections (Jewell 1986).

Case studies of legislative party campaign committees have been done in California, Connecticut, Wisconsin, Illinois, Pennsylvania, and New York. A report published by the California Commission on Campaign Financing (1985) describes in detail the activity of California legislative parties in campaign finance. In the 1984 general election, the Democrats transferred $3,009,506, or 24 percent of all funds raised in legislative elections, through leadership PACs to candidates, and the Democrats raised and distributed $124,359, or 1 percent of all legislative campaign funds, through caucus committees. The Republican figures were $1,359,355 in transfers, or 12 percent of all funds raised, and $1,100,180 through caucus committees, or 10 percent of all funds raised. Obviously, the legislative party campaign committees are a major force in state legislative campaigns in California. These funds are even more significant in that the distribution of the funds is often held up until the last possible minute of a race, flooding it with money just before election day (California Commission on Campaign Financing 1985).

Legislative party campaign committees in California became a major force in campaign finance as a result of a battle for the Speakership of the Assembly between Majority Leader Howard Berman and Speaker Leo McCarthy. As part of their campaigns for the position, they both began to raise and distribute money to candidates who would support their candidacies for the Speakership position. This process has since then evolved into a vehicle for electing party members in a state where interparty competition, or divisiveness, has seen a significant increase. And it is now expected that party leaders will raise and distribute campaign money as part of the responsibilities of their positions (California Commission on Campaign Financing 1985).

As for the purpose of the legislative party campaign activity today, legislative staffers interviewed by the California Commission on Campaign Financing (1985) claim that the sole purpose of the distribution of the money is to elect party members. It is, according to staffers, not used to enforce party unity.

The passage of Proposition 73 in June of 1988 changed these campaign finance practices in the California legislature. The proposition outlawed the transfer of money between candidates and put a $5,000 cap on contributions by political parties (Alexander 1988).

In Connecticut, Rose (1987) found that substantial proportions of victorious candidates' total campaign funds in state senate races came from the campaign caucus committees of the state legislative parties. The contributions from the caucus committees overshadowed the contributions made by the state parties but remained a relatively small proportion of total contributions. Rom and Aoki (1987) present evidence of legislative party campaign committees in Wisconsin. Under state law legislative party campaign committees' classification as parties gives them an advantage in that they do not have to adhere to the contribution limits placed on PACs. Legislative caucus committees in Wisconsin were found to play an important role in some races: some candidates received up to 20 percent of their funds from the legislative party campaign committees (Rom and Aoki 1987).

In Illinois, legislative campaign committees—the Republican Senate State Campaign Committee, the Committee to Re-Elect a Democratic Senate, the House Republican Campaign Committee, and the Illinois House Democratic Majority Committee—have rapidly expanded their role in elections since 1974 (Johnson 1987). Such committees' funds accounted for 23 percent of all funds raised in Illinois legislative races for the 1984–85 period. The committees rely heavily upon large interest group donors: Republicans rely upon business and individual donors and Democrats on labor and professional group donors. The committees also receive money from the national and state party organizations and from party leaders (Johnson 1987).

Legislative party campaign committees were responsible for 8.6 percent of all the funds raised by legislative candidates—12.2 percent of all the funds raised by nonincumbents—in the 1982 Pennsylvania legislative elections. These party committees were found to give a greater proportion of their funds to close races, their funds making up about 20 percent of the funds raised by legislative candidates in close races (Eisenstein 1984).

In New York, the Democratic campaign committee in the Assembly raised and spent $758,868 in 1984, the figure for the Assembly Republicans was $377,029 (Stonecash and D'Agostino 1987; Stonecash 1989). The committees spent the money on in-kind services, such as mailings, assistance with advertising in print and electronic media, and transfers of funds. Stonecash (1989) found that the resources of the legislative parties were concentrated on close races, regardless of incumbency status. This pattern contrasts sharply with the distribution pattern of campaign contributions from other sources that are raised by the individual legislators (i.e., contributions go mostly to incumbents). Stonecash found that party money was more likely to go to challengers, while individual fund-raising gave incumbents the advantage, leading Stonecash to conclude that without the party money incumbents would have a much greater advantage in campaign resources. The difference between the Democrats and Republicans in terms of the types of candidates funded, incumbents versus nonincumbents, also suggests a possible effect of party status and party popularity on the party strategy.

In summary, our knowledge of the campaign activities of legislative parties is based upon studies of the congressional parties and a number of case studies in a handful of states. This literature suggests that the legislative parties use their campaign resources mainly to fund candidates in close races. It also suggests the possibility that the parties also take into account trends in party popularity and candidates' status in the legislature, with majority party committees funding mainly incumbents, in a defensive posture, and minority party committees pursuing an offensive strategy of funding nonincumbents. The research in this chapter takes a comparative look at the way legislative parties and legislative leaders distribute the resources available to them and how these patterns vary from state to state.

A Theory of Legislative Party Resource Allocation

Our expectations about the distribution of legislative party resources need to be put into a theoretical framework to provide some organization of and linkage between propositions and ultimately to lead us to some expectations as to what would be found in the research. The framework used in this chapter is based upon previous research on political parties (legislative and other) and legislative behavior. The underlying assumption is that legislators and party leaders are rational decision makers.[1] That legislators are rational decision makers means simply that they act to maximize benefits and minimize costs in pursuing their goals. An examination of the goals of the actors involved in the legislative party campaign committee decisions, then, led us to some expectations about the behavior of the legislative party campaign committees.

Legislative party campaign committees may pursue the goals of individual legislators or the collective goals of the party. Which they pursue depends upon the level of input that individual legislators have in the decisions of the committee. If legislators dominate it, the committee should be found to pursue their goals. If the committee is insulated from individual legislators, it should be found to pursue the collective goals of the party. In fact, evidence of this difference was found by Herrnson (1986) between the DCCC, dominated by incumbent legislators, and the RNCC, which is more insulated from the incumbent Republican representatives. Leadership PACs (i.e., individual legislative leaders who distribute excess funds out of their own campaign committees) will obviously pursue the leaders' goals, a difference to be explored in future research.

What should the distribution of resources be if the legislative party campaign committees pursue the individual goals of legislators? Conventional wisdom, as well as rational choice research on distributional politics (i.e., pork-barrel politics) (Shepsle and Weingast 1981) would lead us to believe that where reelection valuable resources are concerned incumbent legislators will fight for and win their fair share of the committees' resources. In fact, according to Shepsle and Weingast (1981) the fear of being in the minority, and losing out on the reelection valuable resources, should lead to a norm of universalism among legislators (i.e., every legislator receiving a share). Legislative party campaign committees, however, have limited resources, limiting their options to (1) distributing token amounts to all legislative incumbents or (2) targeting close races, including those involving nonincumbent candidates, to build or maintain a legislative majority.

Given that the game of legislative elections is one of multiple repetitions, at least for most players, legislators should opt for the second strategy, the targeting of resources, for two reasons. First, safe incumbents may be willing to pay the cost of forgoing the token benefit, in exchange for the greater benefit they would accrue in the future if they faced a stiff challenge and their

---

[1] This assumption is often questioned in the literature. Its use in developing models to explain elite behavior is more readily accepted in that elites are more likely to meet the qualifications of rational decision makers. An example of the use of this assumption can be found in Aldrich's study of the calculus of running for presidential nominations in *Before the Convention*.

legislative parties targeted races. This discounting of future benefits can be seen as a type of insurance policy that incumbents may be willing to buy into. The second reason legislators would opt for a strategic distribution is that the benefits derived from being in the majority party, in terms of favorable committee assignments and favorable outcomes on public policy, should also be greater than the benefits derived from the token amount that an equal distribution of legislative party resources would bring. This should also lead the legislative party campaign committee to pursue the best strategy to gain a majority. If the party is in the minority, acceptance of funding nonincumbents, the only way to build a majority, should be greater. If the party is enjoying a surge in popularity, acceptance of an offensive strategy of funding nonincumbents should also be more acceptable to incumbent legislators, since the possible payoffs, in terms of gaining or maintaining a majority, are higher. In cases where the legislature is dominated by one party, and the hopes or fears of a change in status are remote, this calculus would obviously be very different.

If the legislative party campaign committees pursue the collective goals of the party, a strategic distribution of resources should also be found. A party's overriding goal is to gain control of government by winning the most votes, and it does this in legislative elections by trying to win a majority of seats. The most effective use of the party's resources to attain this goal is to concentrate the resources on races where the recources will make the most difference (i.e., close races). Furthermore, if the party is trying to build a majority, it will need to fund nonincumbent candidates to increase the size of the party's legislative contingent. If the party holds a large majority, it should be found to concentrate its resources on defending weak incumbents.

Thus, whether pursuing individual legislators' goals or the collective goals of the political party, legislative party campaign committees should be found to distribute their resources strategically. From these arguments, we derived a number of hypotheses regarding the distribution of legislative party campaign committee resources:

H1: Legislative party campaign committees will target their resources to close races.

H2: Legislative party campaign committees will be more likely to fund nonincumbent candidates than incumbent candidates.

H3: Legislative party campaign committees whose party holds a minority of seats in the legislature should be more likely to fund nonincumbent candidates than legislative party campaign committees whose party holds a majority of seats.

In summary, we hypothesized that, contrary to conventional wisdom and research on distributional politics, legislative party campaign committees will act like real parties, not just as collectives of individual legislators who pursue their own fair share of the resources.

Data and Analysis

Most states now require that campaign finance information, including itemized revenues and expenditures for candidates, PACs, and party committees, be filed with a state agency. Data on legislative caucus campaign contributions were collected from seven states—California, Indiana, Minnesota, New York, Oregon, Washington, and Wisconsin—to test our hypotheses.[2] The data include individual contributions, in-kind and cash, to state house or assembly candidates from legislative caucus committees and leadership PACs for the election of 1986.[3]

Some of the descriptive statistics for these party committees are presented in tables 1 and 2. Large differences in the amount of funds allocated are obvious, especially when comparing California and New York to Washington and Oregon. It is reasonably safe to say that these differences mainly reflect the different costs of winning legislative seats in these states. The relative size of the standard deviations vis-à-vis the means indicates that the committees must be concentrating resources on a selective number of legislative candidates, with many candidates receiving no assistance. And, finally, the percentage of nonincumbents receiving assistance provides some initial support for the second hypothesis (legislative party campaign committees should be willing to fund nonincumbents). The data show that it is not just that some nonincumbents receive assistance but, for most cases, that a greater proportion of nonincumbents receives help than incumbents.

Tests of the hypotheses outlined above require that the analysis turn to the individual-level patterns of legislative party campaign committees' resource distribution.

Targeting

To test the targeting hypotheses (H1 and H2) a multiple regression analysis was performed on the 1986 data. Regressions were run for each party commit-

---

[2] States were selected based upon a number of criteria. They were first selected based upon whether or not a significant level of legislative party campaign committee activity existed. Then they were selected to provide variation in types of legislative party campaign committee practices and to include as much regional variation as possible. We would like to thank Jeffrey M. Stonecash for his generosity in making his New York data available to us.

[3] Leadership PACs' contributions were defined as contributions or transfers from a current legislature (from the same chamber). Thus, contributions from statewide officials, from nonincumbents, or from legislators in the other chamber are not included in these figures.

TABLE 1. State House Legislative Caucus Committee Funds, 1986

	Democrats	Republicans
California		
Total funds allocated	$2,518,068.00	$1,256,872.90
Mean level of support	33,574.24	15,909.78
Standard deviation	103,346.52	47,169.17
Percentage incumbents funded	7.5%	3.7%
Percentage nonincumbents funded	22.9%	37.3%
Indiana		
Total funds allocated	$76,950.00	$74,500.00
Mean level of support	905.29	846.59
Standard deviation	1,667.41	1,180.20
Percentage incumbents funded	20.0%	78.6%
Percentage nonincumbents funded	34.0%	40.6%
Minnesota		
Total funds allocated	$45,000.00	$28,300.00
Mean level of support	362.90	231.97
Standard deviation	723.43	347.60
Percentage incumbents funded	15.1%	26.7%
Percentage nonincumbents funded	65.1%	48.4%
New York		
Total funds allocated	$944,042.00	$632,984.00
Mean level of support	6,890.82	4,620.32
Standard deviation	13,746.04	9,056.37
Percentage incumbents funded	29.9%	26.9%
Percentage nonincumbents funded	46.0%	23.5%
Oregon		
Total funds allocated	$40,111.00	$102,151.98
Mean level of support	691.57	1,792.14
Standard deviation	1,559.82	3,326.23
Percentage incumbents funded	24.1%	4.3%
Percentage nonincumbents funded	51.7%	58.8%
Washington		
Total funds allocated	$46,206.99	$39,145.00
Mean level of support	481.32	425.49
Standard deviation	1,017.51	959.41
Percentage incumbents funded	17.6%	12.1%
Percentage nonincumbents funded	33.3%	40.7%
Wisconsin		
Total funds allocated	$56,680.00	$41,415.00
Mean level of support	682.89	440.59
Standard deviation	1,087.35	712.54
Percentage incumbents funded	23.9%	32.6%
Percentage nonincumbents funded	67.6%	74.5%

Sources: State of California Fair Political Practices Commission 1987; Indiana State Election Board 1986; Minnesota Ethical Practices Board 1986; Oregon Secretary of State 1986; Washington Public Disclosure Commission 1986; Wisconsin State Board of Elections 1987.

Note: These are the funds distributed to candidates, in-kind and cash. Because they do not include operating expenses, they do not reflect the total expenditures made by the committees.

tee in each state, regressing the level of assistance provided each candidate on a measure of the closeness of the race and incumbency status. An analysis of each state party's contributions was included for the sake of comparison. The margin of defeat or victory for the party's candidate in the previous election was used as an indicator of the closeness of the race. This was done for two reasons. First, using the previous margin avoids the causality problem associated with using the final outcome of a race as the measure of closeness. This is especially critical when dealing with money in campaigns where the question arises as to whether the money was given to races that were close or the contributions made the races close. And, second, this type of information is

TABLE 2.   State House Legislative Leadership Committee Funds, 1986

	Democrats	Republicans
California		
Total funds allocated	$722,708.00	$200,095.00
Mean level of support	9,636.11	2,532.85
Standard deviation	22,043.54	6,931.64
Percentage incumbents funded	27.5%	1.4%
Percentage nonincumbents funded	40.0%	29.4%
Minnesota		
Total funds allocated	$38,492.00	$60,775.00
Mean level of support	310.42	498.16
Standard deviation	611.54	1,229.52
Percentage incumbents funded	28.3%	25.0%
Percentage nonincumbents funded	49.3%	35.5%
Oregon		
Total funds allocated	$57,275.00	$18,872.00
Mean level of support	987.50	331.09
Standard deviation	2,017.12	792.68
Percentage incumbents funded	27.6%	21.7%
Percentage nonincumbents funded	41.4%	32.4%
Washington		
Total funds allocated	$101,231.00	$49,323.00
Mean level of support	1,054.49	536.12
Standard deviation	1,775.34	1,231.39
Percentage incumbents funded	25.5%	15.2%
Percentage nonincumbents funded	46.7%	39.0%
Wisconsin		
Total funds allocated	$4,451.00	$4,000.00
Mean level of support	53.63	42.56
Standard deviation	164.12	191.75
Percentage incumbents funded	47.8%	25.6%
Percentage nonincumbents funded	13.5%	29.4%

Sources: State of California Fair Political Practices Commission 1987; Minnesota Ethical Practices Board 1986; Oregon Secretary of State 1986; Washington Public Disclosure Commission 1986; Wisconsin State Board of Elections 1987.

part of what is available to the decision makers in the legislative party campaign committees when they have to make their allocational decisions. The specific measure for the previous margin is a folded scale using the candidate's party percentage in the previous election, subtracting the absolute value of fifty minus the vote percentage from fifty:

previous margin = 50 − (50 − previous vote percentage) .

Incumbency status was included in the regression in the form of a dummy variable that equaled one if the candidate was not an incumbent and zero if the candidate was an incumbent. This allowed us to test the campaign committees' willingness to fund nonincumbents. The regression model, thus, is as follows:

$$\text{LPCC\$} = b_0 + b_1(\text{Margin}) + b_2(\text{Nonincumbent}) , \qquad \text{(eq. 1)}$$

where "LPCC$" is the level of assistance provided to a candidate from the legislative party campaign committee, in dollars, "Margin" is the margin in the previous election, and "Nonincumbent" is the dummy variable for incumbency status.

If legislative party campaign committees' decisions are strategic, we would expect to find that b_1 and b_2 are both greater than zero. That is, we would expect to find a positive relationship between the closeness of the race and the level of assistance provided and a positive relationship between the status as a nonincumbent and the level of assistance provided.

The results of the regression analyses, presented in table 3, provide support for both of the targeting hypotheses (each line in the table is the result of a separate regression analysis using eq. 1).[4] All of the legislative caucus committees were more likely to give greater assistance to candidates in closer races. For example, for each .1 percent increase in the closeness of the previous margin, the California Assembly Democrats were likely to give an extra $2,371.16; the figure for the Republicans was $832.65. All of the leadership PACs, with the exception of both parties in Wisconsin, were likely to give more money the closer the race was in the previous election. The state party organizations in a few cases demonstrated evidence of targeting. The poor showing of the state parties may be explained by the low levels of assistance most of them provide (a finding significant in itself, since it demonstrates that in these states the dominant party actor in legislative elections has become the legislative party).

The results also demonstrate that most legislative campaign committees

---

[4] Though significance levels are provided, they are not very relevant since the samples in this case are the populations.

TABLE 3. Analysis of Campaign Resource Distribution, 1986

Committee	Margin	Nonincumbent	Constant	R^2	Percentage of Seats[a]	Mean Contribution[b]
California						
D LCC	2,371.16*	48,289.81*	−555,211.34*	.18	59	($33,574)
R LCC	832.65*	23,968.72*	−22,356.06*	.12	41	($16,323)
D LPAC	638.01*	5,458.62	−10,737.26*	.19	59	($9,636)
R LPAC	189.36*	2,642.13	−4,337.25*	.17	41	($2,599)
D State	26.12	613.00	−317.31	.03	59	($698)
R State	183.37*	4,206.33	−4,674.65	.10	41	($3,133)
Indiana						
D LCC	42.83*	936.26*	−1,144.22	.18	39	($1,026)
R LCC	24.12*	−209.82	104.39	.08	61	($918)
Minnesota						
D LCC	22.58*	124.75*	−528.77*	.15	49	($381)
R LCC	10.16*	147.33*	−211.45	.13	51	($242)
D LPAC	17.33*	134.27	−397.17*	.13	49	($325)
R LPAC	30.44*	353.88	−820.17*	.09	51	($491)
R State	6.18*	205.04*	−192.68	.12	51	($144)
New York						
D LCC	487.73*	3,132.12	−7,070.18*	.28	63	($6,890)
R LCC	333.91*	1,091.08	−481.42*	.29	37	($4,620)
Oregon						
D LCC	19.61	532.19	−210.01	.07	57	($692)
R LCC	6.24	2,983.04*	−198.84	.21	43	($824)
D LPAC	24.83	11.65	176.87*	.04	57	($988)
R LPAC	7.68	141.96	−10.09	.03	43	($337)
D State	1.50	−49.47	2.50	.03	57	($26)
R State	−7.34	981.89*	242.08	.09	43	($589)
Washington						
D LCC	31.60*	389.41	−889.27	.11	54	($374)
R LCC	16.08	450.22*	−475.00*	.08	46	($425)
D LPAC	66.13*	759.04*	−1,782.71	.15	54	($1,054)
R LPAC	30.06*	431.48	−883.69	.08	46	($536)
D State	19.86	904.16*	−462.81	.08	54	($749)
R State	24.69	967.37*	−856.85	.09	46	($721)
Wisconsin						
D LCC	29.35*	291.46	−317.93	.24	53	($709)
R LCC	16.73*	174.99	−118.20	.11	47	($512)
D LPAC	0.42	2.53	39.31	.00	53	($53)
R LPAC	0.49	−115.10*	104.04	.08	47	($47)
D State	4.33	−51.85	−40.05	.02	53	($68)
R State	11.27*	142.78	−103.69	.08	47	($366)

Notes: Multiple regression—campaign committee contributions regressed upon previous margin and incumbency status.

Abbreviations: "D" for Democratic committee, "R" for Republican committee, "LCC" for legislative caucus committee, "LPAC" for leadership political action committee, and "State" for state central committee.

[a]Seats held by the party before the election.

[b]Average contribution from committees to all candidates.

*Significant at the .05 level or better.

are willing to fund nonincumbents, providing support for the second hypothesis. This is especially true for the legislative caucus committees, all of which, with the exception of those of Indiana Republicans, were more inclined to give assistance to nonincumbents. In Minnesota, for example, the mean contribution from the Democratic-Farmer-Labor House Caucus Committee was $124.75 higher for nonincumbents (controlling for the closeness of the race). For independent Republican nonincumbent candidates, the mean contribution from their house caucus committee was $147.33 higher than that for incumbents. In the Republicans' caucus in Indiana greater emphasis on incumbents is most likely due to the fact that they hold a large margin in the house, leading them to operate in a more defensive posture, with more incumbents to defend. Eight out of twelve leadership PACs give a greater emphasis to nonincumbents. The results for the state parties are more mixed.

The low R^2s for most of the equations indicate a model specification problem. Presented in table 4 are the results of the model with the addition of the square of the previous margin. This was done to model the expected exponential increase in assistance as competition increased. The specific form of the equations was

$$y = b_0 + b_1(\text{Margin}) + b_2(\text{Margin})^2 + b_3(\text{Nonincumbent}) , \quad \text{(eq. 2)}$$

where "Margin" is the previous margin, "(Margin)^2" is the previous margin squared, and "Nonincumbent" is the dummy for incumbency status. The results are presented for the cases in which the model represents an improvement over the previous model.

As the R^2s demonstrate, the curvilinear form improves the variance explained by the model. The greatest improvement in explained variance is for those committees that are the wealthiest (i.e., those in California and New York). A California Democrat whose party came within 5 percentage points of winning or losing in the previous election could on average, ceteris paribus, expect $135,586.25, while one who came within only 15 points of victory or defeat last time could on average expect $82,626.25 this election year.

These results provide substantial support for the targeting hypotheses. Legislative party campaign committees, especially the legislative caucus committees, were shown in the analysis to target resources to close races and were likely to give more to nonincumbent candidates. In fact, in some cases they acted more like parties (utilizing resources to gain control of the government) than the state parties did.

Offensive versus Defensive Strategies

To test the offensive/defensive hypotheses (H3), the same regression model was used with a different dependent variable. To make the results comparable

TABLE 4. Exponential Model

Committee	Margin	Margin^2	Nonincumbent	Constant	R^2
California					
D LCC	−6,364.94*	193.34*	58,101.35*	3,423.09	.34
D LPAC	−1,209.62*	40.89*	7,533.94	216.88	.35
R LPAC	−295.96	11.26*	1,380.76	−815.63	.29
Indiana					
D LCC	−106.94*	3.13*	901.55*	−449.29*	.29
R LCC	−30.75	1.13*	−106.25	281.56	.14
Minnesota					
D LCC	−47.41*	1.27*	93.05*	170.14	.27
R LCC	−17.26*	0.50*	157.60*	39.30	.22
D LPAC	−41.37*	1.07*	103.44	192.94	.25
R LPAC	−37.66	1.23*	307.07	−102.34	.12
New York					
D LCC	−987.31*	32.42*	1,033.31*	3,551.44	.50
R LCC	−791.95*	24.79*	1,863.91	2,023.93	.61
Oregon					
D LCC	−80.89	2.14*	615.17	144.02	.16
D LPAC	−124.27*	3.18*	134.76	702.13	.16
Washington					
D LCC	−47.58	1.28*	473.97*	129.32	.16
D LPAC	−96.36	2.64*	939.71*	285.99	.22
Wisconsin					
D LCC	−50.81*	1.72*	364.66	54.28	.36
R LCC	−16.35	0.73*	256.44	−41.30	.18

Notes: Multiple regression—regressing level of assistance from legislative party campaign committee on the square of the closeness of the race and on incumbency status.

Abbreviations: "D" is Democratic committee, "R" is Republican committee, "LCC" is legislative caucus committee and "LPAC" is leadership political action committee.

*Significant at the .05 level or better.

across parties, committees, and states, the regression analysis this time involved regressing the proportion of the committee's total funds received by each candidate on the previous margin and incumbency status.[5] If the status of the legislative party has an impact on the way the legislative party resources are distributed, as hypothesized in H3, minority legislative party campaign committees should be found to be more likely to fund nonincumbents than the majority parties.

The results from the regressions are presented in table 5. The committees are labeled according to party status in the legislature. A comparison of the

---

5 The specific formula used was $\dfrac{\text{LPCC contributions}}{\text{LPCC total funds}} \times 100$. The coefficients should thus be interpreted in terms of percentage. This was done to avoid extremely small coefficients.

TABLE 5. Analysis of the Effect of State Legislative Party Status on State Legislative Party Campaign Committee Assistance

Committee	Margin	Nonincumbent	Constant	R^2 Percentage	Seats
California					
Majority LCC	.094*	1.918*	−2.913*	.18	59
Minority LCC	.066*	1.907*	−1.779	.12	41
Majority LPAC	.088*	0.755	−1.486*	.19	59
Minority LPAC	.095*	1.320	−2.168*	.17	41
Indiana					
Majority LCC	.032*	−0.282	0.140	.09	61
Minority LCC	.056*	1.217*	−1.448	.18	39
Minnesota					
Majority LCC	.036*	0.521*	−0.747	.13	51
Minority LCC	.050*	0.277	−1.175*	.15	49
Majority LPAC	.050*	0.582	−1.350*	.09	51
Minority LPAC	.045*	0.349	−1.031*	.13	49
New York					
Majority LCC	.052*	0.332	−0.749*	.28	63
Minority LCC	.053*	0.172	−0.760*	.29	37
Oregon					
Majority LCC	.049	1.327	−0.524	.07	57
Minority LCC	.006	2.920*	−0.195	.21	43
Majority LPAC	.043	0.020	0.309	.04	57
Minority LPAC	.041	0.752	−0.053	.03	43
Washington					
Majority LCC	.068*	0.843	−1.925	.11	54
Minority LCC	.041	1.150*	−1.213	.08	46
Majority LPAC	.065*	0.750*	−1.761*	.15	54
Minority LPAC	.061*	0.875	−1.792	.08	46
Wisconsin					
Majority LCC	.052*	0.514	−0.561	.24	53
Minority LCC	.040*	0.423	−0.285	.11	47
Majority LPAC	.009	0.057	0.883	.00	53
Minority LPAC	.012	−2.878*	2.601	.08	47
Mean coefficients for all states					
Majority LCC		0.74			
Minority LCC		1.15			
Majority LPAC		0.43			
Minority LPAC		0.08			

Notes: Multiple regression—proportion of committee funds received by a candidate regressed upon previous margin and a dummy variable for incumbency status.

Abbreviations: "LCC" is legislative caucus committee and "LPAC" is leadership political action committee.

*Significant at the .05 level or better.

means of the "nonincumbent" coefficients of the legislative caucus commit-tees provides some support for the notion that minority parties are more likely to allocate a greater proportion of their resources to nonincumbent candidates. The mean of the nonincumbent coefficients for the majority party committees is .74 and the mean for minority parties is 1.15, meaning that, on average, the minority caucus committees were likely to allocate 1.15 percent of their resources to a nonincumbent candidate, while the majority parties were likely to allocate .74 percent of their resources to a nonincumbent candidate. The means for the leadership PACs provide little support for the hypotheses. At .43 and .08 for majority and minority leadership PACs, respectively, they actually represent the direct opposite of what was hypothesized—that minor-ity parties put a greater emphasis on nonincumbents. Caution is advised in interpreting these results since these means may mask relationships at the individual state level.

A state by state comparison of the campaign committees' willingness to fund nonincumbents shows that the expected pattern is found among caucus committees in only three out of seven states: Indiana, Oregon, and Wash-ington. The expected pattern of minority party committees giving a greater proportion of their funds to nonincumbents is found among leadership PACs in three out of five states: California, Oregon, and Washington. In 1986 in Indiana, for example, the mean proportion of the majority Republican caucus committee resources received by a nonincumbent was .282 percent less than what an incumbent would receive (controlling for the closeness of the race). For the minority Democrats, a nonincumbent candidate was on average likely to receive 1.217 percent more of the caucus committee resources than incum-bents were. The similarity between the coefficients for the rest of the states is probably either due to the fact that these legislatures are already closely divided or due to idiosyncratic state factors. The Wisconsin leadership PAC results are the most peculiar, with the minority party refusing to a great extent to fund nonincumbents. This may be attributable to the fact that there are not many resources involved in leadership PAC transfers in Wisconsin, a fact attributable, in turn, to the strict campaign finance laws in that state. In Wisconsin, leadership PACs are treated like other political action committees, and if candidates accept public funding, they may not accept any PAC money. Note that a greater proportion of campaign committee funds from both the caucus committees and the leadership PACs goes to close races, providing additional support for the targeting hypothesis.

Thus, the analysis provides some support for the hypothesis that party status in the legislature is one factor affecting the distribution of legislative party caucus campaign committee and leadership PAC resources in a few states. Further research is needed to determine why all of these states do not fall into this pattern. Possible explanations include the fact that these legislatures are already closely divided and the possibility that national or state party trends have an impact on the distribution of resources.

Discussion

Marginality

For each of the state caucus committees and leadership PACs, there is a large variation in the amount of funds given to each candidate, and there are large numbers of candidates who receive no funding. We found that the closeness of the previous race in most cases has a significant impact on the allocation of resources. For most of the state caucus committees and leadership PACs, the previous margin contributes more than incumbency to explaining variance, as measured by the size of the standardized regression coefficients (not shown here). The Wisconsin leadership PACs are among the few exceptions. It would be surprising if there was not a strong relationship between the previous margin and the level of funding by these groups. We believe that legislative caucuses and leaders concentrate funds in the marginal races, those that are close enough so that the better-funded campaigns can make a difference. In contrast to the interest group PACs, which usually want to support probable winners, the caucus committees and leadership PACs both have strong reasons for trying to influence the outcome of marginal races.

There are several reasons why the statistical relationship between the previous margin and level of funding is not any stronger than what we found. In deciding which races are likely to be close, legislators take into account the previous margin, which we can measure. They may also take into account national and/or state partisan trends, though we found the evidence of this is thin and inconsistent (Gierzynski and Jewell 1989).

But caucuses and leaders presumably take into account some other variables that we cannot measure. In the two years since the previous election, the incumbent may have made mistakes and be perceived as weaker or may have been highly successful. The quality of the challenger varies greatly from one election to the next. Party leaders may recognize that they have a much stronger challenger than in the previous election and thus sink funds into supporting the incumbent. It is also true that when an incumbent is perceived as losing strength it is easier to recruit a strong challenger.

Campaign events may affect the flow of money late in the campaign. A challenger may turn out to be a much weaker or much stronger campaigner than expected. A new issue may have been raised or a mistake made by a candidate during the campaign that changes expectations concerning the outcome.

There is also a technical reason why the statistical relationship between the previous margin and the level of spending is not any higher. A number of incumbents and nonincumbents receive no financial support, a fact that reduces the strength of the correlation. If, for example, a caucus committee were to donate an extra $1,000 to a candidate for every percentage point increase in the candidate's competitiveness, this very high correlation would be reduced if the party also decided to allocate no funds to any district that was won or lost in the last election by more than an eighty to twenty margin. The increase in the variance explained in the exponential model—in terms of the R^2s—over the linear model indicates that this is what is going on.

Incumbency

It is perhaps surprising to find that most caucus committees and leadership PACs are more willing to fund nonincumbents than incumbents, although this is what we hypothesized should happen. But it would not be surprising to find that in some legislative parties the rank-and-file members are unwilling to extend caucus financing to outsiders. Also, it is interesting to find that there are substantial differences among states, among parties, and among types of committees in the priority assigned to funding nonincumbents. These differences are not very well explained by our theories about how majority and minority legislative parties should behave nor how they should react to national political trends.

We have two quite different measures of the incumbency effect. The simplest (tables 1 and 2) is merely a measure of the proportion of incumbents and of nonincumbents who receive any funding at all from each caucus committee and leadership PAC. It is striking that almost every unit funds a larger proportion of nonincumbents. One exception is the Indiana caucus committees (the Republicans both years and the Democrats one year). The other exceptions, by a narrow margin, are the Republican caucus committee in New York and the Wisconsin Democratic leadership PACs (in sharp contrast to the Wisconsin Democratic caucus committee).

One difference between caucus committees and leadership PACs stands out. The caucus committees are more likely than the leadership PACs to fund a much higher proportion of nonincumbents than incumbents. Individual leaders are apparently less willing than the caucus committees to ignore the requests of incumbents for funding assistance. One good example is the Minnesota Democratic caucus committee, which funds a large proportion of nonincumbents and relatively few incumbents, while the leadership PACs fund the two categories more equally.

The other measure of the incumbency effect is very different. In table 3 we are measuring whether or not the *amount* of funding is affected by incumbency and we are also controlling for the size of the previous margin. In some cases the results are similar. For the California caucus committees, for example, nonincumbency has almost as much effect on spending level as does the previous margin. But for the caucus committees in New York and (for Republicans) Oregon, nonincumbency is much less important than the size of margins.

We found that, when we consider only the proportion of candidates who receive funding, most caucus and leadership groups favor nonincumbents. But, generally speaking, when we consider the amount of spending and we control for the previous margin, there is less consistent evidence that these groups give priority to nonincumbents. To some extent this means a larger proportion of nonincumbents is being funded but at a relatively low level.

Conclusion

The research presented within this chapter demonstrates that legislative party campaign committees target their resources to close races, are likely to fund nonincumbent candidates, and in some instances take into account their party's status in the legislature in determining what type of candidates to support. Concentrating their resources where they will be the most effective increases the importance of legislative party campaign committees above and beyond what the raw dollar figures indicate. It means that these legislative parties have come to play an important role in state legislative elections, a role that may have major implications for legislative behavior, in terms of party unity and interest group influence; state political parties, in terms of the role they play in elections; and the strength of legislative leaders.

The role played by legislative party campaign committees, given the strategic distribution of their resources, also has implications for the careers of individual legislators. The member or successful candidate who receives substantial assistance from the legislative party campaign committee may be less dependent on large donations from interest group PACs. Consequently, he or she may be less obligated to those interest groups on legislative issues. This may be particularly true of interest groups that are not strong in the member's district and whose influence over the member is based solely on campaign funds.

On the other hand, legislative party campaign committees might make the legislator more dependent on the legislative party and its leadership. This would be particularly true if the legislative party had made a large contribution to the member's last campaign or the member anticipates strong opposition in the next election. The legislator from a safe district would be less affected. A freshman legislator might feel particularly indebted to the legislative party for strong support. If funding assistance comes from a leadership committee rather than a caucus committee, the member may believe that personal loyalty to that leader is essential. Moreover, if the legislative party raises much of its funds from particular interest groups, members may be asked by party leaders to vote a certain way on bills in order to support the alliance between the party and an interest group that has contributed generously to the party.

The growth of legislative party campaign funding, and particularly the strategy of concentrating such funds on close races, has several other implications for legislators' careers. These trends have little effect on members who represent relatively safe districts; they still have to organize their own fundraising efforts. The member in a close race, or one who faces an unusually strong opponent, can expect substantial assistance from the legislative party in the form of campaign funds and/or in-kind services. This assistance would appear to reduce the incumbent's chances of defeat. On the other hand, because most legislative parties are also financing the campaigns of serious challengers, assistance certainly does not guarantee security for the incumbent. From the perspective of the legislative leader who is making the decisions for the caucus campaign committee, or for the leader's own campaign committee, the practice of distributing funds has implications for the leader's career. The strategic distribution of funds may allow leaders to strengthen their positions or advance their careers in the leadership hierarchy by building support among legislators. On the other hand, if legislators have come to expect their leaders to raise large sums of money for campaigns, the failure to meet these expectations may be damaging to the leaders—as the Speaker of the California Assembly discovered a few years ago.

The data presented here leave a number of questions unanswered, partly because they cover a single year but in large part because we can only speculate and hypothesize about the reasons for the variations we found. In order to understand these reasons better, we are now engaged in interviewing legislative leaders and their staffs in these states. This should help to explain why these results differ by state, by party, and by type of committee. It may also shed light on additional variables that ought to be added to our analysis—though data may not be readily available on all of them.

CHAPTER 8

Midsession Vacancies: Why Do State Legislators Exit and How Are They Replaced?

Keith Hamm
and
David M. Olson

At the outset of the 1988 Hawaii legislative session, fully 13 percent of the seventy-six members of the House and Senate had not attained their positions via the electoral process but instead had been appointed as midsession replacements by Governor John Waihee (Lee 1988). A considerable number of these "replacements were due to [part-time] legislators accepting full-time positions in the new administration" (Lee 1987, 7). While this example may be considered atypical due to the sheer number of appointments, it does spotlight interesting issues that have not been addressed in existing research on state legislative careers and turnover.

The current study attempts to fill in some of these gaps by focusing on midsession resignations and replacements during the 1981–86 period in eighty-eight state legislative chambers. Five major research questions are addressed. First, to what extent do legislators abandon legislative service before completing their terms? The second question focuses on the reasons for members voluntarily vacating their elected positions. A key issue is whether or not the factors associated with legislators voluntarily retiring at the end of their terms are sufficient to explain the midterm exits. We expect significant differences. Third, what factors, if any, account for the rate of early voluntary departures across the state legislatures? The fourth inquiry focuses on the legal procedures for replacing the resigners and tries to link the importance of a political party's organizational strength to the method of replacement that is used. Finally, the analysis traces the success of the replacement legislators in keeping their seats. The impact of the type of selection procedure on retention rates is examined.

We wish to thank Lydia Andrade for her significant effort in obtaining and coding the data on which this paper is based. Also, we wish to thank James Nowlin of Knox College for his very helpful information on the Illinois legislature.

Literature Review

Available evidence indicates that state legislative turnover is continuing to decline relative to that found in earlier periods, reaching its lowest levels in the last fifty years during the 1981–85 period (Niemi and Winsky 1987, 115). Members are more apt to seek reelection and their chance of being defeated is quite low (e.g., see Grau 1981b; Jewell 1982; Tucker and Weber 1985; Hamm and Olson 1987; Jewell and Breaux 1988). If electoral defeat is not the only major reason for legislative turnover, what additional factors account for it?

A growing body of research has focused on several variables (Rosenthal 1974b; Hain 1974; Bernick and Wiggins 1978; Miller and Smith 1978; Calvert 1979; Blair and Henry 1981; Francis and Baker 1986). Yet no single explanation accounts for why legislators leave voluntarily. The recent conclusion by Francis and Baker, in their study of legislators in Indiana and Missouri, highlights the multiplicity of factors:

> To summarize, legislators who voluntarily vacate their seat do so for various reasons, the most common of which are the opportunity costs associated with their private occupation and the prospects for career advancement in public office. Important also are opportunity costs associated with the family, dissatisfaction with legislative experience, health-or-age-related considerations, and electoral considerations. (1986, 124).

Should we expect the same set of factors to be prominent for the midsession vacancies? The answer is partially yes since in several of the previously cited studies the authors contacted legislators who did not seek reelection, a subset of whom also quit midterm. On the other hand, it is anticipated that certain factors will be more prominent. The key difference from what Francis and Baker found is that to depart midterm probably indicates the emergence of important and significant "opportunities" or "costs." On the positive side, legislators departing midterm are thought to be more open to advancing career ambitions, particularly those that involve seeking higher elected offices but do not require the legislators to resign their current seats unless an electoral victory is forthcoming. Thus, when midsession vacancies occur in the U.S. House of Representatives, state legislators may be more likely to enter the special replacement elections because they do not jeopardize their state legislative seats. At the same time, it is anticipated that the constellation of items related to the family factor discussed by Blair and Henry (1981) would not be as responsible for midterm resignations. Perhaps, at least in a relative sense, those factors somewhat out of the immediate control of the legislator will be more influential.

Data Sources

The information on midsession resignations and replacements between 1981 and 1986 was acquired via a questionnaire that was mailed to all ninety-nine house and senate clerks in June 1987, with a follow-up mailing sent about six weeks later. A clarifying questionnaire was mailed in January 1988 to resolve any ambiguities. If questions still remained, telephone calls were made to the appropriate state legislative offices, including those of chief clerk, Speaker, president of the senate, and legislative reference bureau. In the end, eighty-eight of the ninety-nine state legislative chambers supplied all or almost all of the requested information.

State laws were consulted to determine the legal method for filling legislative vacancies. Knowledgeable individuals in the various states were called to clarify ambiguities.

The fourth aspect of this study, the electoral success of the replacement legislators, was undertaken by consulting primary and general election results from 1981 to 1987 for these eighty-eight chambers. In those few cases where we did not have the appropriate election data, telephone calls were placed to either legislative personnel or election officials to obtain the missing bits of information.

Data Analysis

Descriptive Analysis

How frequently do members resign before the completion of their terms? According to the responses from legislative personnel, 651 vacancies occurred from 1981 to 1986, or on average, 217 legislators left early during every two-year period. Why do legislators not complete their terms? To answer this question, the reasons for leaving were first dichotomized into involuntary or voluntary categories. The involuntary category taps reasons that basically were beyond the legislator's control. Included were death, problems with the criminal justice system (e.g., arrest, indictment, or conviction), and being recalled by constituents. The voluntary category includes seven major reasons—sought elective office, appointed to a government position, concerned with occupation, had personal reason, suffered from ill health, moved out of district, and defeated for next term—along with several subcategories. In the findings in table 1 a major difference can be found between those exiting before their terms are complete and those who finish their terms but do not continue in the legislature. Almost three in ten midsession leavers did so involuntarily. They had relatively little ability to control their fates. Economic, family, and career factors were not at issue here. In fact, six out of every seven legislators who involuntarily departed midsession died while in office. Throughout the six-year period examined, at least one sitting legislator passed away in fifty-eight of the eighty-eight chambers for which we have information. Perhaps not unexpectedly, the greatest contingent ($N = 24$) came from just the New Hampshire House, a legislative body known for having a high percentage of older members. Conviction for lawbreaking or the legal accusation of such behavior constituted a small percentage of the total, although at least one legislator resigned for these reasons in twenty-two chambers. It is unclear from the questionnaires and telephone interviews if there

TABLE 1. Reasons State Legislators in Eighty-eight Chambers Quit before Completing Their Terms of Office, 1981–86

Reason	Percentage	Number of Cases ($N = 651$)
Involuntary Reasons	28.7	187
Death	(23.8)	(155)
Arrested/indicted/convicted of crime	(4.6)	(30)
Recalled	(0.3)	(2)
Voluntary Reasons	69.5	464
Elected office (sought)[a]	(21.1)	(137)
Federal office	(4.5)	(29)
State office	(10.4)	(68)
Executive office		(25)
State senator[b]		(29)
State judge		(14)
Local office	(6.1)	(40)
Appointive position	(30.4)	(198)
Federal agency	(4.2)	(27)
State	(24.7)	(161)
Agency/governor's cabinet		(108)
Senator[b]		(22)
Legislative administrator		(3)
Judge		(28)
Local government	(1.5)	(10)
Occupational position	(6.8)	(44)
Private sector business		(33)
Lobbyist		(11)
Moved out of legislative district	(4.9)	(32)
Ill health	(2.6)	(17)
Personal/retired/schooling	(3.1)	(20)
Defeated or did not run for reelection	(0.6)	(4)
Not listed	1.8	(12)

[a]It is unclear how many individuals won their try at another position.
[b]Applies only to members of the lower houses.

was any underreporting of this type of activity. It is apparent, though, that legislative personnel were sometimes hesitant to provide this type of information. The final subcategory, recalled via election, occurred only to two members in the Michigan Senate after the passage of a tax increase in the early 1980s.

The greatest number of legislators left voluntarily. Accepting appointive office was the largest general category, about 30 percent of total reasons. Roughly one in seven legislators who resigned during the term did so to be affiliated with a state agency or to work in the governor's office. For example, former Senator Peter Danton resigned to become Administrative Assistant to Governor Joseph Brennan in 1985, former Delegate Lorraine Sheehan was appointed Maryland's Secretary of State in 1983, while former Senator Louis Bergeron was appointed New Hampshire's Insurance Commissioner. When and why types of appointments were made are topics for future research. For example, how many appointments occur at the time a new governor is putting together a "team" and how many are, in effect, a "reward" for helping with legislation crucial to the governor's program?

Federal appointments, while less frequent, still accounted for roughly one in every twenty state legislators who left their legislative positions early. For example, in 1981 Ohio Representative Donna Pope left to become director of the U.S. Mint, while former Colorado Senator Steven Durham resigned to become, as a presidential appointment, regional director of the Environmental Protection Agency. Three legislators gave up their seats to accept administrative-political positions within the legislature.[1]

Legislators also resigned early to seek other elective offices or because they had already won them. One major opportunity was the chance to win election to the U.S. House of Representatives. Examples of special election victors to the U.S. House include Ohio's Michael G. Oxley, Wisconsin's Gerald Kleczka, and New York's Gary Ackerman, while general election winners include Ohio's Michael DeWine, Pennsylvania's George Gekas, and Virginia's Norman Sisky and Owen Pickett. Over 40 percent of the winners resigned after the state legislative session was already completed, usually in November or December of the second year.

While election to Congress is the highlight of major midterm political opportunities, a far more prevalent opportunity involves state office, be it that of a state senator, an executive officer, or a state judge. Some legislators gave up their state legislative seats early in order to enhance their chances of

---

[1] Former West Virginia Delegate Donald Kopp was chosen Clerk of the Delaware House in 1983, former Texas Representative Gordon Arnold left his elected position to become executive assistant to Speaker Gib Lewis, and former Representative Dennis Heck became Chief Clerk of the Washington House in 1985.

securing statewide elective offices. Included are unsuccessful gubernatorial candidates such as former Iowa Senator Lowell Junkins and former Florida Representatives Steve Pajcic and Barry Kutun. Several lower house members won special elections to the state senate. If the appointive senators are also included, then fifty-one, or roughly 12 percent, of all the house members who resigned during the six-year period did so to advance to the smaller, but more prestigious, state senate chambers.

However, just as many members resigned after winning election to local-level positions. Examples are legislators elected to the city councils of major U.S. cities, including those of New York, Chicago, Los Angeles, Honolulu, and New Orleans, and local elected executives, including the mayors of Provo, Utah, Biloxi, Mississippi, and Stamford, Connecticut, along with several Maryland County executives. In these cases, the state legislative position was a stepping-stone to what was possibly a more visible political office. Progressively ambitious legislators don't always follow a logical route from local to state to federal office.

Direct occupational factors had significantly less import in these data. However, they may have been masked in the categories "moved out of district" and "personal," although more in-depth analysis will be necessary before it can be determined the extent to which the occupational considerations entered into those latter reasons. Also, it may be that several former legislators who accepted state-level appointments did so hoping to enhance their financial situations.

Perhaps the question is not whether or not the legislator resigned before the completion of his or her term, but instead whether or not this action took place while the legislature was still in session, when crucial votes could still be cast. There would be no discernible impact on the legislative process if a legislator resigned after the session adjourned but before the scheduled start of the next session. The early exit, however, may affect the ability of the legislator's replacement to establish a concrete record on which to subsequently run as an incumbent. Whether or not the legislature was still in session when the incumbent left office was determined by examining the duration of session data in the *Book of the States* (Council of State Governments 1984, 1986) for 1981–85 and by calling state legislative clerks to ascertain dates the legislatures met in regular and special sessions during 1986. Roughly four out of five vacancies occurred while there was still some time left in the session, even if it only involved a special session.[2]

In summary, just as with the studies that investigate the general reasons

---

[2] A certain amount of caution must be taken in citing these percentages since they focus on the time period the legislature was officially in session, even if the sessions temporarily recessed for several months in the second year.

legislators do not return to the legislature, no one factor seems preeminent in the reasons for midsession vacancies. However, there is a difference in the relative importance given to specific reasons. The next research question is whether or not the voluntary/involuntary distinction tends to vary systematically across the state legislative chambers.

Chamber Variations: Description

As expected, the house chambers with the largest number of legislators tended to have the greatest number of vacancies, being led by the New Hampshire House (52), Illinois House (29), Massachusetts House (24), Ohio House (24), and the South Carolina House (23). The simple correlation between chamber size and total number of midsession vacancies over the six-year period is .803, statistically significant at the .001 level.

The aggregate midsession turnover rate (i.e., total departures 1981–86 divided by membership size) is 10.3 percent or roughly 3.4 percent every two years (see table 2). However, there is significant variation among these eighty-eight chambers, with the range being between zero (i.e., the Arizona Senate,

TABLE 2. Distribution of Voluntary and Involuntary Reasons for Midsession Exits in Eighty-eight State Legislative Chambers, 1981–86

Exiting Percentage[a]	Percentage of Voluntary Reasons	Percentage of Involuntary Reasons	Percentage of Total Reasons[b]
0	11.4[c]	25.0	3.4
.1–5.0	33.0	59.1	19.3
5.1–10.0	36.4	12.5	38.6
10.1–15.0	10.2	3.4	22.7
15.1–20.0	4.5	0.0	8.0
20.1–25.0	3.4	0.0	4.5
25.1–30.0	0.0	0.0	2.3
30.1–35.0	1.1	0.0	0.0
35.1–40.0	0.0	0.0	1.1
Mean	7.07	2.96	10.25
Standard deviation	5.99	2.96	6.74

Note: $N = 88$

[a]*Percentage* refers to the percentage of membership that left during midsession. For example, if ten legislators between 1981 and 1986 exited early, then the percentage of early departures in a fifty-member chamber would be 20 percent.

[b]Voluntary plus involuntary reasons. The total percentage is less than 100 percent due to rounding.

[c]Entry refers to the percentage of eighty-eight chambers that had the exiting percentage shown in the left-hand column.

California Senate, and the Oregon Senate) and thirty-six percent (i.e., the Ohio Senate). On average, midsession turnover rates are higher in state houses (mean = 10.58) than in the state senates (mean = 9.39).

An interesting variation emerges among the chambers when the types of reasons for leaving are taken into account. As shown in table 2, the mean chamber value for voluntary departures is more than twice as large as that for involuntary departures, with a score of zero for only ten chambers for the former but twenty-two chambers for the latter. A more relevant comparison may be obtained by calculating the percentage of total early resignations due to voluntary factors for each chamber. On average, two-thirds of the resignations per chamber are done voluntarily, with the minimum being zero in seven chambers and with the maximum being 100 percent in nineteen. For example, tremendous differences exist between two states—Texas and Arkansas—from the same region of the country that only meet in biennial sessions. In the Arkansas House and Senate, involuntary reasons (for example, death) were responsible for nine of the eleven vacancies, while only two of twenty-one resignations from the Texas House and Senate were attributable to these factors.

Explaining the Number of Voluntary Departures

What accounts for the variation in the number of early voluntary departures? Ten possible factors are examined in this paper. The most obvious one is the size of the legislative chamber; the greater the size, the greater the number of early voluntary departures. In addition, membership in the lower house, rather than the senate chamber, should increase the likelihood of early departure. Not only are house chambers generally larger than state senates, but also members of the lower house usually have less stature in the legislative process, thus decreasing their attachments to the institution and thereby increasing their chances of early departure.

Four measures tap the benefits and costs of legislative service (see Francis 1985a). The higher the legislative salary, the less incentive members should have for leaving the institution in midsession, all other factors being equal. If the legislature meets on an annual basis, the longer it is in session over the two-year period, particularly in terms of special sessions, the more likely members are to seek an early exit due to a host of excessive costs with which they must deal. Of course, legislators may weigh the relative benefit-cost ratios of completing their terms. That is, the greater the salary relative to the number of days in session, the less incentive members would have to depart early.

Significant differences exist across the state legislatures in the extent to which legislators identify themselves as being "full-time" legislators, with the range being from 0 percent to 66 percent in 1986 (see National Conference of State Legislatures 1987).[3] Squire shows that career legislatures, those with high salary and low to moderate advancement prospects, have a significantly greater percentage of members identifying themselves as full-time legislators than do dead-end or springboard legislatures (1988a, 75). Therefore, the expectation is that the greater the percentage of self-identified full-time legislators, the lower the number of early exits from the state legislature. On the other hand, the expectation is that the greater the percentage of retired individuals in the chamber, the greater the number of early voluntary exits.

Among the ninety-nine state legislative chambers, terms of office vary: two-year terms, four-year terms with 50 percent of the membership chosen every two years, and four-year terms with all members chosen in one election every four years. What impact does the term of office have on midsession vacancies? If members are chosen every two years, they may be more willing not to resign early since they know that it is a relatively short period of time until the next election. On the other hand, if members are selected for four-year terms, the probability increases that a midsession exit may occur since members have no other opportunity to leave throughout this time period. Finally, in a few states (i.e, Virginia, Kentucky, New Jersey, and Mississippi), legislative elections are held in odd-numbered years, thus providing members with the chance to seek a congressional seat without risking their present positions.

The simple correlations presented in table 3 offer only marginal support for the hypothesized relationships. The strongest relationship involves the size of the chamber variable, and it is in the expected direction. In addition, state house chambers have a higher rate of early departures than senates, partially due to the aforementioned size factor. However, the other two significant relationships are the opposite of the direction hypothesized. The greater the percentage of the membership elected to four-year terms, the lower the number of departures. More surprisingly, the greater the percentage of the membership that identifies itself as full-time legislators, the greater the number of early departures. In addition, salary, while not statistically significant, is positively, not negatively, related to voluntary departures.

Partial clarification is provided by a multivariate analysis. The most "parsimonious" regression model contains just two significant variables: size of the chamber and percentage of full-time legislators (see table 4). The greatest number of voluntary midsession vacancies occurs in larger chambers and in those in which "full-time" legislators predominate. Why would the more "professional" legislatures produce higher numbers of voluntary vacan-

---

[3] Squire, using data gleaned directly from member biographies, provides similar information for twenty-five lower houses for the late 1970s and early 1980s (1988a, 75).

TABLE 3. Correlations between Independent Variables and Number of Midsession Voluntary Departures and Voluntary Departure Ratios

Independent Variable	Number of Voluntary Departures	Voluntary Departure Ratio × 100
Size of chamber	.701***	.070
Senate chamber	.476***	.069
Salary	.183	.155
Length of session	.122	.154
Biennial session	.039	−.063
Benefit ratio	.066	.025
Percentage of full-time legislators	.300**	.274*
Percentage of retired legislators	.012	
Off-year elections	.024	−.076
Four-year terms	−.243*	.069

*p < .05.   **p < .01.   ***p < .001.

cies? To answer this question, the voluntary reasons were dichotomized into public sector and private reasons. The former category includes those elected or appointed to other government positions, while the latter is composed of the remaining voluntary reasons.

The parsimonious regression analyses for these two variables are shown in tables 5 and 6. While size of the chamber is positively associated with both variables, the percentage of full-time legislators is only related to the public sector variable. It would appear that in legislatures with a higher percentage of members who consider their legislative jobs as full-time there is a greater propensity for members to seek or accept other governmental positions. However, there is no impact on the number of members who leave for occupational, health, or personal reasons.

Splitting the voluntary reasons into public and private categories permits the uncovering of the opposite effects of two additional variables. While

TABLE 4. Parsimonious Model of Number of Midsession Voluntary Departures in Eighty-eight State Legislative Chambers

Independent Variable	Unstandardized Coefficient	Standardized Coefficient	t-value	Significance
Constant	−.322			
Size of chamber	.068	.667	8.675	.000
Percentage of full-time legislators	.055	.165	2.149	.034

Note: $R^2 = .517$, adjusted $R^2 = .506$.

TABLE 5. **Parsimonious Model of Public Sector Reasons for Early Exiting from Eighty-eight State Legislative Chambers**

Independent Variable	Unstandardized Coefficient	Standardized Coefficient	*t*-value	Significance
Constant	−0.931			
Size of chamber	0.027	.366	2.572	.012
Percentage of full-time legislators	0.054	.221	2.229	.029
Percentage of retired legislators	−0.167	−.250	−2.225	.029
House chamber	1.976	.242	2.039	.045

Note: R^2 = .381, adjusted R^2 = .351.

increases in the percentage of retired in a legislative chamber increases the number of midsession vacancies due to private reasons, the opposite effect occurs for the public sector category. Even controlling for size, house chambers are more likely to have a greater number of members exit early in order to seek other public sector positions, while fewer exit for private reasons.

State Laws and Practices on Filling Vacancies

The states have adopted a plethora of approaches for filling midterm vacancies. This analysis focuses on four key aspects: (1) the timing for filling a vacancy, (2) whether the selection method is appointment or special election, (3) the possibility for a partisan seat change, and (4) the importance of political parties.

An initial issue is whether or not the vacancy has to be filled no matter when it occurs. In several states, there is no requirement to replace the departed legislator if the legislature will not reconvene before the legislator's term expires. For example, there is no need to fill the vacancy in the Indiana legislature if no subsequent legislative session is scheduled before the next

TABLE 6. **Parsimonious Model of Private Reasons for Early Exiting from Eighty-eight State Legislative Chambers**

Independent Variable	Unstandardized Coefficient	Standardized Coefficient	*t*-value	Significance
Constant	−0.363			
Size of chamber	0.039	.748	7.771	.000
Percentage of retired legislators	0.159	.337	4.596	.000
House chamber	−1.724	−.300	−3.473	.001

Note: R^2 = .663, adjusted R^2 = .651.

general election. In other cases, no action is taken once the legislative session has progressed beyond a certain point. No special election is necessary in California if the vacancy occurs during the final year of the term of office and if it is after the close of the nomination period for the next election. If the vacancy occurs after February 2 of the second year of the term in Rhode Island, the position is not filled. On the other hand, in some states (e.g., South Carolina) the vacancy must be filled by special election irrespective of the length of the legislator's term that remains.

If the position must be filled, the next major issue is who is vested with the legal responsibility for choosing the successor. Two main options are for the successor to be chosen in a special election or to be appointed by a designated actor, be it the legislature, an elected official (e.g., governor), a local party organization, a unit of local government, or some combination thereof. The general outline of the process for each state is shown in table 7. Compared with the special election replacement procedure for the U.S. House of Representatives, the states display a greater variety of options. Perhaps the most surprising finding is that as of 1987 twenty states rely exclusively on an appointive method, twenty-eight states utilize only the special election approach, and two states—Tennessee and Washington—employ a combination of these two options.[4] In one sense then, the example of the midterm appointees to the Hawaii legislature is not as atypical as originally anticipated. The upshot, however, is that any study of state legislative special elections would be severely restricted in terms of generalizability. An example of the potential divergence of impact between the appointive versus the special election method of replacement is analyzed in the next section of this chapter.

One possibility is that in either the special elections or the appointive process a change in which party controls the seat may occur. Sigelman, for instance, found that in roughly 21 percent of the U.S. House special elections the party that had previously controlled the seat lost out in the special election, with the bulk of the losses being sustained by the president's party (1981, 580–82). In terms of state legislative replacements, this possibility of party turnover obviously exists in those states opting for special elections to choose successors. However, the opportunity is significantly reduced in the states relying on an appointive procedure because in seventeen of the twenty-two states (including Tennessee and Washington) the appointee must be of the same political party as the person who resigned. Change in party control of the seat, if it is going to occur, must be found in the states using special elections. The extent to which this happens will be explored in a future paper.

---

4. In Arizona, the procedure until 1987 was that a special election had to be held in order to fill a vacancy. The new law now emphasizes an appointive approach involving the county board of supervisors.

TABLE 7. State Laws Regarding the Method for Filling Midterm State Legislative Vacancies

State	Election				Appointment			
	Party Appointment/ Convention	Primary	Special General	Same Party	Governor	Local Party	Local Officials	Legislative Party
Alabama			X					
Alaska				X	X	X		X
Arizona				X(1) (1987)			X(1987)	
Arkansas	X	X	X					
California		X	X					
Colorado				X		X		
Connecticut	X		X					
Delaware	X		X					
Florida		X	X					
Georgia		X	X					
Hawaii				X	X			
Idaho				X	X	X		
Illinois				X		X		
Indiana				X		X		
Iowa	X		X					
Kansas				X		X		
Kentucky	X	X						
Louisiana		X	X					

Continued on next page

Table 7—*Continued*

State	Election				Appointment			
	Party Appointment/ Convention	Primary	Special General	Same Party	Governor	Local Party	Local Officials	Legislative Party
Maine	X							
Maryland				X	(2)	X		
Massachusetts		X	X					
Michigan		X	X					
Minnesota		X	X					
Mississippi			X					
Missouri	X		X					
Montana				X		X	X	
Nebraska					X			
Nevada				X			X	
New Hampshire		X	X					
New Jersey		X	X					
New Mexico					X(3)		X	
New York	X		X					
North Carolina				X		X		
North Dakota			X					
Ohio				X		X		X

State							
Oklahoma		X	X				
Oregon			X	X		X	X X
Pennsylvania	X		X				
Rhode Island		X	X				
South Carolina							
South Dakota					X		
Tennessee		X	X(4)				X
Texas			X				
Utah				X	X		
Vermont					X		
Virginia			X				
Washington		X	X(5)	X		X	
West Virginia			X	X	X	X	
Wisconsin		X	X				
Wyoming				X			X

Notes: (1) = The Arizona law before 1987 mandated that a special election be held. Starting in 1987 the procedure is to have the county board of supervisors appoint someone of the same political party as the person who resigned.

(2) = If among the local party central committees a tie exists in which more than one county is involved, then the governor makes the appointment.

(3) = If the legislator represents more than one county, then the governor chooses from the names presented by the county commissioners of each county represented.

(4) = If more than twelve months remain in the term, then the county court appoints an interim appointment and a special election is called, along with the party primary.

(5) = The political party recommends three names to the county commissioners, which may take any one of the names.

The final point to be made from an examination of table 7 is the extent to which the replacement process is left as a local political decision. The legislature or a political party within the legislature appears to have a significant say in only two states, while the governor is a major factor in only a handful of states, excluding those cases where the governor simply appoints the choice of another decision-making authority (e.g., the local political party). In fact, by our count, the governor has complete and free choice, at least in a legal sense, in only three states—Nebraska, South Dakota, and Vermont—while the governors of Utah and Hawaii are only limited in that appointees must be of the same political party as those who resigned. In Alaska, Idaho, and New Mexico (in some cases), the governor makes a selection from among a limited number of choices offered. A complicating factor in Alaska is that this decision must be confirmed by the political party of the chamber vacated by the legislator. In Maryland, the governor plays a major official role only when a tie vote exists among the local party central committees when more than one county is involved. In summary, in most states the governor is not delegated a major legal role in the selection process.

Role of Political Parties

A key actor, particularly in the appointive process states, is the local political party. In six states—Colorado, Illinois, Indiana, Kansas, Maryland, and North Carolina—the key appointive decision is made strictly by the local party leaders. In addition, local party leaders structure the choice of elected decision makers in six other states. For example, in Idaho the governor may select only from the list of three names provided by the local political party committee from the resigner's district. In Oregon local county commissioners from the district represented by the former legislator select a replacement from a list of three to five names supplied by the appropriate local political party commission. Local party control also carries over into some of the states that utilize special elections. In only a handful of states may anyone simply enter the special general election process. Parties are given the opportunity to select their candidates by holding a primary in sixteen states. More importantly, in nine states the local party nominates a candidate either via convention or by some other appointive process. Taken together, these laws tend to provide political parties major roles in the selection process to fill these midterm vacancies.

A question is whether or not there is any relationship between local party organizational strength and the reliance on parties to select the replacement. To test the conjecture that the strong, rather than weak, local party organizations are more likely to be given major roles in the selection process, we utilized the average strength rankings of local party organizations as developed by Gibson et al. (1985, 154–55). Each state was placed into one of two categories—strong or weak—based on the averages of Democratic and Republican local party scores.[5] The impact of local parties on the replacement process for midterm vacancies was also used to dichotomize states. Local parties with major impact either made the decision as to the replacement or significantly limited the options that subsequent decision makers had. In terms of special elections, states were scored in the major impact category if the political parties chose the nominees for the special elections through conventions or some other appointive methods. The results are displayed in table 8. As can be seen the relationship is as conjectured, albeit the support is not overwhelming. Perhaps, a more important question is whether or not the method of replacement is related to the probability of electoral success by the replacement.

Electoral Success of Legislative Replacements

How successful are those legislators who acquire their seats in midsession or after the legislature has already adjourned? In these cases, but particularly in the latter, the typical advantages often attributed to incumbency in the literature may be reduced substantially.

Roughly three in four vacancies were filled in a such a way that the opportunity existed between 1981 and 1986 for the replacement legislators to seek reelection (see table 9). Among these 490 legislators, almost nine in ten did take this opportunity to return to the legislature, and about 87 percent of this group was reelected. Legislators who fill midterm vacancies do not appear to be any less likely to relish the opportunity to establish legislative careers, at least for one additional session, and they are about as successful in their electoral quests as those members who won their last general election.

What impact does the selection method have on the electoral fortunes of these new legislators? The argument can be made that a majority of these members who are seated in midsession initially won their way into the legislature via a special election, which in some cases also required their winning a primary election. Therefore, even though these elections may have smaller turnouts than those associated with general elections, the new incumbents still have been forced to successfully compete for votes. The expectation regarding those who were appointed initially is less clear-cut. It may be that the appointees are individuals chosen with an understanding that they will not seek reelection. They are, in effect, temporary stand-ins. A few examples can be found in these data where the spouse of a deceased legislator performed just

---

[5] If the average score was greater than zero, the state was placed into the strong category; otherwise it was assigned to the weak category.

TABLE 8. Relationship between Strength of Local Party Organizations and Role of Local Party in Filling State Legislative Vacancies

Role of Local Party in Filling Legislative Vacancies	Strong Local Party Organizations		Weak Local Party Organizations	
	Percentage	Number of Cases ($N = 28$)	Percentage	Number of Cases ($N = 22$)
Major	50	(14)	19	(4)
Minor	50	(14)	81	(18)

Note: X = 5.28, df = 1, p < .05, N = 50.

such a role. However, if the spouse does decide to stand for office at the next election cycle, he or she is competing electorally, in effect, as a novice, at least for that office. It is assumed that name recognition will be lower among appointees than for those originally selected in special elections. Therefore, the expectation is that legislators who acquire their positions by a special election will have a higher success rate at the next general election than those who are initially appointed.

The relevant data are reported in table 10. The hypothesis regarding the impact of the selection method is confirmed using both a trichotomous and dichotomous dependent variable (i.e., electoral outcome). Overall, approximately seven out of every eight special election replacements are subsequently victorious at the polls while only two out of every three appointed replacements win the next election. The difference is not due solely to differences in rates of electoral defeats. Rather, appointees are almost three times as likely

TABLE 9. Subsequent Electoral Outcome for Vacancies in Eighty-eight State Legislative Chambers, 1981–86

Electoral Outcome	Total Vacancies		Electoral Decision (in Percentage)	Election Outcome (in Percentage)
	Percentage	N		
Opportunity to seek reelection	78.7	513		
Sought reelection		454	88.5	
Reelected		(394)		86.8
Defeated		(60)		13.2
Did not seek reelection		59	11.5	
Appointments too recent for reelection/elected before short-term appointment	8.7	56		
Vacancy not filled	12.6	82		

Note: Total N = 651.

TABLE 10. Relationship between Method of Selecting Replacments for Midterm State Legislative Vacancies and Subsequent Electoral Outcome, 1981–86

	Appointment		Special Election	
Electoral Outcome	Percentage	Number of Cases ($N = 218$)	Percentage	Number of Cases ($N = 295$)
Reelected	62.8	137	87.1	257
Defeated for reelection	19.3	42	6.1	18
Primary defeat		11		7
General election defeat		31		11
Did not run for reelection	17.9	39	6.8	20

Note: Statistical tests: Method of selection by electoral outcome (reelected, defeated, did not run)— $X = 41.64$, $df = 2$, $p < .001$. Method of selection by electoral outcome (reelected, defeated)—$X = 27.05$, $df = 1$, $p < .001$.

as the special election winners not to stand for reelection. Although in neither case is the percentage excessively high, there is an indication that appointees are somewhat less interested in developing a legislative career.

If those who decided not to seek another term are excluded, a better indication of the impact of the selection method can be gauged. While nineteen out of every twenty special election winners are reelected, only about four in every five appointees are successful. For whatever reasons, legislators who first attain office by special election are somewhat more likely to be able to retain the seats than if they acquired them by political appointment. It also should be stated that the reelection rates for both the special election winners and the appointees compare favorably with the comparable scattered data that do exist for regular incumbent reelection rates for the 1981–86 period.

A final question involves the relationship between the extent of party control over the appointees and their subsequent electoral success. The hypothesis is that if the legislators are chosen initially by the local party hierarchy, loosely defined, then they have a better chance of being successful with the voters in the next electoral cycle than legislators selected by another political actor (e.g., the governor or local elected officials). No support, however, is found for this hypothesis, there being roughly the same probability of electoral success from either method of appointment.

Conclusion

A guiding purpose of the research presented in this chapter was to determine the extent to which, if any, generalizations and explanations about midterm vacancies and subsequent replacements differ from the current state of knowledge about (1) why legislators do not return to the legislature and (2) the success rates of incumbents in the electoral process. In other words, what modifications must be made to the existing body of knowledge to accommodate those individuals who opt for an early exit from the legislature? If none, then there would be no compelling reason for substantial additional analysis on the set of research questions discussed in this chapter.

This preliminary study covering a six-year period highlights several interesting observations that suggest that additional research is warranted. The findings regarding at least the publicly stated reason for legislators resigning early suggest that greater attention could be given to the importance of "chance" opportunities in the development of political careers. It would be interesting to know how many of the various decisions were planned versus being made due to unanticipated events.

The second area requiring further research focuses on any additional impacts that the method of selecting legislators to fill vacancies may have on the newly chosen legislator's behavior or career and on the legislative process. In the latter case, using the example cited at the outset of this paper, the key question is what difference does it make in the legislative process that roughly one in seven legislators in the Hawaii legislature attained their position via gubernatorial appointment?

PART 3

Careers inside the Legislature

Legislative careers consist of at least two components: the electoral career and the career in the institution (Fenno 1978, 171). In the previous section, we explore some of the issues involving the electoral career. In this section two important components of the institutional career are analyzed. In chapter 9, Ronald Hedlund takes a look at the committee assignment process in several state legislatures. This is a topic that has received very little attention in the literature on state legislatures. Hedlund first examines the research on congressional committee assignments and then tests these congressional "models" against his state legislative data. Hedlund's data set is quite unique; it is based on the actual committee request slips of the state legislators in Wisconsin, Iowa, Maine, and Pennsylvania.

It is likely that committee assignments are increasingly important to state legislators as the legislature professionalizes. As Hedlund points out, "From an individual legislator's point of view, service on the 'right' committee(s) can materially affect a legislative career. For example, service on certain committees is typically seen as a 'pathway' to increased recognition and responsibility (e.g., becoming a chairperson) and eventually perhaps even a leadership position." It may also be important in a reelection effort.

Hedlund notes several important differences between congressional and state legislative assignment procedures, but it is our contention that the procedures will become more similar over time, as state legislatures continue to professionalize. Essentially, we would argue that it is in the career-minded legislator's interest to standardize and formalize the committee assignment process as much as possible. If the legislator's career is built in part because of his or her committee work, then the careerist legislator would prefer as much control over that process as possible. While this has yet to be formalized in most state legislatures, Hedlund shows that "legislative leaders do appear to accommodate members' committee requests to a large extent." Indeed, he notes that over 50 percent of all legislators receive their first choice of committees, and three-fourths receive either their first or second-most preferred committee choice. A second important finding by Hedlund is that the "state legislative committee assignment process seems to foster continuity of members on committees. Once appointed to a committee, a member is very likely to remain *on that committee* in future sessions if he or she so requests."

Peverill Squire examines leadership patterns in state legislatures. Squire argues that increased state legislative professionalization should lead to more stable leadership structures, in which leaders serve longer terms and are more likely to serve "apprenticeships" in assistant majority or committee chair positions. Relying on data from California, Iowa, and New York, Squire concludes, "The overall impression these figures leave is that Speakers are serving progressively longer terms; indeed tenure now is greater than at any other time this century." He also indicates that more experience is needed before a legislator ascends to the Speaker's position, but that there isn't a well-defined pattern of specific stepping-stone positions as of yet.

Squire notes two other important trends. First, it appears that there is less gubernatorial influence than previously existed in the selection of legislative leaders. This is an important indicator of the "institutionalization" of the legislature (Polsby 1968). Second, Squire observes that the *function* of the legislative leaders is changing. He argues that professionalization has led members to alter their needs in regard to leadership. They no longer desire policy guidance (which the professional legislators or their staffs are capable of providing on their own) but "Instead, members want leadership to maintain the organization so as to provide them an environment in which they can seek their own goals and to supply them with the means with which to protect or improve their current positions."

This last observation by Squire is especially significant, because it again points out that the internal dynamics of state legislatures are changing. Leadership is increasingly viewed as a device to provide the proper stable environment in which the individual legislator can pursue his or her career.

In the final chapter the coeditors provide a summary of the research findings in the various chapters. The essays in this particular volume answer many important questions about numerous aspects of the changing patterns in state legislative careers. But there are many questions unanswered and areas left unexplored. The final chapter offers some suggestions about future research avenues in this increasingly important area of state legislatures.

CHAPTER 9
Accommodating Member Requests in Committee Assignments: Individual-Level Explanations

Ronald Hedlund

Studies of U.S. legislatures have long identified the important role played by committees both in the legislative process and in the career development of individual members. Committees are described as one of the organizational features affecting *how* the legislature works and *what* it accomplishes. Specifically, committees are a primary organizational device for handling the legislative work load while achieving division of labor, specialization, and expertise development (see Hedlund and Powers 1987; Jewell and Patterson 1986; Keefe and Ogul 1985; Shepsle 1978; Rosenthal 1974a; Fenno 1973). Indeed, committees are seen as an important locus for policy-making by about one out of every four state legislators responding in a recent survey, second only to legislative leaders (Francis and Riddlesperger 1982).

From an individual legislator's point of view, service on the "right" committee(s) can materially affect a legislative career. For example, service on certain committees is typically seen as a "pathway" to increased recognition and responsibility (e.g., becoming a chairperson) and eventually perhaps even a leadership position (Rosenthal 1981; Fenno 1973; Jewell 1969; Clapp 1963). Further, service on a committee whose subject is important to a legisla-

A number of individuals have played key roles in the completion of this study. Without the assistance of Speaker Tom Loftus, former minority leader Betty Jo Nelsen, Senate President Fred Risser, former Speaker Ed Jackamonis, all from Wisconsin; Speaker Don Avenson of Iowa; Speaker John Martin of Maine; and former Speaker Leroy Irvis of Pennsylvania, this study would not have been possible. Also important were Sue Meyer, Dave Dunwiddie, and Terry Donohue of Wisconsin and Clancey Myer of Pennsylvania. In addition, the Wisconsin Legislative Reference Bureau, the State Historical Society of Wisconsin, and numerous senators and representatives in the study's states who provided important information must be acknowledged. Also noteworthy from the University of Wisconsin-Milwaukee were Linda L. Hawkins (Social Science Research Facility), the Graduate School, and the College of Letters and Science. Comments from Professor Malcolm Jewell (University of Kentucky), and Keith Hamm (Rice University) provided numerous insights into the data analysis. Funding for the collection of some of the data used in this report was provided by a National Science Foundation grant (SES-8411353).

tor's district is often viewed as building the member's relationship with his or her constituents (e.g., a rural member's service on the agriculture committee) (Rosenthal 1981; Fowler, Douglas, and Clark 1980; Ray 1980; Fiorina 1977; Mayhew 1974a; Fenno 1973; Masters 1961). Thus, seeking to serve on certain committees becomes an important career decision for legislators because of "door-opening" and advancement possibilities, as well as potential effects on reelection.

As a result, the process and consequences of the committee assignment process have been an important concern among legislators, as well as political scientists. While much is known about committee assignments in the U.S. House and Senate, less is known about those in state legislatures. This chapter, is a modest effort to aid our knowledge of state committee selection. The analysis contained herein is based on longitudinal data collected for two states (Wisconsin, seven legislative sessions, and Iowa, two) and on single-session data in two additional states (Maine and Pennsylvania). While data from these states *do not* constitute a random sample of states nor of the assignment processes used, they do provide both cross-state and longitudinal perspectives on the assignment process at the state level.

Prior Research on Legislative Committee Assignments

Committees are an integral part of the legislative process. Permitting relatively large and generalist-oriented legislative bodies to scrutinize increasing amounts of complex technical legislations creates a division of labor that facilitates member and small group specialization, competes with the growth and sophistication of executive agencies and interest groups, strengthens leaders' power by sharing decision-making responsibilities, provides a "proving ground" for activities and members' advancement, facilitates compromise and negotiation, and incorporates members' competence and continuity into the decision-making process. By playing these roles in the legislative process, committees serve important functions for the operations of legislative organizations and the evolution of individual members' careers.

Literature on the committee assignment process in the United States focuses almost exclusively on the U.S. House of Representatives and more recently on the Senate. A recent review by Eulau (1985) evaluates findings on the committee assignment process and seniority, members' occupational and social backgrounds, members' electoral margins and subsequent reelection, constituencies' concerns, geographical balancing of committees, interest groups' pressure on committees, members' goals, leaders' strategies, and committees' subsequent policy-making. Eulau concludes that a great deal of information and theory formulation is evident regarding committee assignments in Congress.

A rigorous study of Democratic committee assignments in the U.S.

House posits an interest-advocacy-accommodation syndrome in which individual members announce their interests in committee assignments as a means of advising decision makers about their own committee preferences (Shepsle 1978). These interests represent policy preferences of members as well as those of their districts. The articulation of interests gives individual members an opportunity to build support for their appointments among influential persons and members of the Committee on Committees. If successful, these relevant others will advocate members' requests during the assignment process.

Working concurrently is the congressional leaders' desire to build a working consensus among party members through the accommodation of requests. Success in meeting expressed committee preferences is expected to advance party harmony and unity. Work by Gertzog (1976), Westefield (1974), Shepsle (1978), and Smith and Ray (1983) on the U.S. House, Bullock (1985) on the U.S. Senate, and Hedlund (1989) on the Wisconsin legislature all provide persuasive evidence regarding the impressive degree to which leader accommodation takes place in committee appointments. Shepsle's work demonstrates how committee assignments affect leaders and their ability to lead, affects members, especially in the development of their careers, and affects the entire committee system in its ability to meet policy expectations.

While Shepsle's work, as well as that of others, is instructive for understanding committee assignments in Congress, many of these explanatory factors do not apply in other legislative settings. For example, in forty-five lower chambers of U.S. state legislatures, a single individual (the Speaker, the majority leader, or the minority leader) has almost complete discretion in making committee appointments (Council of State Governments 1986), so decision making rests more in the hands of a single individual than in the hands of a committee. Secondly, formal representation by geographical areas (zones) for the assignment process is found in only one state, Nebraska. While attention may be given toward balancing appointments across geographical areas of the state, as in California, these appointments are rarely as formally implemented into decision making as is done in the U.S. House. The role of seniority is also generally less formal than found in Congress. In spite of the importance given to experience, senior state legislators in some states are more likely to undergo shifts in committee assignments, contrary to their requests, than is true in Congress.[1] While these generalizations do not apply

---

[1] One example of this occurred after the 1988 general election in Wisconsin. The assembly Speaker, *before* being reelected by the Democratic caucus for his fourth term as Speaker, announced his intention to replace the current two-time cochair of the powerful Joint Finance Committee. Although the incumbent cochair, a nine-term veteran with four terms of service on this committee, protested the decision in public, no serious effort was made to challenge that reassignment by the Speaker.

uniformly across all states, the assignment process typically varies from that found in the U.S. House.

Models of Legislative Committee Assignments

In his very extensive literature review of prior studies on committee assignments, Eulau (1985) discusses different models of the committee appointment process. While the number of studies cited and the range of variables included is extensive, four models based on congressional studies predominate.

Reelection or the Masters-Clapp Model

Much of the early discussion of committee appointments in Congress dealt with the relationship between such assignments and the reelection of individual members. Starting in the early 1960s, several authors provide interview evidence to support the proposition that assignments were intended to help ensure reelection of members, especially those from marginal districts. The assignment process was thus a means for assisting members in solidifying relationships with their districts and in their reelection. Committee assignments reflected reelection "needs" (Clapp 1963; Masters 1961). Subsequent research by Bullock (1972, 1973), Fowler, Douglas, and Clark (1980), and Smith and Ray (1983) raises questions about the appropriateness of this model, given other factors.

Constituency Interests

Concurrent with findings regarding the importance of reelection, several researchers note the impact of constituency interests on the assignment process. It is argued that a member's constituency can "suggest" certain committee requests so that a member can be involved in policy decisions of interest to his or her district. According to this approach, members, cognizant of their districts' interests, would seek assignments on committees whose interests were compatible with those of their districts. While several different rationales for this relationship have been provided, substantial findings support the validity of the constituency interest model (Davidson 1981; Ray 1980; Rohde and Shepsle 1973; Bullock 1972, 1973; Masters 1961).

Member Motivations, Preferences, and Goals

The most extensive research has taken place with regard to the motivations, preferences, and goals pursued by individual members. While much of the original work was based on Fenno's statement about individual goals sought by members, a variety of research approaches and analysis strategies have characterized this research. Basically, the hypothesis being tested concerns the effects of individual members and their orientations on the assignment process (Smith and Deering 1983; Perkins 1981; Shepsle 1978; Bullock 1976; Fenno 1973). The most persuasive analysis is that of Shepsle whose application of a social choice-based theory to the assignment process provides important information regarding committee assignments in the U.S. House.

Norms, Rules, and Practices

Like all organizations, U.S. legislatures are characterized in their operations by the applicability of norms, rules, and practices. A fourth set of studies investigates the impact of these factors on the assignment process. For example, norms of seniority, conformity, and apprenticeship have been the most common themes. This research posits that norms, informal rules, and practices prescribe committee selection and therefore affect committee appointments (Hinckley 1978; Shepsle 1978; Asher 1975; Bullock 1970; Swanson 1969; Masters 1961).

Recent research tends to combine factors from more than one of these approaches, thus providing a means for evaluating the comparative applicability of more than one alternative. The result has been a complex view of the assignment process in which the revealed preferences for committee assignments reflect a complex combination of individual members' motivations and experiences, together with the nature of the districts being represented. These revealed preferences reflect compromises and "discounting" of real preferences due to the realities of the legislative appointment process and the necessity for reelection. Revealed preferences are then subjected to the selection process in which leaders seek to accommodate members so as to build a workable coalition in pursuing public policy decisions (Shepsle 1978).

The research described in this chapter builds on this approach and explores the applicability of two sets of factors investigated in numerous studies of the committee assignment process in the U.S. House. Specifically, this research focuses on the appropriateness of *member background* variables and the *choice strategy* used on the success members achieve in their overall committee appointments. In the analysis, these two sets of variables are first treated as separate models and then combined for exploring a parsimonious model of success in committee assignments. The goal is to assess the applicability of congressional models and findings to legislative settings in which the appointment process is quite different from that found in Congress. Also, this research provides information on committee assignments and the legislative career development of state legislators.

Data on Standing Committee Assignments

While collecting information on committee memberships in eighteen state legislatures, I was able to obtain information regarding the committee requests of legislators in four states. These request data varied somewhat in completeness and specificity. For example, data were available from one or both parties for seven sessions in Wisconsin, from Democrats for two sessions of the Iowa House, from both parties for one session of the Maine House, and from Democrats for one session of the Pennsylvania House. While I attempted to get information for both chambers, and from Republicans as well as from Democrats, success was entirely dependent on the individuals who control access to these data. Typically, legislative leaders have been reluctant to provide access to information like this; however, the appearance of new leadership styles and personalities at the state level has resulted in greater openness and willingness to discuss and provide such information.

In these fourteen instances, I was provided, or was able to obtain through historical records, the original committee request sheets filed by individual members or extensive notes recorded by individuals involved in the assignment process. Conversations with individuals involved in the assignment process as well as the nature of the request information indicate that these request forms and notes are valid representations of the requests made by individual legislators.[2]

With one notable exception, these data take the form of individual preferences provided by members for committee requests. Typically, the instruction to members was to list, in order, their top three to six committee assignment requests. Thus, for each legislator for whom data are available, there is a one to N preference listing of committee assignments. In Pennsylvania, however, a more complicated request was made of legislators. On the committee request form, all twenty-one major standing committees were listed. In one column, committees were grouped into five major categories, and in the other, they were listed in an ungrouped fashion. First, members were asked to rank preferences *within* each group. Then, they were asked to rank all twenty-one committees. While all twenty-one preferences were recorded, only the *top nine* are relevant for the purposes of this chapter, in order to provide comparability in the cross-state analysis.

Because assignments to subcommittees of the Appropriations Committee in Iowa were requested in the same fashion and on the same form used to

---

[2] It was also apparent from interviews with leaders and members that informal discussions among the principal actors frequently precede the submission of formal requests. This seemed especially evident for new members of the chamber and for experienced members seeking a major "improvement" in committee assignments. Evidence persists, however, that these data constitute the formal requests made for committee assignments.

request assignments on standing committees, these Iowa subcommittee requests and assignments *are included*. For all committee measures in Iowa, then, assignments to and requests for the Appropriations subcommittees are treated like those for standing committees.

For analysis, these request data were then merged with committee assignment and personal background data. The resulting data file contains information on background characteristics, committee requests, and committee appointments (for both the prior session and the session of interest). A variety of analyses and comparisons are possible using original and derived variables in an across-session framework.

Variables

Personal background information on four variables is available for legislators in all four states. In most instances, this information was obtained from official publications.[3] *Age* is the respondent's age during the first year of the biennial session. *Education* is a six-fold categorization of the education level achieved. The respondent's *sex* is the third background variable. Because of the importance attached to seniority in the legislature, the number of *previous sessions* served is also included.[4]

The second set of variables relates to the choice strategy used by the individual legislator in making his or her committee requests. For these variables, I was concerned with the nature of the choices made—the "discounting problem" facing legislators (Shepsle 1978, 63). When discounting, a legislator is presumed to alter his or her "true" committee preferences to reflect the realities of the assignment situation. Given that committee assignments are a scarce resource, members may adjust their requests by anticipating demand levels for the more popular committees, targeting a small number of committees, and returning to the same committee assignments held previously, if they are veteran legislators. Thus, the committee choice strategy variables reflect the decisions legislators make regarding the number of choices to include in their preferences, the anticipated demand level for committees chosen, and remaining on the same committees from last session.[5]

---

[3] Typically, these sources were the "Red Book" or "Blue Book." For Maine, information was also taken from *A Citizen's Guide to the Maine Legislature*, Maine People's Resource Center.

[4] The "age" variable is actual age. For "education," the higher the value, the greater the level of education. Males were recorded as 1, females as 2. "Previous sessions" is the number of previous sessions.

[5] The actual number of requests made, up to a maximum of nine in Pennsylvania, was coded. The demand level for a committee is the proportion of legislators requesting a committee, which means a higher value indicates greater demand. Same committee requests is the proportion of committee requests this session that correspond with committee assignments held last session.

The number choice strategy variable may be viewed in two ways: a larger number of requests will provide leadership greater latitude in accommodating members' requests and also provide a member with a greater probability for receiving a requested committee, or a small number of requests may be to the members' advantage if leaders are really committed to accommodating members' requests.

Demand levels that exist for differing committees require a different choice strategy variable. While some modification of committees' sizes may take place, it is unlikely that legislative leaders will adjust committees' sizes so as to accommodate *all* of the demands for the most popular committees. Thus, requesting a committee in high demand may affect a member's overall success. In this study, two stops were used to determine demand levels. First, each committee was assigned a "popularity" score, indicating the proportion of all requests made for that committee. Second, each member was given the average of scores for all committees he or she requested. This individual demand score has the advantage of permitting the value of the variable to reflect the actual demands made for that person's committee choices during the specific session under study.[6] The higher the demand level for committees requested, the higher the value for this score. The third choice strategy variable relates to the degree to which legislators serving in the prior session requested the same assignments as previously held. A high value for this variable designates many members requesting committees on which they had prior service.

Committee Assignment Process

Two factors related to the committee assignment process as it affects these variables must be noted. While the requester(s) in each state asked legislators to provide a ranking of preferences, legislators did not have to rank all committees. Thus, variation occurred in the number of requests made. In addition, legislative chambers differed in the number of requests legislators were to make and in the number of assignments members could expect. These factors, together with systematic appointment process differences associated with each state/chamber/session/party, requires that each state/chamber/session/party combination be treated as a separate case in this analysis. Thus, there are fourteen combinations included here.

Although several different operational measures of committee assignment success are possible, the concern here is with the overall success achieved for each combination. Two characteristics of overall assignment

---

[6] In congressional research, demand for committee assignments was frequently operationalized into a perception of committee status.

success are appropriate for analysis. The first relates to the percentage of success legislators achieved in their requests, while the second relates to the rank of the choices received. In this latter instance, the lower the number for the variable, the higher the ranking of the choice received.[7]

While committee assignment processes have many similarities across the four states for the time period covered, there are some differences. In each state, information regarding committee choices is solicited from individual members shortly after the November general election. In Iowa, Pennsylvania, and Wisconsin, this is done separately by each political party. In Maine, while the minority Republicans have been responsible for assigning their members to committees, some of the requested information has been forwarded to the Democratic Speaker. In each instance, however, the party is responsible for making assignments. There are also considerable discussions between members and leadership regarding committee assignments. In the Pennsylvania House and the Wisconsin Senate, the ultimate decisions are made by a Committee on Committees; thus, members discuss assignments with more than one person, and the numbers of contacts appear extensive. The goal for such contact is to help ensure that leaders know the rationale for the choices being made and are convinced about the value of supporting members.

After reviewing the two measures of success in committee appointments, this chapter evaluates the adequacy of the background and committee choice strategy models for each of the fourteen cases. Also included is an analysis of the most parsimonious models for explaining the percentage of success and the choice received variables.

Findings

This chapter's initial concern is with the overall degree to which members obtain the committees requested. Since these success variables also serve as the dependent variables here, basic information about the distribution of responses is provided.

Success in Obtaining Committee Requests

One dominant theme in all previous studies of committee assignments is the degree to which leaders are able to meet the committee requests made by individual members. In table 1 comparable information for the fourteen study sites is provided, and the substantial degree to which members in each state have received committee assignments they requested is indicated. The lower

---

[7] Since, in each of the two sessions for the Iowa House, all members received their first choice assignment, no variability exists for this variable for this state.

TABLE 1. Percentage of Standing Committee Requests Received by Legislators of Those Requested, by State, Chamber, Session, and Party (percentage by row)

State/Chamber/ Session/Party	Percentage Requests Received of Requested						Total		Overall Percentage Received
	0%	1–24%	25–49%	50–74%	75–99%	100%	Percentage	Number of Cases	
Wisconsin assembly									
1975–76 Democrats	1.8	1.8	10.7	42.9	3.6	39.3	100.1	56	64.8
1979–80 Democrats	0.0	1.7	8.6	37.9	17.2	34.5	99.9	58	67.0
1981–82 Democrats	3.5	1.8	14.0	31.6	14.0	35.1	100.0	57	65.5
1983–84 Republicans	0.0	5.1	33.3	38.5	0.0	23.1	100.0	39	50.3
1985–86 Democrats	6.5	0.0	10.9	37.0	15.2	30.4	100.0	46	63.5
1985–86 Republicans	0.0	11.6	37.2	41.9	0.0	9.3	100.0	43	45.5
1987–88 Democrats	3.8	1.9	13.5	42.3	11.5	26.9	99.9	52	63.2
1987–88 Republicans	0.0	10.5	18.4	39.5	13.2	18.4	100.0	38	53.3
Wisconsin senate									
1987–88 Democrats	7.7	0.0	7.7	30.8	0.0	53.8	100.0	13	77.5
Iowa house									
1985–86 Democrats	0.0	0.0	39.0	61.0	0.0	0.0	100.0	59	48.0
1987–88 Democrats	0.0	0.0	37.5	62.5	0.0	0.0	100.0	56	48.0
Maine house									
1987–88 Democrats	6.7	8.0	37.3	22.7	0.0	25.3	100.0	75	39.4
1987–88 Republicans	13.3	6.7	53.3	13.3	0.0	13.3	99.9	15	39.4
Pennsylvania house[a]									
1987–88 Democrats	1.6	18.8	53.1	7.8	4.7	14.1	100.1	64	39.7

Note: Total percentages are slightly more or less than 100 percent due to rounding.

[a] Since Democratic members of the Pennsylvania House were asked by their leaders to rank their preferences for twenty-one committees, only the first nine listed were included in these calculations.

percentages of requests received in states other than Wisconsin can be traced, in part, to the assignment process itself. In Maine, members are assigned, typically, to one or, rarely, to two committees, while request sheets averaged more than 2.5 requests. Similarly, in Iowa, members provided requests for up to six standing committees and three appropriations subcommittees. No one was assigned to more than one appropriations subcommittee nor to more than four standing committees. As already noted for Pennsylvania, the data provided rankings for up to nine committees, and most members received three or four assignments. In Wisconsin, suggestions regarding requests varied a great deal. Thus, cross-state comparisons in table 1 should be initiated with care. Nevertheless, the degree to which legislative leaders *do accommodate* members' requests is evident from the percentages receiving *none* of their requests. In only one instance (Maine Republicans, 1987–88) does the number denied exceed 10 percent. In six of the fourteen cases, all legislators received at least one of their requests.[8] As shown in the "Overall Percentage Received" column in table 1, a minimum average of about 40 percent of a member's requests were received in these fourteen instances. Thus, legislative leaders do appear to accommodate members' committee requests to a large extent.

This conclusion about leaders' accommodation is reinforced by table 2, in which the degree to which members received their first choice committee requests is shown. At least half, and in most instances two-thirds or more, received their first choice request. This is true regardless of party status (minority or majority), session, or even state. When combining first and second choices, almost three out of every four members received their first or second. Again, most state/chamber/session/party combinations substantially exceed this 75 percent threshold. The lone exception is 1987–88 Republicans in the Maine House; however, generalizations about this group must be tempered in light of the small number of cases and the fact that the information used here was in the form given to the Democratic Speaker, while the Republican Minority Leader had the responsibility for these assignments. Data from these two tables underscore the degree to which state legislative leaders do accommodate members' requests for committee assignments.

Background Model Explanation

For testing the proposed explanatory models of committee appointment success, a regression analysis approach was selected. In table 3 the findings are summarized for each of the fourteen cases using the four background variables previously discussed to explain the overall percentage of assignments

---

[8] Since the data in Pennsylvania, as used here, included only the first nine stated choices, presumably this 1.6 percent in table 1 received an assignment, but the choice was below their first nine.

TABLE 2. Highest Priority of Standing Committee Requests Received by State Legislators, by State, Chamber, Session, and Party (percentage by row)

State/Chamber/ Session/Party	Priority of Committee Request Received						Total	
	No Choice Received	Fifth or Lower Choice	Fourth Choice	Third Choice	Second Choice	First Choice	Percentage	Number of Cases
Wisconsin assembly								
1975–76 Democrats	1.8	0.0	0.0	3.6	21.4	73.2	100.0	56
1979–80 Democrats	0.0	1.7	0.0	3.4	12.1	82.8	100.0	58
1981–82 Democrats	3.5	0.0	0.0	5.3	17.5	73.7	100.0	57
1983–84 Republicans	0.0	0.0	0.0	2.6	20.5	76.9	100.0	39
1985–86 Democrats	6.5	0.0	0.0	0.0	17.4	76.1	100.0	46
1985–86 Republicans	0.0	2.3	0.0	7.0	16.3	74.4	100.0	43
1987–88 Democrats	3.8	0.0	0.0	3.8	28.8	63.5	99.9	52
1987–88 Republicans	0.0	2.6	0.0	7.9	39.5	50.0	100.0	38
Wisconsin senate								
1987–88 Democrats	7.7	0.0	0.0	0.0	15.4	76.9	100.0	13
Iowa house								
1985–86 Democrats	0.0	0.0	0.0	0.0	0.0	100.0	100.0	59
1987–88 Democrats	0.0	0.0	0.0	0.0	0.0	100.0	100.0	56
Maine house								
1987–88 Democrats	6.7	1.3	0.0	6.7	13.3	72.0	100.0	75
1987–88 Republicans	13.3	0.0	0.0	13.3	13.3	60.0	99.9	15
Pennsylvania house[a]								
1987–88 Democrats	1.6	3.1	1.6	7.8	21.9	64.1	100.1	64

[a]Since Democratic members of the Pennsylvania House were asked by their leaders to rank their preferences for twenty-one committees, the only members who could receive none of their choices were those who provided only a partial list of committee preferences.

received. As table 3 indicates, for seven of the fourteen cases *none* of the four explanatory variables has a statistically significant regression coefficient at the .1 level. In those seven cases where statistically significant coefficients exist, prior legislative service is the most frequent (Republicans in the Wisconsin Assembly for 1983–84, 1985–86, and 1987–88 and in the Pennsylvania House, 1987–88) followed by two instances for age and education and one for sex. The amount of variance explained is relatively small (adjusted R^2 less than .25) in ten of the fourteen cases. Thus, the background model is of limited utility in explaining one measure of overall committee appointment/request success.

These relatively few instances of a sizable relationship were expected, given prior findings for Congress (Smith and Ray 1983; Shepsle 1978). If committee assignments were based primarily on members' background characteristics, legislative leaders would be charged with bias, would face hostile members, and would probably lose their leadership posts. The two instances where age has a significant impact are both in a positive direction, indicating that older members tended to experience higher success levels in

TABLE 3. Regression Analysis Summary of Background Model Explanation for Percentage of Committee Requests Received, by State, Chamber, Session, and Party

State/Chamber/ Session/Party	R^2	Adjusted R^2	Statistically Significant *t*-ratio Explanatory Variables
Wisconsin assembly			
1975–76 Democrats	.261	.203	Sex***/age*
1979–80 Democrats	.062	−.009	None
1981–82 Democrats	.117	.048	None
1983–84 Republicans	.205	.111	Previous service**
1985–86 Democrats	.109	.022	None
1985–86 Republicans	.462	.403	Education**/previous services**
1987–88 Democrats	.143	.067	None
1987–88 Republicans	.401	.328	Previous service**
Wisconsin senate			
1987–88 Democrats	.586	.431	Education*
Iowa house			
1985–86 Democrats	.085	.018	None
1987–88 Democrats	.205	.142	Age**
Maine house			
1987–88 Democrats	.130	.063	None
1987–88 Republicans	.287	−.120	None
Pennsylvania house			
1987–88 Democrats	.292	.244	Previous service****

$*p < .1.$ $**p < .05.$ $***p < .01.$ $****p < .001.$

their assignments. With regard to education, one relationship is in the positive direction (Wisconsin Senate Democrats, 1987–88) and the other in the negative (Wisconsin Assembly Republicans, 1985–86). There is also a negative direction for the relationship with sex, indicating that women in the 1975–76 Wisconsin Assembly experienced lower rates in the percentage of committee assignments received. All four relationships with prior service are in the positive direction; thus, the longer one serves in the legislature, the greater the percentage of requested appointments received. Again, this finding is consistent with expectations based on the congressional literature.

Turning to the highest-priority committee choice received (table 4), one again finds relatively few instances in which background variables seem to have much impact. In fact, the pattern of the relationship is more "meager" than that found for the percentage of requests received. Seven out of the twelve cases show no statistically significant regression coefficients ($p < .1$) for the background variables. Of the five instances where background variables result in statistically significant coefficients, the respondents' sex is an explanatory variable in three, and in all three, the relationships are positive,

TABLE 4. Regression Analysis Summary of Background Model Explanation for Highest-Priority Committee Request Received, by State, Chamber, Session, and Party

State/Chamber/ Session/Party	R^2	Adjusted R^2	Statistically Significant t-ratio Explanatory Variables
Wisconsin assembly			
1975–76 Democrats	.154	.088	Sex***
1979–80 Democrats	.175	.113	Sex***
1981–82 Democrats	.018	−.058	None
1983–84 Republicans	.040	−.073	None
1985–86 Democrats	.086	−.003	None
1985–86 Republicans	.105	.008	None
1987–88 Democrats	.204	.137	Sex**/education*
1987–88 Republicans	.162	.060	None
Wisconsin senate			
1987–88 Democrats	.238	−.016	None
Iowa house			
1985–86 Democrats			
1987–88 Democrats			
Maine house			
1987–88 Democrats	.067	−.005	Age*
1987–88 Republicans	.349	−.023	None
Pennsylvania house			
1987–88 Democrats	.136	.077	Previous service**

*$p < .1.$ **$p < .05.$ ***$p < .01.$ ****$p < .001.$

indicating that women were more likely to receive a lower-priority committee choice than were men.

Committee Choice Strategy Model

Table 5 is a summary of the regression analyses when the three committee choice strategy variables plus previous legislative service are used as explanatory variables, with the percentage of committee appointments received being the dependent variable. Only two sites show *no* statistically significant regression coefficients: $p < .1$ for 1985–86 Wisconsin Democrats and 1987–88

TABLE 5. Regression Analysis Summary of Committee Choice Strategy Model Explanation for Percentage of Committee Requests Received, by State, Chamber, Session, and Party

State/Chamber/ Session/Party	R^2	Adjusted R^2	Statistically Significant *t*-ratio Explanatory Variables
Wisconsin assembly			
1975–76 Democrats	.600	.556	Same requests****/number of requests****/demand for choices**
1979–80 Democrats	.602	.567	Number of requests****/same requests****
1981–82 Democrats	.506	.459	Same requests***/number of requests***/demand for choices**
1983–84 Republicans	.745	.681	Number of requests****
1985–86 Democrats	.259	.149	None
1985–86 Republicans	.641	.579	Same requests*
1987–88 Democrats	.428	.368	Same requests***/number of requests**
1987–88 Republicans	.654	.605	Same requests**
Wisconsin senate			
1987–88 Democrats	.912	.842	Same requests***
Iowa house			
1985–86 Democrats	.252	.187	Same requests***
1987–88 Democrats	.140	.045	None
Maine house			
1987–88 Democrats	.649	.623	Same requests****/number of requests****
1987–88 Republicans	.765	.631	Same requests**
Pennsylvania house			
1987–88 Democrats	.759	.740	Number of requests****/same requests****/demand for choices**

$^*p < .1.$ $^{**}p < .05.$ $^{***}p < .01.$ $^{****}p < .001.$

Iowa Democrats. This is very different from table 3. In addition, sizable adjusted R^2s are noted for many cases—nine of the fourteen exceed .5. These findings suggest that the strategies used when making committee choices offer substantially better explanations for the percentage of committee appointments received than do members' background variables. While this result is expected, given prior findings, the extent of the difference is striking.

Eleven of the fourteen cases have statistically significant coefficients for members requesting the same assignments as held in the previous session, seven for the number of requests made and two for the level of demands made for the committees sought. In each case, the direction of the relationship is as expected—the higher the percentage of requests for the same committees, the higher the percentage of requested assignments received; the higher the number of committee requests made, the lower the percentage of requests received; and the higher the demand level for committee assignments, the lower the percentage of success.

Considering across-state differences, Iowa has adjusted R^2s that are lower than those of the other states, suggesting state variation in the effects of these variables. Further, in the two most recent sessions, the adjusted R^2s for the Wisconsin Assembly Democrats are lower than in earlier sessions. Although the same Speaker made the appointments during these recent sessions, one cannot determine if these differences are traceable to that or to other factors. Nevertheless, there are differences across states and across sessions in a state.

Turning to the highest-priority committee choice received, one again finds many fewer statistically significant regression coefficients in table 6 than in table 5. The adjusted R^2s are substantially lower for choices received in table 6, than those found in table 5, and the signs of the relationships are not as consistent as those noted above.

Parsimonious Model

Due to the interrelationship among background and committee choice variables, one final analysis step was initiated. This involved combining the seven explanatory variables and then removing them one at a time until a model was derived in which all remaining explanatory variables had a regression coefficient with a $p < .1$. The results for the percentage of committee appointments received are found in table 7. The signs of the relationship are generally consistent with those noted above for the choice strategy model variables. The sole exception occurs among senate Democrats in Wisconsin where a higher number of requests is associated with a higher percentage of appointments received. This finding may reflect the nature of the choice process in the senate and the carryover of members across sessions.

TABLE 6. Regression Analysis Summary of Committee Choice Strategy Model Explanation for Highest-Priority Committee Request Received, by State, Chamber, Session, and Party

State/Chamber/ Session/Party	R^2	Adjusted R^2	Statistically Significant t-ratio Explanatory Variables
Wisconsin assembly			
1975–76 Democrats	.252	.169	Same requests**/demand for choices*
1979–80 Democrats	.307	.246	Number of requests****
1981–82 Democrats	.160	.080	Same requests**/number of requests*
1983–84 Republicans	.398	.247	Same requests**
1985–86 Democrats	.151	.025	None
1985–86 Republicans	.132	−.019	None
1987–88 Democrats	.292	.221	Same requests*
1987–88 Republicans	.333	.237	Demand for choices**
Wisconsin senate			
1987–88 Democrats	.322	−.130	None
Iowa house			
1985–86 Democrats			
1987–88 Democrats			
Maine house			
1987–88 Democrats	.116	−.050	Same requests**
1987–88 Republicans	.818	−.714	Same requests***/number of requests***/demand for choices**
Pennsylvania house			
1987–88 Democrats	.161	.097	Previous service**

$*p < .1.$ $**p < .05.$ $***p < .01.$ $****p < .001.$

The pervasiveness of statistically significant regression coefficients involving committee choice variables is very apparent. One major conclusion that can be drawn from these tables, then, is the great impact that the committee choice strategy used by a member has on the overall percentage of committee assignments received. This is affected only in relatively minor ways when the potential influence of background variables is considered simultaneously.

In table 8 the regression analysis summary is shown for the parsimonious models of the highest-priority committee request received. As previously noted, the adjusted R^2s are generally lower than those found for the percentage of committee requests received. Further, the number of statistically significant regression coefficients is smaller. Again, the committee choice strategy variables are more numerous than are personal background variables. The signs are consistent for the same choice as last session, committee demand,

TABLE 7. Regression Analysis for Parsimonious Model of Percentage of Committee Requests Received in Five State Legislative Chambers, by Session and Party

Background/Committee Choice Variables	Unstandardized Coefficient	Standardized Coefficient	t-ratio	Significance
	Wisconsin Assembly Democrats, 1975–76			
Intercept	133.15			
Number of committee requests	−13.11	−.53	−4.54	.0001
Same committee requests	33.20	.37	2.97	.0053
Demand for committee choices	−130.22	−.28	−2.53	.0159
Sex	−21.06	−.22	−1.81	.0789
$N = 41$, $R^2 = .63$, adjusted $R^2 = .59$				
	Wisconsin Assembly Democrats, 1979–80			
Intercept	77.26			
Number of committee requests	−7.11	−.46	−4.22	.0001
Same committee requests	33.72	.42	3.87	.0003
$N = 50$, $R^2 = .598$, adjusted $R^2 = .581$				
	Wisconsin Assembly Democrats, 1981–82			
Intercept				
Same committee requests	39.76	.48	3.90	.0004
Number of committee requests	−7.84	−.41	−2.85	.0069
Demand for committee choices	−155.57	−.33	−2.63	.0121
Education	−6.63	−.27	−2.59	.0133
Previous service	−1.91	−.19	−1.73	.0905
$N = 47$, $R^2 = .576$, adjusted $R^2 = .524$				
	Wisconsin Assembly Republicans, 1983–84			
Intercept	121.03			
Number of committee requests	−12.93	−.83	−6.58	.0000
$N = 21$, $R^2 = .695$, adjusted $R^2 = .679$				
	Wisconsin Assembly Democrats, 1985–86			
Intercept	44.57			
Same committee requests	34.86	.42	2.52	.0169
$N = 32$, $R^2 = .176$, adjusted $R^2 = .148$				
	Wisconsin Assembly Republicans, 1985–86			
Intercept	70.89			
Number of committee requests	−8.66	−.43	−2.59	.0159
Same committee requests	31.78	.41	2.49	.0197
$N = 28$, $R^2 = .602$, adjusted $R^2 = .571$				

Table 7—*Continued*

Background/Committee Choice Variables	Unstandardized Coefficient	Standardized Coefficient	*t*-ratio	Significance
	Wisconsin Assembly Democrats, 1987–88			
Intercept	68.13			
Same committee requests	36.67	.51	4.28	.0001
Number of committee requests	−5.71	−.39	−3.27	.0022
$N = 43$, $R^2 = .427$, adjusted $R^2 = .398$				
	Wisconsin Assembly Republicans, 1987–88			
Intercept	23.18			
Same committee requests	65.13	.78	6.94	.0000
$N = 33$, $R^2 = .609$, adjusted $R^2 = .596$				
	Wisconsin Senate Democrats, 1987–88			
Intercept	9.46			
Same committee requests	66.95	1.06	7.54	.0001
Number of committee requests	8.76	0.29	2.05	.0790
$N = 10$, $R^2 = .897$, adjusted $R^2 = .868$				
	Iowa House Democrats, 1985–86			
Intercept	30.07			
Same committee requests	40.12	.47	3.89	.0003
Sex	6.61	.28	2.27	.0275
$N = 51$, $R^2 = .289$, adjusted $R^2 = .259$				
	Iowa House Democrats, 1987–88			
Intercept	34.87			
Age	.29	.36	2.38	.0222
$N = 41$, $R^2 = .127$, adjusted $R^2 = .105$				
	Maine House Democrats, 1987–88			
Intercept	55.12			
Same committee requests	42.11	.50	4.87	.0000
Number of committee requests	−8.90	−.39	−3.83	.0003
$N = 56$, $R^2 = .644$, adjusted $R^2 = .631$				
	Maine House Republicans, 1987–88			
Intercept	8.73			
Same committee requests	89.60	.81	4.42	.0013
$N = 12$, $R^2 = .661$, adjusted $R^2 = .627$				

Continued on next page

Table 7—*Continued*

Background/Committee Choice Variables	Unstandardized Coefficient	Standardized Coefficient	*t*-ratio	Significance
Pennsylvania House Democrats, 1987–88				
Intercept	60.85			
Number of committee requests	−6.15	−.59	−6.20	.0000
Same committee requests	32.19	.29	3.28	.0018
Previous service	1.97	.13	1.89	.0649
Education	2.97	.11	1.80	.0771
$N = 57$, $R^2 = .800$, adjusted $R^2 = .784$				

TABLE 8. Regression Analysis for Parsimonious Model of Highest-Priority Committee Request Received in Five State Legislative Chambers, by Session and Party

Background/Committee Choice Variables	Unstandardized Coefficient	Standardized Coefficient	*t*-ratio	Significance
Wisconsin Assembly Democrats, 1975–76				
Intercept	1.24			
Same committee requests	−1.49	−.36	−2.51	.0163
Demand for committee choices	6.40	.29	2.06	.0464
$N = 41$, $R^2 = .242$, adjusted $R^2 = .202$				
Wisconsin Assembly Democrats, 1979–80				
Intercept	−.15			
Number of committee requests	.22	.46	3.89	.0003
Sex	.58	.31	2.57	.0134
$N = 50$, $R^2 = .362$, adjusted $R^2 = .334$				
Wisconsin Assembly Democrats, 1981–82				
Intercept	4.58			
Number of committee requests	−.50	−.41	−2.56	.0140
Same committee requests	−1.99	−.38	−2.34	.0242
$N = 47$, $R^2 = .153$, adjusted $R^2 = .115$				
Wisconsin Assembly Republicans, 1983–84				
Intercept	1.74			
Same committee requests	−.93	−.58	−3.13	.0055
$N = 21$, $R^2 = .340$, adjusted $R^2 = .305$				

Table 8—*Continued*

Background/Committee Choice Variables	Unstandardized Coefficient	Standardized Coefficient	*t*-ratio	Significance
Wisconsin Assembly Democrats, 1985–86				
Intercept	3.10			
Same committee requests	−.34	−.25	−1.39	.1759
$N = 32$, $R^2 = .060$, adjusted $R^2 = .029$				
Wisconsin Assembly Republicans, 1985–86				
Intercept	1.91			
Same committee requests	−1.02	−.36	−1.94	.0629
$N = 28$, $R^2 = .127$, adjusted $R^2 = .093$				
Wisconsin Assembly Democrats, 1987–88				
Intercept	−1.34			
Demand for committee choices	7.98	.41	2.98	.0047
Sex	1.03	.25	1.87	.0685
$N = 45$, $R^2 = .291$, adjusted $R^2 = .257$				
Wisconsin Assembly Republicans, 1987–88				
Intercept	−.55			
Demand for committee choices	6.05	.40	2.61	.0138
Number of committee requests	.22	.33	2.16	.0391
$N = 33$, $R^2 = .316$, adjusted $R^2 = .271$				
Wisconsin Senate Democrats, 1987–88				
Intercept	−2.47			
Demand for committee choices	11.67	.55	1.95	.0826
$N = 11$, $R^2 = .298$, adjusted $R^2 = .220$				
Iowa House Democrats, 1985–86				
No Variation in Highest Committee Choice Received				
Iowa House Democrats, 1987–88				
No Variation in Highest Committee Choice Received				
Maine House Democrats, 1987–88				
Intercept	3.19			
Same committee requests	−1.96	−.33	−2.46	.0171
Age	−.03	−.29	−1.90	.0629
Previous service	.36	.27	1.69	.0968
$N = 56$, $R^2 = .158$, adjusted $R^2 = .109$				

Continued on next page

Table 8—*Continued*

Background/Committee Choice Variables	Unstandardized Coefficient	Standardized Coefficient	*t*-ratio	Significance
Maine House Republicans, 1987–88				
Intercept	29.08			
Same committee requests	−20.22	−1.78	−5.27	.0008
Demand for committee choices	−45.67	−0.95	−3.50	.0080
Number of committee requests	−3.11	−0.80	−3.47	.0084
$N = 12$, $R^2 = .781$, adjusted $R^2 = .699$				
Pennsylvania House Democrats, 1987–88				
Intercept	2.53			
Previous service	−.31	−.36	−2.85	.0061
$N = 57$, $R^2 = .129$, adjusted $R^2 = .113$				

and sex variables, as noted previously, but they are more mixed for the others. The greater the degree to which similar assignments are requested, the more likely it is for an individual to receive the high-priority committees requested. The greater the demand level for committees requested, the less likely it is that an individual will be assigned to these committees. Additionally, women are less likely to receive a higher-priority choice than are men in the two instances where a statistically significant regression coefficient is identified.

Elaboration on Committee Choice Strategy Model

The overwhelming nature of the evidence presented regarding the impact of a member's choice strategy indicates that additional attention must be paid to the variables of this strategy, especially to the requests for committee assignments from the last session. For this reason, those individuals who served in the previous session of the chamber were selected for additional analysis. Presented in table 9 are the standing committee requests of these experienced legislators and the average number of requests made, as well as the percentage of requests that were for the same committees as served in the last session and the percentage of requests for different committees. These figures show the degree to which experienced members requested the same committee assignments as previously held. The low percentage of requests for the same committee positions from Iowa House Democrats in 1985–86 probably reflects the shift that took place at the beginning of the 1983–84 session from the Democrats being a minority to becoming the majority party in the chamber. Among Wisconsin Assembly Republicans, the 1983–84 session reflects a change in leadership. The sizable degree to which experienced state legislators request assignment to "new" committees is indicated in table 9.

A follow-up analysis for these same legislators regarding the assignments received is provided in table 10. The percentage of assignments received shows the degree to which members' committee positions reflect the coalescing of previous service plus requests for continued service on committees. In all cases except two (the 1985–86 Wisconsin Assembly Democrats and the 1985–86 Iowa House Democrats), a majority of the assignments received by individual legislators were for committees they had served in the previous session and requested for this session. In Wisconsin, experienced legislators appear more likely to be assigned to committees *not* requested than to those requested but on which they had not previously served—evidence that leadership uses assignments for purposes other than accommodating members.

Also in table 10 are data for the percentage of requests for new appointments that were received and the percentage of requests for positions that were previously held and subsequently received. Experience in the Wisconsin

TABLE 9. Standing Committee Requests for State Legislators Who Served in Previous Session, by State, Chamber, Session, and Party

State/Chamber/ Session/Party	Average Number of Requests	Percentage of Requests for Same Assignments as Had Last Session	Percentage of Requests for Assignments Different From Last Session	Total Percentage	Total Number of Cases
Wisconsin assembly					
1975–76 Democrats	2.58	59.5	40.5	100.0	111
1979–80 Democrats	3.38	55.0	45.0	100.0	169
1981–82 Democrats	3.38	51.5	48.5	100.0	169
1983–84 Republicans	4.00	47.6	52.4	100.0	84
1985–86 Democrats	3.54	50.8	49.2	100.0	124
1985–86 Republicans	4.07	41.8	58.2	100.0	122
1987–88 Democrats	3.51	55.7	44.3	100.0	158
1987–88 Republicans	3.88	46.5	53.5	100.0	128
Wisconsin senate					
1987–88 Democrats	3.08	59.5	40.5	100.0	37
Iowa house					
1985–86 Democrats	7.87	21.4	78.6	100.0	425
1987–88 Democrats	7.98	41.9	58.1	100.0	327
Maine house					
1987–88 Democrats	2.68	36.7	63.3	100.0	158
1987–88 Republicans	2.92	31.4	68.6	100.0	35
Pennsylvania house					
1987–88 Democrats	7.51	34.6	65.4	100.0	428

TABLE 10. Standing Committee Assignments for State Legislators Who Served in Previous Session, by State, Chamber, Session, and Party

State/Chamber/Session/Party	Average Number of Assignments	Percentage of Assignments Requested Last Session	Percentage of Assignments Requested This Session	Percentage of Assignments Received but Not Requested	Number of Cases	Percentage of Requests for New Assignments Received	Percentage of Assignments Requested and Received Both Sessions
Wisconsin Assembly							
1975–76 Democrats	2.40	64.1	12.6	23.3	103	28.9	100.0
1979–80 Democrats	3.06	60.8	14.4	24.8	153	28.9	100.0
1981–82 Democrats	3.44	50.6	13.4	36.0	172	29.3	98.9
1983–84 Republicans	3.14	60.6	22.7	16.7	66	34.1	100.0
1985–86 Democrats	3.74	48.1	15.3	36.6	131	37.7	95.2
1985–86 Republicans	2.83	60.0	11.8	28.2	85	14.1	100.0
1987–88 Democrats	3.87	50.6	6.9	42.5	174	17.1	100.0
1987–88 Republicans	3.15	57.7	13.5	28.8	104	20.6	100.0
Wisconsin Senate							
1987–88 Democrats	3.25	56.4	17.9	25.7	39	60.0	90.9
Iowa House							
1985–86 Democrats	4.22	39.9	49.1	11.0	228	33.5	100.0
1987–88 Democrats	4.24	78.7	12.6	8.7	174	11.6	100.0
Maine House							
1987–88 Democrats	1.37	71.6	9.9	18.5	81	11.0	96.6
1987–88 Republicans	1.42	64.7	17.6	17.7	17	12.5	100.0
Pennsylvania House							
1987–88 Democrats	3.61	71.8	16.0	12.2	206	11.8	100.0

Assembly indicates that between 14 and 38 percent of requests for new appointments will be granted. In other states, with the exception of the 1985–86 Iowa House, the percentages are more modest—11 to 13 percent. These percentages, however, are quite different from those for the requests received for assignments held in the prior session. In this case, it is virtually guaranteed that if a member requests service on a committee on which he or she had prior service, the member can expect to receive that assignment again. In Pennsylvania, this outcome was expected since interviews indicated that prior service was an informal guide governing the assignment process. In the other states, however, prior service was reported to be a consideration but not necessarily the preeminent one. Regardless, these findings indicate the degree to which prior service on a committee together with a request to continue service on that committee virtually assure an experienced member, regardless of party, of reappointment to that committee.

Conclusions and Implications

This cross-state and cross-session study of committee appointments in four states indicates the following:

1. A substantial degree of members in all states and of both parties receives a high percentage of committee assignments that are requested and the highest choices in the priority of assignments requested.
2. Variables related to the committee choice strategy have great utility in explaining variance in the percentage of committee requests received and the highest-priority committee requests received.
3. A more adequate explanation of variation in the percentage of committee requests received is possible using these choice variables than is true for using the priority of the request received.
4. Cross-state and cross-time differences affect the ability of these variables to explain the percentage of success and priority received, which is *perhaps* related to the specific leaders making the appointments.
5. The variables relate to the selection strategies of experienced members: they request the same committee assignments as held in the previous session and request assignments to a smaller number of committees.
6. Reappointment is virtually guaranteed for experienced members to committees held in the last session, if requested at the next.

These findings have several implications for the career development of individual members. The state legislative committee assignment process seems to foster continuity of members on committees. Once appointed to a committee, a member is very likely to remain on that committee in future sessions if he or she so requests. This trend contributes to issue continuity as well as to development of a committee's expertise and to facilitating a member's specialization in issue areas. Such a pattern, however, may restrict a member's movement to new committees. In fact, the evidence indicates a much lower "success rate" for experienced members receiving assignments to "new" committees requested than to maintaining existing assignments. The procurement of new appointments is thus more difficult than maintaining the status quo. Indeed, it seems especially important that first-term members obtain "good" initial appointments.

Leadership in all states, regardless of majority or minority party status, seems committed to accommodating members' requests. This works to the advantage of members in building their careers, within limits. The "judicious" use of requests for new committee assignments, especially when coupled with external factors like committee vacancy patterns, offers *some* opportunity to develop new interests and expertise.

The choice strategy a member uses in seeking committee appointments appears to be more influential than the member's background. For example, seeking reappointment to previous committee assignments, focusing requests on a fewer number of committees, and carefully selecting the committees of interest to avoid exclusive requests for high-demand committees seem to increase the likelihood of overall success.

Further investigations should consider (1) the degree to which members from different backgrounds have common choice strategies in making their committee requests, (2) the strategies used by new members in obtaining appointments, and (3) the applicability of variables related to election success in explaining state committee appointments. Such analyses will provide additional insights regarding committee appointments at the state legislative level.

CHAPTER 10

Changing State Legislative Leadership Careers

Peverill Squire

Over the last three decades state legislatures have changed dramatically (Rosenthal 1989). Members' salaries have increased substantially, sessions have grown longer, and facilities have greatly improved. As a general result of this professionalization, membership stability has increased and state legislatures have, on the whole, increased both their influence in the political process and stature relative to the governor. As documented in other chapters in this volume, state legislative careers have changed, with important implications for members and institutions. In this chapter, I assess the consequences of professionalization on the career patterns of legislative leaders.

Leadership is an important but little understood concept. The focus in this chapter is on formal positions of leadership, primarily speakers and majority and minority leaders in lower state houses. After reviewing the existing literature, I examine the career patterns of legislative leaders to determine if, as we might expect, professionalization leads to more stable leadership structures.

Professionalization, Leadership, and Careers

In their text on U.S. legislatures, Keefe and Ogul observe, "There has been little research on state legislative leaders" (1985, 240n). Likewise, Jewell notes, "Among the most neglected topics in state legislative studies is leadership. We know almost nothing about leadership selection and turnover" (1981, 8). Peabody's (1985) chapter on leadership in the *Handbook of Legislative Research* evidences little work in this area. If, as Arnold (1982) asserts, there are undertilled and overtilled fields in political science, then a plow has rarely broken the earth in the study of state legislative leaders.

This is not to claim there is no research to provide guidance. Works on the politics of particular states (Zimmerman 1981; Bell and Price 1984) or legislatures (Jewell and Miller 1988; Rosenthal 1986; Rodgers, Sittig, and Welch 1984; Dauer 1984; Swanson 1984; Muir 1982; Squire and Scott 1984;

175

Kirkpatrick 1978) can provide useful information on leadership, but typically, it is incidental to a larger task. Perhaps the single best source of information on state legislative leadership selection processes is a 1980 survey covering all fifty states, compiled by Jewell in the *Comparative State Politics Newsletter* (1986). Synthesis of these essentially short case studies has been rare, Rosenthal's (1981) and Jewell and Patterson's (1986) insightful discussions being the notable exceptions.

Theories explaining the number of leadership positions in a body or how they are filled are in even shorter supply. Chaffey and Jewell (1972) examined leadership posts in eight lower state houses from 1945 to 1970 to link the process by which they were filled to the legislature's level of professionalization. They conclude that leaders in more professionalized bodies tended to have longer apprenticeships before achieving those positions and longer tenures once in them. They also suggest that clear patterns of succession were found in more professionalized legislatures. More recently, Squire (1988a), in a study of lower houses in California, Connecticut, and New York, claims that the career opportunity structure in each body determined the use of seniority as a criterion for gaining positions of power. In the case of California this means that the Assembly's undisputed professional status does not necessarily result in leadership patterns of the sort Chaffey and Jewell (1972) found because such patterns do not meet the needs of politically ambitious members of that body. But, taken together, these two studies suggest that we should expect differences among legislative bodies in leadership acquisition patterns and tenures and that these differences are strongly related to the professional characteristics of the legislature and career needs of the membership.

Leadership Positions and Career Patterns

Positions

The focus of this chapter is on formal leadership positions: speaker, president pro tem, majority leader, assistant majority leaders, and the like. The number of these positions by state and chamber for 1976 and 1988 is provided in table 1. Of the ninety-nine legislative bodies, sixty-eight experienced some change in the number of leadership posts by 1988. Overall, the number of positions increased in both the upper and lower houses, and the number of chambers adding offices was greater than those eliminating them. These trends seem consistent with the increasing level of professionalization if we assume that members who serve longer desire and agitate for more leadership positions in order to fulfill their own career ambitions. In most state houses the increases were modest, the creation of a caucus leader or another assistant minority leader or two. Several bodies, such as the Connecticut and Rhode Island lower

TABLE 1. Change in Number of State Legislative Leadership Positions

State	Upper House[a]			Lower House		
	1976	1988	DIFF	1976	1988	DIFF
Alabama	1	1		2	2	
Alaska	5	3	− 2	4	5	+ 1
Arizona	7	8	+ 1	7	7	
Arkansas	3	1	− 2	4	7	+ 3
California	5	7	+ 2	9	8	− 1
Colorado	8	8		7	8	+ 1
Connecticut	12	19	+ 7	13	30	+17
Delaware	5	5		5	5	
Florida	7	7		8	12	+ 4
Georgia	11	7	− 4	11	8	− 3
Hawaii	14	10	− 4	20	14	− 6
Idaho	5	7	+ 2	7	7	
Illinois	5	13	+ 8	13	17	+ 4
Indiana	6	9	+ 3	9	10	+ 1
Iowa	7	8	+ 1	10	12	+ 2
Kansas	4	9	+ 5	9	8	− 1
Kentucky	8	7	− 1	8	8	
Louisiana	2	2		2	2	
Maine	5	5		5	5	
Maryland	6	7	+ 1	5	7	+ 2
Massachusetts	7	9	+ 2	7	7	
Michigan	17	13	− 4	23	30	+ 7
Minnesota	11	13	+ 2	10	12	+ 2
Mississippi	1	1		1	1	
Missouri	4	6	+ 2	12	10	− 2
Montana	6	6		6	7	+ 1
Nebraska	1	1				
Nevada	4	3	− 1	4	4	
New Hampshire	7	8	+ 1	7	7	
New Jersey	10	10		10	14	+ 4
New Mexico	5	8	+ 3	5	9	+ 4
New York	4	9	+ 5	10	6	− 4
North Carolina	3	4	+ 1	5	4	− 1
North Dakota	7	7		7	7	
Ohio	6	7	+ 1	7	8	+ 1
Oklahoma	9	10	+ 1	15	17	+ 2
Oregon	8	6	− 2	13	9	− 4
Pennsylvania	13	7	− 6	13	7	− 6
Rhode Island	10	14	+ 4	11	20	+ 9
South Carolina	1	1		8	5	− 3
South Dakota	5	5		6	6	
Tennessee	18	10	− 8	26	15	−11
Texas	1	1		2	2	
Utah	5	5		7	5	− 2
Vermont	3	5	+ 2	5	5	
Virginia	3	4	+ 1	5	5	

Continued on next page

Table 1—*Continued*

State	Upper House[a]			Lower House		
	1976	1988	DIFF	1976	1988	DIFF
Washington	14	10	− 4	16	9	− 7
West Virginia	4	5	+ 1	6	7	+ 1
Wisconsin	9	7	− 2	14	8	− 6
Wyoming	4	5	+ 1	4	6	+ 2
Total	326	343	+17	423	434	+11

Sources: Book of the States 1976–1977; Book of the States 1988–1989.
[a]Does not include the lieutenant governor as presiding officer.

houses, saw significant increases; seventeen posts—mostly assistant majority and minority leaders—and nine posts respectively. A few legislatures, notably both houses in Pennsylvania, Tennessee, and Washington, streamlined their leadership structures.

The first point to make about these data is that leadership structures are not stable, at least on the margins. Almost every chamber has a core set of leaders—a presiding officer and party floor leaders. Only the Alabama Senate, Mississippi Senate and House, Nebraska Unicameral, South Carolina Senate, and Texas Senate operate with a single formal leader. These particular bodies are unusual in that they are either dominated by a single party or, in the case of Nebraska, nonpartisan. In most other legislative bodies there is a strong tendency for the number of leadership positions to fluctuate. There is no obvious explanation for this phenomenon. Large and small, more and less professional bodies have all added, subtracted, or kept the same number of positions. Rather than looking to structural characteristics for an explanation, what is more likely to be the case is that the size of the leadership cadre is increased by major party leaders to secure support and stabilized or decreased when their own situations are less tenuous.

Occasionally, the general membership forces the addition of new offices. One example of this is the creation of a speaker pro tem by the Tennessee Senate in 1985 (Williams 1985), a post designed to provide for a presiding officer in the absence of the speaker. The speaker (the lieutenant governor elected by the senate) did not want the position because he feared it might challenge or reduce his powers. He accepted it after it was changed to a position whose occupant the speaker selects, but the minority Republicans worried that over time the office would acquire the extra staff and other benefits associated with powerful leaders. Another example is the creation in 1989 of a majority floor leader by the Democratic caucus in the North Carolina House after a minority of the party's members joined with Republicans to elect the speaker. The new position, empowered by and responsible to the caucus, not the speaker, could become an important office in the legislature (Christensen 1989, 19).

Although all of the data in table 1 represent formal leadership positions, obviously the positions do not exercise equal power or influence. Some posts, like the Tennessee Senate speaker pro tem, are considered ceremonial. As the Republicans in that state feared, however, any leadership office has the potential to become significant. When Tom Hannigan became the California Assembly majority leader in 1987, it was speculated that many of the important functions his predecessor had performed would be transferred to the previously mostly ceremonial posts of Speaker pro tem and assistant speaker pro tem (Block 1987, 150). Other traditionally important posts can be stripped of their powers, as happened in 1989 to the Rhode Island Senate majority leader (Sullivan 1989). Ambitious and skilled politicians can exploit a title and transform a minor position into a major one or weaken another. Thus leadership structures are, in most states, in flux, both in numbers and in powers exercised by particular posts.

Pay and Perks

The main reason members covet leadership positions is, of course, because their occupants can exercise some amount of political power. These posts do, however, have other benefits, which add to their attraction. In nine states, including Arizona, California, and Washington, legislative leaders do not receive any additional compensation, but in the other forty-one they do. A few legislative bodies only provide trivial amounts: Alabama, for example, gives its House Speaker $2 per day. The level of remuneration in other legislatures varies, from a little over $7,000 per year for presiding officers in Florida, Iowa, and Maryland to over $30,000 per year in Massachusetts and New York. The speaker of the Mississippi House, the body's only formal leader, gets $34,000 annually. Leaders below majority and minority leaders receive additional compensation in fourteen states. Although taken alone none of these sums may seem overwhelming, when added to the regular base pay the result is a salary that can make service financially worthwhile.

There are other perks that can have important ramifications. Leaders are, in many cases, entitled to additional staff. Because of the paucity of staff in many legislatures, having such assistance increases the power leaders may exercise over followers. Influence over the legislative process results in another benefit of leadership: increased publicity. Legislative leaders, like their congressional counterparts, become spokespersons for their parties and institution. In 1987, for example, California Assembly Speaker Willie Brown was prominent in 23 *Los Angeles Times* stories, his senate counterpart, pro tem David Roberti, in 21. These numbers were far less than Governor George

Duekmejian's 243 stories but far more than those for any other members of the legislature.[1] Indeed, in a 1984 *California Poll* survey 73 percent of the respondents could offer an opinion on Willie Brown's performance as speaker, and 54 percent gave a rating to Roberti.[2] Legislative leaders become important and well-known people.

Who Are the Leaders?

While much has changed about legislative careers over the last two decades, women and minorities are still underrepresented, despite some impressive gains. The same is true at the leadership level. Data reported by Simon (1987a, 247) show that, from 1977 to 1987, women increased their overall numbers from over 6 percent to almost 16 percent. By 1987, eighteen women held leadership posts, up from four ten years earlier. Several women had achieved the highest position in their legislatures, including the speakerships in North Dakota, South Dakota, and Oregon. According to McClure (1987), women hold important leadership positions in fourteen states. Compared to women, blacks hold far fewer state legislative seats: 5 percent in 1987, representing only a slight increase over 1977. Only five blacks held leadership positions in 1987, with Willie Brown and Leroy Irvis serving as lower house speakers in California and Pennsylvania, respectively. Hispanics and Asians held ten posts, mostly in Arizona, Hawaii, and New Mexico. Overall, then, white males still dominate the state legislative leadership ranks.

Stability, Selection, and Apprenticeships

Turnover in state legislatures has decreased markedly over the last eighty years. The extremely high rates found early in the century (Hyneman 1938) have, in most states, been replaced by far lower ones (Niemi and Winsky 1987; Shin and Jackson 1979; Ray 1974). How, if at all, have these trends changed leadership tenures? Longer leadership tenures are considered important because they potentially increase the power wielded by leaders, especially relative to the executive (Jewell and Patterson 1986, 119).

Although it is not logically necessary, short service among the general membership must translate into short leadership tenures. In fact, leaders in the past have tended to serve only one or two terms. Indeed, in many states, by tradition, leadership positions were regularly rotated. For example, Campbell (1980, 43), in a study of the lower houses in Illinois, Iowa, and Wisconsin during the late 1800s, found that thirteen speakers served during the fifteen

---

[1] These data were collected from the *Los Angles Times* index (1987). An examination of the *Des Moines Register* index reveals similar numbers.

[2] These data were originally collected by the Field Research Corporation and were provided by the University of California State Data Program, Berkeley.

legislative sessions he examined. This system has held in many states: according to the 1980 leadership survey (Jewell 1980) thirteen lower houses had a new speaker every term or two. The same procedure was followed, but with a single exception, in eight additional states (Jewell 1972, 133, 138). The only lower houses where one leader served six or more terms were in one-party states—Georgia, Mississippi, South Carolina, and Virginia.

Increased professionalization should result in state legislatures where leaders serve longer terms, as in the U.S. Congress. There is some evidence that rotation systems are fading (Jewell 1980). One study (Wunnicke and Randall 1986, 28) claims only Arkansas, Florida, North Dakota, South Dakota, and Wyoming place limits on the length of leaders' service. In New Jersey, Rosenthal observes, "Until 1971 new presiding officers were chosen every year, and from 1971 to 1979 they normally were chosen every two years. Today, members may serve successive two-year terms, and several have done so" (1986, 124). Similarly, an examination of the Nebraska Unicameral notes, "In 1981, the trend toward institutionalization of the speakership became clear when the tradition of not reelecting top officers was ended and the incumbent speaker . . . was unanimously re-elected" (Rodgers, Sittig, and Welch 1984, 68).

It can be inferred from figures 1–13 how widespread this trend is. Presented here are Speakers' tenures from 1901 to 1987 (or 1985 or 1989) in thirteen states for which such information was available. Although not chosen randomly, these states represent a good cross section, with houses from every region, population size, and level of professionalization. The overall impression these figures leave is that speakers are serving progressively longer terms; indeed tenure now is greater than at any other time this century. In Connecticut, Idaho, Iowa, Maine, Maryland, Michigan, North Carolina, Oregon, and West Virginia, the trend seems particularly clear. In the other states—California, Illinois, New York, and Rhode Island—rotation either never took hold or vanished long ago, and speakers have always been able to serve unlimited terms.

Why have speakers been able to serve longer in office? Rotation systems may have withered because of changes elsewhere in the political system, which had implications for the political career ambitions of legislative leaders. Laws allowing governors to serve longer are thought to impede political advancement opportunities for legislative leaders, putting them in a position of wanting to remain in office while waiting for a chance to move up the ladder (Jewell and Patterson 1986, 119). In North Carolina, for example, voter approval in 1977 of a constitutional amendment removing the one-term limit on governors convinced members of the state house to allow their speaker to serve more than two years (Beyle 1989, 4). Lengthening the gubernatorial term appears to have increased legislative leadership tenures in other states, including Texas and Louisiana (Jewell 1980, 10).

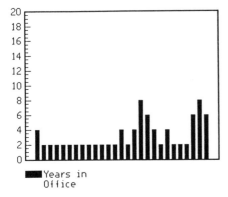

Fig. 1. Tenures of Speakers of Michigan
House, 1901–87

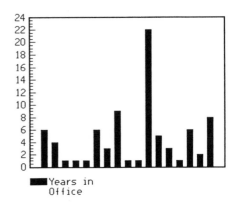

Fig. 2. Tenures of Speakers of New York
Assembly, 1901–87

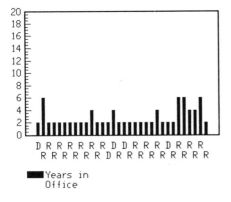

D R R R R R R D D R R R D R R R
R R R R R R D R R R R R R R R

Fig. 3. Tenures of Speakers of Idaho
House, 1901–87

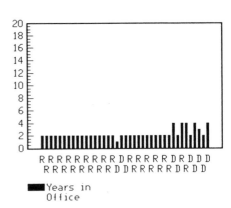

R R R R R R R R D R R R R R D R D D D
R R R R R R R D D R R R R R D R D D

Fig. 4. Tenures of Speakers of Oregon
House, 1901–87

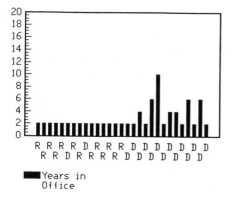

Fig. 5. Tenures of Speakers of West Virginia House, 1901–85

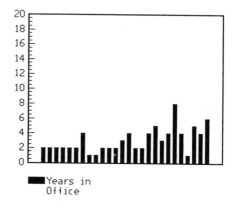

Fig. 6. Tenures of Speakers of Maryland House, 1901–87

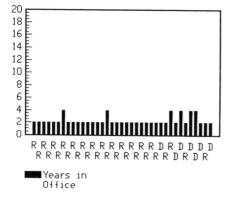

Fig. 7. Tenures of Speakers of Connecticut House, 1901–87

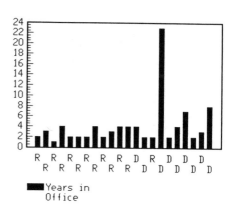

Fig. 8. Tenures of Speakers of Rhode Island House, 1901–87

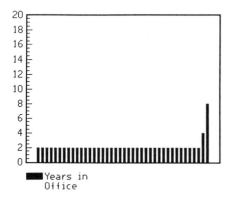

Fig. 9. Tenures of Speakers of North
Carolina House, 1901–87

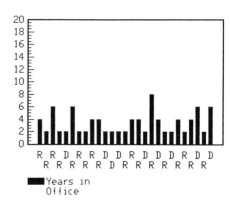

Fig. 10. Tenures of Speakers of Illinois
House, 1901–87

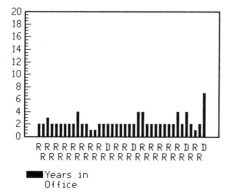

Fig. 11. Tenures of Speakers of Iowa
House, 1901–89

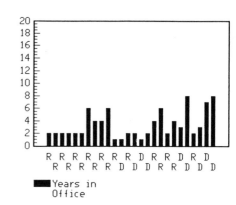

Fig. 12. Tenures of Speakers of California
Assembly, 1901–89

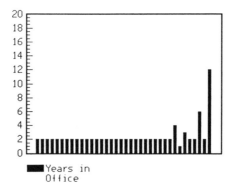

Fig. 13. Tenures of Speakers of Maine
House, 1901–87

A second factor in explaining longer leadership service is the unusual political skill of a particular leader who breaks tradition for those who follow him or her. Examples of such speakers may be Don Avenson of Iowa and John Martin of Maine. It should be kept in mind, however, that the shift away from a rotation system is not irreversible. Beyle (1989, 15) notes that the recent successful revolt against the North Carolina House's four-term speaker, Liston Ramsay, may herald a return to the rotation system. Similarly, Connecticut House Speaker Irving Stolberg's expected election to a third term in 1989 was thwarted in part by some members' resistance to breaking a two-term limit (Jacklin 1989).

The evidence presented here demonstrates that, at the speaker level, leaders are serving longer tenures, which is consistent with our expectations given increasing professionalization. Chaffey and Jewell (1972) also assert that increased professionalization ought to result in longer apprenticeships before members attain high positions. Data collected by Simon (1987a, 248) tend to support this hypothesis. Examining the experience of the ninety-nine elected presiding officers in 1987, Simon found that thirty-five had been either majority or minority leaders immediately before winning the top positions. Another eleven were assistant leaders just before becoming the presiding officers, and forty-four had been committee chairs. Only five were elevated directly from the rank and file.

This evidence demonstrates that presiding officers have leadership experience before assuming their positions, but we must be cautious in inferring either the existence of a leadership ladder or the use of seniority as an important criterion in selection. On the former, Simon notes, "In a handful of states, notably Massachusetts, Pennsylvania and Wyoming, the path to leadership runs through the ranks of lower-level leadership positions" (1987a, 247). On the latter, we can only speculate using Simon's data. Moreover, these data tell us nothing about possible change over time. The information presented in table 2 offers a better handle on these questions. Table 2 shows the top leaders—speaker and majority and minority leaders—for the lower houses in California, Iowa, and New York from 1961 to 1987. Aside from the obvious regional distribution of these legislatures, they also represent different career opportunity structures (Squire 1988b). New York is more career-oriented, and seniority ought to count for more there than in California, where most members seek to move to higher office, or Iowa, where legislators serve for a few terms and then retire from political life (Squire 1988a). Thus, New York ought to evidence longer apprenticeships and more senior leaders than the other two bodies.

A cursory examination of table 2 tends to support these expectations. The New York Assembly has had more continuity and fewer members holding

TABLE 2. Leadership Patterns in Three State Lower Houses, 1961–87

Year	Majority Leader	Speaker	Minority Leader
		California	
1961			
1963	Waldie (4)	Unruh (8)[a]	Conrad (16)
1965			Monagan (4)[b]
1967	Zenovich (4)		
1969+	Biddle (4)	Monagan	Unruh
1971+	Karabian (4)	Moretti (6)	Monagan
1973	Fenton (8)[b]		Beverly (6)
1975	Berman (2)[b]	McCarthy (6)[c]	
1977			Priolo (10)
1979			Hallett (2)[b]
1980	Brown (15)[b]		
1981	Roos (3)[b]	Brown[b]	
1983			Naylor (4)
1985			Nolan (6)[b]
1987	Hannigan (8)[b]		
		Iowa	
1961	Naden (6)	Nelson (6)[b]	
1963	Mowry (6)	Naden	Eveland (6)[b]
1965	Maule (8)	Steffen (2)	Edgington (14)
1967	Millen (4)	Baringer (6)	Gannon (2)
1969	McCartney (2)[b]	Harbor (2)[d]	
1971	Varley (4)		Cochran (6)
1973	Holden (6)	Varley	
1975+	Fitzgerald (2)	Cochran	Millen (12)[b]
1977			
1979+	Halvorson (4)	Millen[c]	Avenson (6)[b]
1981	Pope (2)[b]	Stromer (14)	
1983+	Norland (10)	Avenson	Stromer
1985			
1987	Arnould (10)		
		New York	
1961	Ingalls (8)	Carlino (16)	
1963			
1965+	Weinstein (6)	Travia (16)	Ingalls
1967			Duryea (6)
1969+	Kingston (9)	Duryea	Steingut (16)
1971			
1973			
1975+	Blumenthal (12)	Steingut	Duryea
1977	Fink (8)		
1979	Walsh (6)	Fink	Emery (14)
1981			

TABLE 2. Leadership Patterns in Three State Lower Houses, 1961–87

Year	Majority Leader	Speaker	Minority Leader
1983			Rappleyea (10)
1985			
1987	Tallon (12)[b]	Miller (16)	

Sources: California Legislature Handbook, Iowa Official Register, New York Red Book, and *Legislative Manual—New York* for various years.

Note: The plus sign represents change in the majority party in the body. Numbers in parentheses indicate years served in state legislature before gaining a leadership position.

[a]Elected September 30, 1961, after Ralph Brown resigned.

[b]Predecessor in the position continued service in the body.

[c]Elected June 28, 1974, after Robert Moretti resigned.

[d]Seniority does not count previous service in the state house and senate.

[e]Resigned March 3, 1980, and replaced until end of the session (April 26, 1980) by former Speaker William Harbor.

major leadership positions than the other two legislatures, even with having experienced three majority party switches. Moreover, the individuals achieving these posts, especially the speakership, have all served a good number of years in the assembly. Indeed, members anticipate gaining seniority before gaining important positions (Squire 1988a). For example, a profile of a Ways and Means Committee chair notes his speakership ambitions and comments, "after 16 years in Albany, Mr. Kremer is willing to wait a little longer for that opportunity" (Herman 1981, 21). There is a tendency for floor leaders to accede to the speakership when it becomes available, with four members having followed that route. Major leadership positions are attained when their current occupants leave the assembly; only Majority Leader Walsh in 1977 was passed over and remained in the body, albeit for only a short period before resigning. Although the leadership career structure in the assembly is not as formalized as that employed by the Democrats in the U.S. House, it very closely resembles that used by the other congressional parties in terms of reliance on seniority and ladders.

California exhibits a somewhat different pattern from New York, despite its similar professionalization level. Only Willie Brown, had substantial seniority when he became speaker, but Brown won under unusual circumstances—as a result of the Leo McCarthy–Howard Berman fight and with Republican votes—and in his third serious run at the position. Others gaining the speakership during this period had a mean of seven-year service in the assembly. Only Robert Monagan and Willie Brown moved from being floor leaders to speakers. The other speakers jumped to the top spot from committee chairs: Unruh from Ways and Means, Moretti from Government Organization, and McCarthy from Labor Relations. The only majority party floor leader to succeed the speaker who appointed him was Brown. In general, floor leaders for the majority and minority have had little seniority when appointed and have replaced people who have remained in the assembly. There is a strong tendency for the minority party to replace leaders who fail to move the party toward majority status; this was what prompted the GOP to remove Robert Naylor in favor of Pat Nolan in 1985 and to supplant Nolan with Ross Johnson in 1989 (Hoover 1989).

As we would expect given its less professional level, the Iowa House has had more leaders who served shorter tenures than the other two bodies have had. A number of legislators without much seniority have been named speaker during this period, but the trend over the twenty-six years covered is clearly toward more house service before reaching the top post and longer tenures once there. The last four speakers had all been in the house for a minimum of five terms when elected. Moreover, unlike California, leadership in the Iowa House appears to use an implicit ladder; five floor leaders have moved directly to the speakership. Ex-speakers, however, are not entitled to special consideration; three who continued to serve in the house after stepping down failed in attempts to regain major leadership posts.

Overall, New York is more structured than California or Iowa in its reliance on seniority and leadership ladders. In the latter two bodies, however, leaders are serving longer tenures. Indeed, the current speakers in those houses have now served longer than any of their predecessors. In these terms the leadership career patterns found in these bodies are consistent with those of an institutionalized legislature (Polsby 1968; see also Squire 1989).

It is harder to ascertain whether or not selection processes have changed over time. Jewell and Patterson observe, "In most two-party legislatures, the presiding officer is selected by the majority party caucus, the members of which will normally unite behind that choice in balloting on the floor of the house or senate" (1986, 119). While that is certainly the case in most legislatures, during the last fifteen years there have been a rash of bipartisan coalitions forming to elect leaders. Legislative bodies in Alaska, California, Connecticut, Illinois, Massachusetts, New Mexico, North Carolina, Tennessee, Vermont, and Washington have experienced coalitions (Rosenthal 1981, 155–56; Jewell and Patterson 1986, 120; Hansen 1989, 11). Why majority party unity dissolves is not clear; examination of such cases suggests strong issue differences can be important, but more typical is deep dissatisfaction with the actions and conduct of an incumbent leader, motivating those who are disaffected to seek an accommodation with the opposition party. Some of these coalitions last over a full term or two; others are, in the words of a Connecticut representative, only "one-day dates" (Jacklin 1989).[3]

---

[3] A minority party member in the Rhode Island senate uses a similar metaphor in assessing the coalition in that body, "This is not a marriage . . . this is a long weekend at the very most" (Sullivan 1989, 21).

Occasionally, equal numbers of Democrats and Republicans are elected to a legislative body. Novel solutions are devised to select leaders in these situations. A tie in the Washington House produced cospeakers, who presided on alternate days, and on equal division of committee chairs and assignments (Jewell 1980, 15). The two parties in the Indiana House reached a similar solution after the 1988 elections produced a tie (Browning 1989). Under the same conditions in 1979, the Minnesota House elected a Republican speaker but agreed on a bipartisan split of committee chairs (Jewell 1980, 15).

The selection of leaders is usually conducted just after an election, at the beginning of a new term. The Florida legislature, however, is an exception. According to Dauer, "The custom in Florida is that a new speaker of the house and new president of the senate are chosen every two years, but this choice is made by the members of the old legislature" (1984, 14). This combination of an odd selection process and a rotation system produces ongoing contests for leadership positions, races that can begin several terms in advance (Rosenthal 1981, 158).

One important change in the selection process has been the decline of gubernatorial influence in the determination of legislative leaders. In Kentucky, for example, the governor traditionally chose his or her party's leaders in both the house and senate. This practice ended in 1979 when newly elected Governor John Y. Brown declined to exercise that power and now legislators select their own officers (Jewell and Miller 1988, 182–91). Gubernatorial influence in leadership selection has also declined in Alabama, Georgia, and Louisiana (Jewell 1980, 15–17).

Reasons for Leaving

Another aspect of legislative institutionalization is that leaders terminate service after long stints and only to retire from political life. That is, they do not seek other political positions (Polsby 1968, 148–53). As I argue elsewhere (Squire 1989), this standard may not be appropriate for state legislatures and their members. Given the place of state legislatures in the political hierarchy it is to be expected that legislators would anticipate moving to higher offices, although the opportunities for doing so vary by state (Squire 1988a, 1988b). State legislative leaders are not immune from these ambitions. Simon's (1987a, 250) examination of the career paths of the ninety-nine state legislative presiding officers serving in 1981 reveals that twenty had sought higher office within six years, although only ten were successful. These data suggest more than that a substantial number of leaders will seek other offices; they also demonstrate that leaders are not necessarily able to exploit their positions to advance their political careers.

More evidence on this last point is presented in table 3, which shows how many higher officeholders in 1987—members of the U.S. Congress and governors—had state legislative experience and served as leaders in speaker, majority or minority leader, or majority or minority assistant positions but were not committee chairs. As can be inferred from the first column, state legislative service is a good springboard to higher office. And as shown in the second column, of the U.S. representatives and senators who previously served in state legislatures, only a small percentage had held any leadership posts. More favorably, of the former state legislators who had made it to the governorship, 33 percent had been a leader in the legislature. The figure against which to compare these percentages is the percentage of state legislators who hold leadership positions—777 out of 7,466, or 10 percent. Thus, state legislative leaders are only trivially more likely to be elected to the Congress than are rank-and-file members, but they do enjoy more success in becoming governor. Assuming that legislative leaders become strongly identified with state issues, this outcome is not surprising.

Of the forty-two former state legislative leaders in higher offices in 1987, only thirteen were former presiding officers—two senate presidents (not lieutenant governors) and eleven lower house speakers. The former senate leaders were Representatives Stump (R-Ariz.) and Hoyer (D-Md.). Former speakers were Governors Hayden (R-Kans.), Kean (R-N.J.), Michelson (R-S. Dak.), McWherter (D-Tenn.), and Bangerter (R-Utah) and Representatives Chappell (D-Fla.), Cardin (D-Md.), Sabo (D-Minn.), Smith (R-Oreg.), Hansen (R-Utah), and Nielson (R-Utah). Apparently, presiding officers have a particularly good shot at becoming governor. Only Utah, however, seems to draw regularly from presiding officers to fill higher posts.

A look back at table 2 reinforces the point that holding an important leadership post is not necessarily the key to higher office. In California, for example, ex-speakers have met with little electoral success. Unruh got the Democratic gubernatorial nomination in 1970 but was soundly beaten by the incumbent, Ronald Reagan. He was later elected state treasurer. Moretti lost a

TABLE 3.   State Legislators and Success in Gaining Higher Office, 1987

Position	State Legislative Experience		State Legislative Leadership Experience	
	Number	Percentage	Number	Percentage
U.S. House	217	50[a]	27	12[b]
U.S. Senate	38	38	5	13
Governor	30	60	10	33
Total	285	49	42	15

Source: Data collected from *The Almanac of American Politics* 1988.
[a]Calculated out of the total number of positions (i.e., 435).
[b]Calculated out of the number of officeholders with state legislative experience (i.e., 217).

gubernatorial nomination fight in 1974. McCarthy was elected lieutenant governor after leaving the assembly but lost a race for the U.S. Senate in 1988. Monagan never sought higher office. Indeed, Unruh and McCarthy are the only speakers to gain other elective offices in California in over fifty years (Squire 1989). Of the floor leaders, Waldie and Berman served in the U.S. House—the former went on to lose a gubernatorial contest. The others either remained in the assembly, moved up to the state senate, or lost their own races for higher offices.

The same disillusioning story can be told for leaders in the New York Assembly and Iowa House. None of the leaders has ever become governor, although a couple have tried, and only a very few have had any other electoral success. Speaker Fink, for example, retired to practice law after deciding an opportunity to run for governor or another high office was unlikely to occur (Simon 1987b). Fink's predecessor, Steingut, suffered a particularly ignominious departure. After achieving his lifetime ambition of becoming speaker as his father had been, Steingut lost in a primary election and failed as a third-party candidate in the general election. Whatever the cause of this failure to capitalize on the leadership office and the attention it generates, the general pattern across states is clear.

Returning to Simon's (1987a) data, what has happened to the other presiding officers of 1981? Consistent with our findings showing increased leadership tenures, thirty-four of the ninety-nine leaders were still holding their positions six years later. But ten were forced out of their leadership posts because of rotation traditions. Another ten lost their positions from internal party challenges. The bulk of the rest had retired; four others left because of legal problems, and three died in office. Thus, state legislative leadership is, for most who achieve it, the apex of their political careers.

The Changing Politics of Leadership

Has the leadership function changed with the increased tenures of leaders? Perhaps the most important trend has been a shift in emphasis from policy leadership to organizational maintenance. The image of state legislative leaders in the past was of politicians who could successfully use the powers of their offices to pursue policy agendas, albeit ones often developed outside the legislature by the governor or party leaders (Wahlke et al. 1962, 190–91; Jewell and Patterson 1966, 162; Wunnicke and Randall 1986). Currently, leaders are spending larger amounts of time and energy tending to the electoral needs of their party's members (Rosenthal 1989, 86–89).

This trend has been initiated by the professionalization revolution; as members serve longer and become more career-oriented, their needs change (Rosenthal 1989). They require less policy guidance from the leadership; their own increased experiences and personal and committee staffs supply them the bulk of the necessary information. Instead, members want leadership to maintain the organization so as to provide them an environment in which they can seek their own goals, and they want leaders to supply them with the means with which to protect or improve their current positions. Simply stated, rank-and-file members want their leaders to raise campaign funds to protect their seats and to keep or put their party in the majority.

According to Rosenthal, "Currently, leaders in more than half of the states have taken on the job of raising funds and allocating money and other forms of support to members of their legislative party" (1989, 87). Moreover, although legislative leaders in California have taken this role to an extreme—Assembly Speaker Willie Brown raises millions of dollars each election—the sums being raised by other leaders are impressive (Wunnicke and Randall 1986; Rosenthal 1989, 87–88).

The costs of this trend can be demonstrated by examination of the recent experience in California. Both the state senate and assembly have been led by the same leaders since 1981. One observer of California politics, Martin Smith of the *Sacramento Bee*, comments, "Both of our houses in Sacramento are led by people who owe their jobs to the sense of dissatisfaction that the majority party members had with the Senate Pro Tem and the previous Assembly Speaker for not raising enough money from single-issue groups to pay for their campaigns" (Center for the Study of Democratic Institutions 1984, 6). Members in each chamber want leaders to focus their energies on the good of their legislative party. Leaders who appear to be pursuing their own political career ambitions at the expense of their supporters are challenged; this was an important motivation in the Berman-led revolt against Speaker McCarthy (Pollard 1980, 198) and in Barry Keene's replacing John Garamendi as majority leader in the senate (Scheidt 1987). And, as noted above, minority party leaders who fail to move their party toward majority status are removed.

The high level of attention given to members' electoral concerns by leaders comes at a cost. First, questions are now raised about any California Assembly speaker's ability to develop and control the policy agenda (Jeffe 1987). One former longtime California staff member notes of Brown:

> the speaker first has to pay close attention to the reelection of his members and the maintenance of the majority. Second, he's got to be a spokesman for the majority and an assistant to the people who are taking the lead in certain areas (Jeffe 1987, 244).

Second, the raising of large sums of money draws the integrity of the legislature into question. Both Proposition 23 (1984), intended to reduce the power of the leadership, and Proposition 73 (1988), intended to ban leaders from transferring campaign funds to other candidates, were successful, no doubt in large part because of public concern about the propriety of leaders raising large sums of money.

To varying degrees, other legislative bodies suffer from these maladies (Wunnicke and Randall 1986; Rosenthal 1989). Rosenthal (1989) suggests that professionalization has produced better legislators but poorer legislatures because individual members pursue their own interests at the expense of the larger good. This fragmentation makes it harder for leaders to formulate coherent policy agendas and forces them to spend more time and energy meeting the other demands of their members. These general developments may explain why members keep getting reelected at high rates (Jewell and Breaux 1988) in the face of the publics' low regard for the institutions in which they serve (Cotter 1986).

Conclusions and Implications for Future Research

Legislative leaders are, in most states and on average, serving longer terms. Rotation systems requiring limited service are being replaced. But in their place we should not expect to find speakers with the longevity of Oswald Heck, (N.Y. 1937–60), Harry Curvin (R.I. 1941–64), or Solomon Blatt (S.C. 1937–73, except four years). Moderate-length tenures are likely for at least two reasons. First, as suggested above, increased apprenticeships in many legislatures mean that it will take longer to reach the highest posts, leaving less time to serve once there. Second, leaders in professionalized legislatures are expected to shoulder an increasingly heavy burden. Chances are that the demands of the job will lead many to resign voluntarily. Moreover, it can also be expected that challenges will be mounted from below, especially as legislatures fill with ambitious, career-minded members.

These trends suggest some inviting leads for future research. For example, at present we can only speculate that longer leadership tenures have important implications for the organization of the body and the legislative process. More work needs to be undertaken to assess exactly what difference longer tenures make. Likewise, a better understanding of the dynamics of leadership contests should be developed. For years students of the legislative process have grappled with the nebulous concept of leadership, with only marginal success. Shifting the focus away from Congress to state legislatures holds more promise as truly comparative studies are conducted on a rich and varied pool of data.

CHAPTER 11

The Evolution of the State Legislature:
Institutional Change and Legislative Careers

Joel A. Thompson
and
Gary F. Moncrief

> For anyone interested in the variety of historical patterns of organiza-
> tion presented by the (U.S.) House and Senate in the nineteenth century,
> the current range of state legislative practices have a quite familiar look.
> One does not need to go, like Darwin, to the Galapagos Islands to
> rediscover long missing species of legislative operation. (Price 1975, 20)

> American state legislatures have changed remarkably in recent years.
> It can be argued that state legislatures have experienced greater internal
> change in the past twenty-five years than any other of our governmental
> institutions and that they have changed more rapidly than during any
> other period in their history. (Pound 1988, 1)

> State legislatures are becoming like the U.S. House of Representa-
> tives. (Rosenthal 1989, 78)

> Modern (state) representatives aggressively pursue political self-
> interest, which usually translates into advancing the interests of their
> district and their political career. (Van Horn 1989, 211)

These observations of state legislative life in the United States, made less than
fifteen years apart, attest to the profound changes that have occurred in state
legislatures in the past three decades. Price's statement was based on his
observation of state legislatures in the mid-to-late 1960s. He found that many
of the characteristics that affected their functioning and operations were similar to arrangements found in Congress at the turn of the century. Pound notes
the rapid and significant changes that have occurred in state legislatures, and
Rosenthal observes that many of these changes mirror those made in Congress. Finally, Van Horn posits a relationship between changes in the institu-

tion and changes in the career orientation of its members. These observations are central to the discussion in this chapter.

This change in the legislative institution has not gone unnoticed. Indeed, a whole literature on state legislative change, often couched in terms of legislative reform and professionalism, has developed. While there is debate as to the policy impact of professionalized legislatures (Moncrief and Thompson 1988), few can deny that the institution itself is very different than it was only two or three decades ago.

While the initial scholarly impetus was to assess either the impact of legislative change on public policy or the impact of change on the internal order of the body, subsequent research efforts have begun to examine changes in those individuals who make up the institution—the state legislators. Just like the institution itself, the job orientation or career of the state legislator has changed dramatically. We believe that these two changes are not independent phenomena. Yet little scholarly work has attempted to connect, in some theoretical way, the relationship between *institutional* change and *individual* change. It is the purpose of this essay to explore this relationship. Specifically, we discuss some theoretical considerations that frame our arguments, review some of the more important institutional changes that relate to individual legislators, and assess the impact of institutional change on state legislative careers.

Legislative Change

The arguments that guide our research are rooted in organizational theory. We assume that legislatures are organizations that are "rational, goal-oriented identities . . . that are created and structured to perform certain functions or tasks" (Cooper 1977, 140). According to this assumption, organizations have discernible structures and exist within a larger social context—an environment.

Legislatures have several structural dimensions. Among these are member recruitment and retention (the electoral dimension), task specialization and the division of labor (e.g., the committee system and staffing arrangements), distribution of authority and modes of decision making (often associated with leadership). Some of these dimensions help differentiate the organization from its environment, one aspect of the process of institutionalization to which we will return later in this chapter (Polsby 1968).

Organizations exist in relation to their environments. As Davidson and Oleszek note, "In order to survive, an organization must adjust both to its external environment and its internal needs. The external environment is in a perpetual state of flux which no organization . . . can entirely contain" (1976, 39). As the environment changes it creates pressures on the organization to change—to adapt. In relation to legislative organizations, terms such as *in-*

stitutionalization, professionalization, and *modernization* have often been used to describe their evolution. These terms fit within the theoretical framework developed by Davidson and Oleszek, who refer to these changes as *adaptation* and *consolidation.* Adaptive and consolidative changes are adjustments that organizations make in relation to external and internal stresses respectively. With regard to state legislatures, there have been many changes in the past two or three decades that have produced external stresses: socioeconomic changes (population growth, urbanization, and migration), political changes (federalism, executive-legislative relations, and party competition), legal changes *(Baker v. Carr* and preclearance provisions of the Voting Rights Act of 1965), and, more recently, the movement to limit legislative terms.

Jewell and Patterson note that

> In the more than 200 years of their existence, American legislatures have undergone significant developmental change as representative bodies. The fact that they have been in existence for a fairly long period of time suggests that these institutions have been relatively adaptable to changing forces in the environment. (1977, 30)

Several analyses of Congress add validity to this observation. Polsby's work on institutionalization (1968), Price's work on professionalism (1975), and Kernell's study of careerism (1976) identify some external and internal stresses leading to congressional adaptation.

Consolidative changes are made to address internal stresses. Internal stresses may be caused by a variety of institutional factors, including members' needs, goals, and motivations; members' relative positions of power and influence; and institutional adaptations to external events that result in unanticipated internal pressures. Environmental changes and adaptive reactions of state legislatures in the past three decades have led to internal stresses on the institution. Most of these stresses relate to individual motivations and needs such as greater electoral security, an efficacious position within the chamber, and career opportunities.

It is our contention that over the past three decades state legislatures have been subjected to significant external stresses and that adaptive changes made to address these external stresses have created additional internal stresses, which subsequently have led to consolidative changes. These consolidative changes have important implications for state legislative careers.

External Stress and Adaptive Changes:
Institutionalization of the State Legislature

Few studies have examined the impact of environmental changes on state-level political institutions in general (Thompson and Lanier 1987) or the state legislature in particular (Moncrief 1985; Brace and Ward 1989). Although these studies used different indicators and time periods, all found linkages between measures of social or economic change and legislative development. Other sources of external stress include political and legal changes.

The *Baker v. Carr* decision served as the legal shock to a system that had already begun to feel the pressures of changing societal forces. Pound notes that "some significant reform trends were evident before [*Baker v. Carr*]" (1988, 1), primarily the development of staff and research capabilities. But the pace of legislative modernization increased dramatically in the mid-1960s. The first sixty years of the twentieth century was a period of rapid growth, increased urbanization and industrialization, and technological change. Societal forces affected state legislatures. For example, Rosenthal and Forth explain the significant increase in the number of bill introductions and enactments in state legislatures as partly a function of the changing political and social environment: "much of what legislators introduce comes in response to conditions in the environment. The more people, the more problems, the more complexity, the greater the amount of legislation proposed" (1978, 287). As a result, governing became a more complex task than at the turn of the century.

Yet state legislatures were ill equipped to meet the demands of a changing society. They had not adapted rapidly enough to changing external stresses and were, in the words of Davidson and Oleszek, operating "on credit," as pressures were "allowed to build up and resolution of the conflict delayed" (1976, 42). This observation was verified by others. Writing in 1966, Heard notes:

> Even if all legislators were models of efficiency and rectitude . . . most state legislatures would remain poorly organized and technically ill-equipped to do what is expected of them. They do not meet often enough nor long enough; they lack space, clerical staffing, professional assistance; they are poorly paid and overworked; they are prey to special interests, sometimes their own; their procedures and committee systems are outmoded; they devote inordinate time to local interests that distract them from general public policy; they sometimes cannot even get copies of bills on which they must vote. They work, in short, under a host of conditions that dampen their incentive and limit their ability to function effectively. (1966, 1–2)

Heard cites the *Baker* decision as a "radical development" that solved the malapportionment problem, considered to be the most serious problem with state legislatures. With reapportionment came "a change in outlook toward the whole future of state legislature" (1966, 2).

The twenty-five-year period following Heard's observations has witnessed a partial fulfillment of the changes that he anticipated and that others advocated. Many of these are similar to changes in Congress during its process of institutionalization (Moncrief 1985; Brace and Ward 1989). In his seminal work on the U.S. House of Representatives, Polsby (1968) identifies factors and trends associated with the process of institutionalization. These include (1) the establishment of political boundaries between the organization and its environment, characterized by membership stability, leadership recruitment, and less turnover; (2) growth in internal complexity, characterized by several factors that enhance the functioning and autonomy of committees (parallel jurisdictions, staff support, and oversight responsibilities) and by various "emoluments and auxiliary aids to members" (office space, salaries, allowances, and staff support); and (3) a shift from particularistic and discretionary to universalistic and automated decision making (growth of the seniority system and decisions concerning contested elections based solely on merit).

Polsby's framework is useful for students of state legislatures for at least two reasons. First, he ties the causes of institutionalization to external forces; greater social complexity places more political demands on the institution that may require adaptive changes in order for them to be facilitated. Second, many of the adaptive changes made by the U.S. House during institutionalization are relevant for monitoring the process at the state legislative level.

Institutionalization is not necessarily the same as professionalization. But as Squire notes, "The two are, however, likely to occur together, because the dynamic element leading to the development of an institutionalized legislature is closely related to the result of professionalization" (1989, 9).

Squire goes on to make an argument that is very similar to ours concerning consolidative and adaptive changes: "A professionalized body is likely to be one where members look on their service as being their career . . . . Legislators who adopt this long-term perspective are likely to try and mold the organization to meet their needs: that is, to institutionalize it" (1989, 9). There may be other differences in the process at the state level as well. Both Moncrief (1985, 1988) and Brace and Ward (1989) conclude that some indicators of environmental change affect institutional changes differentially. In a similar vein, Squire shows that the career needs in the California Assembly are not the same as in Congress, and therefore, some of the norms and structures are different (1989). These findings suggest that there is more than a single path that leads to professionalization of the state legislature.

There is, however, an apparent consensus on what factors constitute the major elements of professionalization at the state legislative level. These factors include increases in session length, members' compensation and benefits, and staffing. These factors contribute to the internal complexity and institutional autonomy of the legislature.

Session Length

As society has become more complex and technical, perhaps no other aspect of legislative performance becomes more paramount than adequate time to gather information, deliberate, legislate, and oversee. In 1940, only four state legislatures (N.Y., N.J., R.I., and S.C.) met in annual sessions. This number grew to nineteen by the early 1960s, thirty-five by 1975, and today, forty-three legislatures meet annually. Twenty-nine states now have the authority to convene themselves in special session. Overall, the average length of legislative sessions has increased and in California averages approximately 250 days. Even states that have maintained biennial or limited sessions have found it increasingly necessary to utilize interim and special committee activities, sometimes to nearly a year-round schedule (Pound 1988).

Compensation

Although salaries remain low in many states, especially for the amount of time spent on legislative matters, they are much improved. It is difficult to compute salary figures for some legislatures because they are tied to the number of session days and daily expense reimbursements. But for thirty-nine of the forty states that have established annual salaries (New Hampshire excluded), the average compensation now approaches $20,000 per year (plus expenses in most cases). Some states still pay extremely low salaries—New Hampshire, $100, West Virginia, $6,500, Texas, $7,200, and Arkansas, $7,500. Others, however, have salaries that are comparable to those in the private sector for requisite education and skills—$57,500 in New York, $52,500 in California, and in excess of $40,000 in Michigan, Ohio, and Pennsylvania. At least ten states now have annual salaries of $30,000 or more. Better legislative salaries should result in a more careerist orientation and, according to Brace and Ward, are "the most important catalyst for stimulating institutional adjustments" (1989, 1a).

Staffing

One way that legislatures become "bounded" is by developing capabilities to obtain information from internal sources, rather than having to rely upon information supplied by external actors such as the governor, administrative personnel, or lobbyists. This is true not only for central staff agencies and committees but personal staff as well. As Kurtz notes,

> The growth of personal staff to members, sometimes in both district offices and the capitol, has a profound effect on the nature of legislatures. Legislators with their own professional staff have more individual re-

sources, less dependence on leadership . . . and great incumbency advantages in election campaigns. (1990, 3)

State legislators have enhanced their capabilities vis-à-vis other political actors by increasing staff resources and research capabilities. The National Conference of State Legislatures estimates that the permanent staff of state legislatures is now between eighteen thousand and twenty thousand persons, compared to about five thousand in the mid-1960s. The number of full-time professional staff now exceeds fifty in all but twelve state legislatures. Thirty-six states hire more than one hundred additional staff members during legislative sessions. Of the fourteen that do not, only four have less than one hundred full-time professionals. In addition, thirty-five states now have full-time staff support for standing committees. Weberg (1988) reports that for all fifty states legislative staffs grew by 24 percent between 1979 and 1988. The largest increases in the past decade have occurred in personal staff. Finally, Pound notes that *every* state legislature has enhanced its research and fiscal capabilities, although some still lag (1988, 16–18). In short, the level of staff and technical support in most state legislatures today is in sharp contrast to that of twenty-five years ago.

The result of these adaptations is greater legislative autonomy and independence. Limitations of time and staff support, coupled with high turnover, and hence little expertise, resulted in the inability of any legislature, except perhaps California's, to carry out its oversight function "with any degree of adequacy" (see Citizens Conference on State Legislatures 1971, 126–27). When oversight was accomplished, it tended to be "episodic, partial, and selective" (Keefe 1966, 46).

But many state legislatures have made adaptive changes to meet the challenges of a strengthened executive branch. One scholar observes that "during the 1970s, state legislatures discovered oversight" (Gormley 1989, 132). Also, they became much more involved in other administrative aspects of governing. For example, in 1967, only two states engaged in administrative rules review. By 1988, at least forty-two states were active to some degree in this process (Pound 1988, 3). Sunset legislation also became a mechanism utilized by approximately two-thirds of the states, and approximately one-third continue to use the legislative veto, although it has been invalidated in at least eight states (Gormley 1989, 132). The result of these and other adaptations may provide "more occasions for legislative oversight and more incentives for individual legislators to engage in oversight" (Gormley 1989, 133).

The results of adaptive changes made by state legislatures have been profound. These changes are perhaps best summarized by Rosenthal:

Thus, the decade from about 1965 to 1975 can appropriately be termed the period of "the rise of the legislative institution." Traditional assemblies became modern ones, and reformed legislatures emerged. They had developed the capacity to do their jobs, to perform the functions that they could be expected to perform. (1989, 70).

Internal Stress and Consolidative Changes:
Implications for Legislative Careers

According to our theoretical framework, byproducts of adaptive changes made by state legislatures include internal tensions, which are "an inevitable concomitant of all organizational innovation" (Davidson and Oleszek 1976, 40). Consolidative changes or innovations are designed to accommodate as much as possible the *individual* needs of members. "Whereas adaptation places priority upon *institutional* arrangements, consolidation is most closely linked to *interpersonal* adjustment" (Davidson and Oleszek 1976, 41, emphasis ours). Thus, subsequent consolidative changes in the state legislature after the rapid period of modernization are more closely linked to the needs, goals, and motivations of individual legislators. If we assume that the goal of some is a legislative career (see Rosenthal 1989), then consolidative changes should enhance this goal.

In addition to the socioeconomic changes chronicled in the literature on institutional change, other political, legal, and structural changes have had profound consequences for the state legislature. The most notable result is the new breed of state legislator—"professionals who want to stay in public office for the long haul" (Rosenthal 1989, 76; also see Loomis 1990, 13). Women constitute a larger proportion of this new breed; Patricia Freeman and William Lyons note in chapter 4 that the number of females serving in the states has quadrupled since 1969. Women hold more than 25 percent of legislative seats in at least five states—New Hampshire, Maine, Colorado, Vermont, and Washington—and make up a sizable contingent in many others (Van Horn 1989, 211). Overall, however, women are still underrepresented. A variety of explanations exist: differential recruitment patterns of political parties, background variables, and cultural differences are a few. Unfortunately, the number of female legislators is so small in many states that we "know virtually nothing about how women's experiences as legislators differ from men's" (chap. 4).

Reapportionment and the preclearance provisions of the Voting Rights Act have had a significant impact on the number of African-Americans and Hispanics elected to state legislatures. Charles S. Bullock notes in chapter 3 that the number of blacks has increased from 172 in 1969 to 400 in 1987. As of 1987, thirty-six states had at least 1 black senator and forty-one states had at least 1 black house member. Sixteen states had at least 10 blacks in the lower house. The number of Hispanic representatives has increased also. By 1988, 120 Hispanics held seats in state legislatures. Hispanics are most predominant in states where they constitute a significant proportion of the population (Va. Horn 1989, 211).

We know very little about the political careers of racial minorities. Some, such as Willie Brown of California, have reached the pinnacle of legislative success. As the numbers of blacks and Hispanics increase, future research should explore this untapped area.

Another difference between the new breed and the old breed relates to occupations. The old breed (lawyers and businesspeople) are being replaced by "career politicians who come from the ranks of unseasoned lawyers, teachers, preachers, spouses of professionals, single people who can live on a legislative salary, public organizers, legislative aides, and others of like ilk" (Rosenthal 1989, 75). Another part of the new breed is made up of "the younger, newer members—men and women alike—who come out of college, graduate school, or law school and go directly into politics" (Rosenthal 1989, 75). They are more mobile and less parochial (see chap. 2). A final contingent of this group has a unique occupation—legislator. Today, more than 10 percent of all state legislators consider their occupation to be legislator, up from 1 percent only a decade earlier (Bazar 1987). In the more professional bodies the proportions are much higher: approximately two-thirds in Michigan and Pennsylvania; half or more in Illinois, Massachusetts, and New York; and only slightly fewer in at least seven other states. Wisconsin is illustrative of the trend (Loomis 1990, 13–15). In 1963 no member listed legislator as his or her primary occupation. By 1969, only about 5 percent were full-time. This proportion grew to about 55 percent by 1983 and today approaches 70 percent (Rosenthal 1989, 71–72).

As a result, the legislature is much less homogeneous than it used to be. Perhaps more importantly though, it is made up of individuals who have few outside interests and distractions. In short, the legislature is their vocation. Thus, to reduce occupational uncertainty, electoral concerns become paramount (Loomis 1990, 20). After all, for the old breed, electoral defeat was a disappointment; for the new breed it may be the end of a career.

Electoral considerations have significantly affected the legislature and the careers of its members. One of the most obvious is money, "the mother's milk of politics." The cost of running for a legislative seat has risen dramatically in the last decade (Alexander 1991, 7). Sorauf (1988, 266) reports that candidates for the Assembly in California spent $56,300,000.00 in 1986, or $3.20 per vote. This figure approaches the average expenditure per vote for Congress that year—$4.59. In Ohio a competitive seat now costs about $300,000.00, in Michigan about $250,000.00, and in Wisconsin about $100,000.00 (Rosenthal 1989, 79). Even in smaller, more rural states where media are not used extensively, competitive campaigns can cost $25,000.00 and more.

As a result of the increase in campaign costs, candidates are forced to seek larger and larger war chests. Quick to fill this void, political action committees (PACs) have proliferated. Jones (1986) reports that the number of PACs has increased significantly: up 500 percent in Arizona, approximately 400 percent in Louisiana and New York, and about 100 percent in Wisconsin. In North Carolina, the number of PACs has increased tenfold since 1974 (Thompson and Cassie 1990).

Of course, there has been a corresponding, almost geometric, increase in the amount of money flowing into electoral coffers. Between 1976 and 1982, the amount of money contributed by PACs increased by 240 percent in Florida, over 400 percent in Montana, and over 1,500 percent in Arizona (Wagner 1986). This money constitutes a substantial proportion of the funds generated and spent by candidates, ranging on the average from about 25 to 75 percent. Studies indicate that PAC contributions go disproportionately to incumbents (Giles and Pritchard 1985; Jones and Borris 1985), giving career legislators another electoral advantage. Although political party organizations may attempt to offset this advantage to some extent (see chap. 7), the proportion of incumbents who are reelected to state legislative seats now approaches that of members of Congress (see chap. 6).

Money has also become a consideration of legislative leaders. Increasingly, leaders are expected to raise and distribute campaign funds for party members. This practice can help insulate individual legislators from PACs and their influence and strengthens the role of the legislative leadership.

Electoral considerations are also a force behind the increase in the proliferation of personal staffs. Approximately twenty states now provide personal staffs for members. In addition, at least ten states have made some type of provisions for district offices, where staffs can maintain close ties with local citizens and provide assistance to constituents. Unlike professional staff, the major function of personal staff is "delivering service to constituents and reelection to members, two very compatible tasks" (Rosenthal 1989, 83).

Increases in money and staff support are related to another aspect of careerism—a decrease in turnover. The steady decline in turnover in state legislatures is well documented (Rosenthal 1974b; Shin and Jackson 1979; Niemi and Winsky 1987). Turnover rates are a product of (1) the relative attractiveness of the position and (2) the relative competitiveness of the district. Salary increases and the availability of personal staff have made the state legislature a more attractive place to work. Large campaign war chests have enhanced the reelection chances of incumbents who run and discourage those who want to challenge.

Stabilization of membership is followed by other consolidative changes like the development of a seniority system, curtailment of the Speaker's power, and the decentralization of power within the chambers. There are surely differences here between the types of changes that occurred in Congress and those that may occur in some state legislatures, because the career opportunity structures are somewhat different (see Squire 1988a, 1989). Nonetheless, the patterns of institutionalization and professionalization are very similar.

The rising costs of campaigns, the proliferation of personal staff, the appearance of district offices, and the increase in the number of full-time legislators are indicative of the "congressionalization" of the state legislature (Van Horn 1989). Whether we call it "reform," "professionalization," "modernization," or "congressionalization," the institution has changed dramatically. And so have those who occupy it.

The most recent external shock to the system—the movement to limit legislative terms—may have profound effects. As we note in the Appendix, some of the short-term effects may be positive ones—positive in terms of making the legislature more representative: women and southern Republicans would likely benefit from the sudden increase in open seats, increasing the possibility that their numbers in the legislature would more accurately reflect their proportion in the general population.

But some of the effects of term limits may adversely affect the evolution of the institution. Certainly leadership positions will change hands more frequently. In some states this may open up the chambers to some of the new breed who may disperse power among the members and open the legislative doors to new ideas and innovative state programs. On the other hand, the departure of those members with long service will result in a substantial loss of legislative and policy expertise, making the remaining members more dependent on lobbyists, the bureaucrats, and the governor. In the long-term, term limits may cause other unintended results: fewer effectively contested elections and an increase in the influence of legislative staff (see Copeland and Rausch 1991 or Moncrief et al. 1992).

We do not know what the ultimate impact will be of term limits. If this movement does not continue to gather momentum in other states, then it may be no more than the evolutionary equivalent of a genetic mutation that briefly effects a partial cohort of the species (i.e., California, Colorado, and Oklahoma). If, on the other hand, it becomes a widespread phenomenon in the states, it could have profound and lasting effects on the evolution of the state legislature.

Conclusions

State legislatures today are very different institutions than before. Changes in the socioeconomic, political, and legal environment generated substantial stresses that required organizational change. Twenty-five years of reform resulted in a stronger, more capable, and more independent branch of government. In Polsby's institutionalization terminology, almost all state legislatures are today bounded and internally complex. Some have developed more universalistic criteria and automated methods for internal decision making. Others continue to employ more particularistic and discretionary methods where the career needs of their members are better met through such systems (Squire 1989). As a result, many state legislatures are becoming more like their national counterpart, the U.S. House of Representatives.

Adaptive changes and system "shocks" (reform, reapportionment, and the Voting Rights Act) have facilitated the election of a new breed of state legislators. The new breed is different from the old in many ways. Its impact has been to make the institution less homogeneous, more representative of its constituents, and more inclined to shape the institution to meet its career needs.

But while some consolidative changes have enhanced the career opportunity structures of state legislatures, others have detracted from the legislative process by contributing to its fragmentation. Members are more concerned with reducing electoral uncertainties than with advancing programmatic or party agendas. As a result, campaign costs have soared, and the pursuit of money has become a time-consuming task. Individual staff members spend more time satisfying constituents' needs and less time researching legislative proposals (see Rosenthal 1989). Citizens are becoming disenchanted with career politicians who give the appearance of placing their electoral welfare over that of the state. These actions and perceptions have contributed to the nascent term limit movement.

These changes carry individual costs as well. The transition from part-time to full-time legislatures has brought with it "a serious source of tension" between public and private affairs (Francis 1985a, 641). For some, the added costs of more time away from family plus more energy directed toward legislative matters outweigh their individual rewards, personal achievements, or desires for a legislative career (Francis and Baker 1986).

An important question for subsequent research is the extent to which state legislatures and legislative careers will continue to evolve in ways similar to Congress. Will they become so fragmented that they lose their capacity to function effectively as governing bodies? Will members become so individualistic and parochial that the public interest becomes lost in a myriad of private interests? "If the case of the U.S. Congress is an indication, then state legislatures . . . face the prospect of an unraveling organizational coherence and approaching paralysis" (Rosenthal 1989, 97). If this prediction comes true, state legislatures will have come full circle, from virtual paralysis due to institutional handicaps and external stress to near paralysis because of individual motivations and internal stress. One is then left with a Darwinian question: Are state legislatures evolving into a stronger species or an endangered one?

APPENDIX

A Note on Term Limits and State Legislatures

A discussion of the term limit phenomenon was not part of the original plan for this volume. However, the issue has such relevance to the subject matter of this book that we felt it would be worthwhile to include a brief discussion of our recent research on the topic.

Because many state legislatures are still part-time, "citizen legislatures," we view the emerging term limit movement with some skepticism. Nonetheless, at this point the movement is attracting considerable interest in some quarters. In late 1990, initiatives were approved by voters in California, Colorado, and Oklahoma. Since then, initiatives or legislative bills have been introduced in about forty other states. The particulars of these bills and initiatives vary by state; in some they apply only to the state legislature, while in others they include congressional term limits and/or statewide offices as well. They also vary in regards to the time in office permitted, generally ranging from six to twelve years.

Reformers have goals in mind when they seek to initiate their changes. These goals may be clear and specific or general and vague. There may or may not be consensus on what is the goal of a specific reform (Moncrief and Jewell 1980). Moreover, reforms almost always have unintended consequences. Presumably, one of the unintended consequences of the legislative reforms of the 1960s and 1970s was the creation of a careerist orientation in some of the more professionalized state legislatures. Also, presumably, the term limit movement of today is intended to eliminate that careerist orientation.

At this point, there is very little research on the effect of term limits on state legislators or state legislatures. Copeland and Rausch (1991) suggest that the consequences might include *less* electoral competition; increased influence for interest groups, legislative staff, and the executive branch; and the general "amateurization" of state legislatures. As Katz notes, "When it comes to term limitation, the possible side effects are endless" (1991, 24).

The problem with analyzing a reform such as the implementation of a term limit is that we don't know the actual consequences until years after the reform is in place. In other words, we can't conduct posttests until the "treatment" (i.e., the imposition of the term limit) has been in effect for a decade or more. We can, however, estimate some of the more immediate impacts by analyzing the present tenures of various groups of legislators today. The questions we want to address here are these: Do state legislators tend to stay in office for lengthy periods? Are certain groups more likely to have extensive tenures compared to other groups? We sought to answer these questions in two recent research projects (Moncrief and Thompson 1991; Moncrief et al. 1992), the results of which are reported below.

Given the apparent popularity of the term limit movement, one might assume that state legislators cling to their seats for decades, truly establishing their offices as careers. But is this the case? Several chapters in this volume (especially chaps. 5 and 6) note that there is less electoral competition, and so we might expect that legislative careers are lengthening. While this is generally true over time, most state legislators do not retain their seats for extended periods (Moncrief et al. 1992). Using the entire 1979–80 cohort of freshmen state legislators ($N = 1,547$), we found that almost half (45.7 percent) of those serving in lower chambers and over one-third (37.7 percent) of state senators had vacated their seats within six years. Only 27.1 percent of house members and 33.6 percent of state senators retained their seats for as long as twelve years.

There is, however, a significant difference in the seat retention rates by *type* of legislature. Using many of the factors discussed by William Pound in chapter 1 of this volume, Kurtz (1990) developed a typology of legislative professionalism. In table A1 we show the retention rates for our original legislative cohort, broken down by type of state legislature. The results are clear; careerism, as manifested by extensive tenure in office, is substantially greater in the handful of professional state legislatures. As shown in the table, 40.2 percent of the house or assembly members and 59.8 percent of the senators in those state legislatures retain their seats for at least twelve years. But for state legislators in the vast majority of states the twelve-year retention rate, in either chamber, is less than 30 percent. It would seem that in most states the term limit movement would actually affect only a small proportion of legislators.

In the other project (Moncrief and Thompson 1991), we used data from the background study reported in chapter 2 of this volume to estimate the effect of term limits on four specific groups of state legislators: women, African-Americans, Repub-

TABLE A1. The Relationship between Cohort Retention and State Legislative Professionalism

Level of Professionalism	Original Cohort (N)	Percentage Remaining for 6 Years	Percentage Remaining for 12 Years
Lower Chambers			
Professional	244	63.5	40.2
Hybrid	691	57.9	29.4
Citizen	616	48.2	19.2
Upper Chambers			
Professional	82	69.5	59.8
Hybrid	274	64.2	29.9
Citizen	147	54.4	25.9

Source: Reprinted from Moncrief et al., *Legislative Studies Quarterly* 18, no. 1 (February, 1992): 43.

Note: Professional: California, Illinois, Massachusetts, Michigan, New York, Ohio, Pennsylvania, and Wisconsin; *Citizen:* Arkansas, Idaho, Louisiana, Maine, Mississippi, Montana, Nevada, New Hampshire, New Mexico, North Carolina, North Dakota, Rhode Island, South Dakota, Utah, Vermont, West Virginia, and Wyoming; all other states are classified as *Hybrid.*

licans in southern state legislatures, and legislative leaders. Not surprisingly, we found that men would be affected initially more than women (since a larger proportion of male legislators has been in office for an extended period of time). For example, while 18 percent of all state legislators in our sample was female, less than 7 percent of those who had served more than twelve years was female. This means that in the first few years after the imposition of a term limit, a larger proportion of male than female incumbents would have to surrender their seats. These seats would then become "open seats." Since female candidates are now about as likely as male candidates to win in an open seat contest, we would expect that the proportion of female state legislators would increase due to a term limit. This effect, of course, would be relatively short-lived, because the proportion of female incumbents who would be forced to give up their seats due to the term limit would increase over time. But for at least the first few years after the implementation of a term limit, we might expect a modest increase (beyond the historical trend) in the percentage of female state legislators. For the same reasons, Democrats in southern state legislatures would feel the effect of term limits more immediately than would southern Republicans.

We did not find, however, that this holds for black state legislators. As described in chapter 3, the percentage of African-American state legislators does not appear to be steadily increasing in the same way it is for women and southern Republicans. Instead, increases for blacks appear in "step-increases," which are usually associated with changes in the electoral districts, often as a result of the reapportionment cycle.

We also found a substantial impact on leadership positions, noting that "As expected, we find a direct relationship between legislative service and leadership. More than half (93 of 179) of the major house leadership positions are occupied by legislators with more than twelve years of service" (Moncrief and Thompson 1991, 5).

There is no doubt that the term limit movement will have an important effect in some states. The data we have presented here, however, shows that term limits may have different types of consequences in different types of state legislatures and may affect different types of legislators in different ways.

References

Adamany, David. 1984. "Political Parties in the 1980s." In *Money and Politics in the United States: Financing Elections in the 1980s*, ed. Michael J. Malbin. Washington, D.C.: American Enterprise Institute.

Aldrich, John H. 1980. *Before the Convention*. Chicago: University of Chicago Press.

Alexander, Herbert. 1988. "Initiatives in California Political Finance." *Impact*, July/August, 1-4.

————. 1991. *Reform and Reality*. New York: The Twentieth Century Fund Press.

Alexander, Herbert E., and Brian A. Haggerty. 1987. *Financing the 1984 Election*. Lexington, Mass.: Lexington.

Alford, John, and John Hibbing. 1981. "Increased Incumbency Advantage in the House." *Journal of Politics* 43:1042-61.

Arnold, R. Douglas. 1982. "Overtilled and Undertilled Fields in American Politics." *Political Science Quarterly* 97:91-103.

Arterton, F. Christopher. 1982. "Political Money and Party Strength." In *The Future of American Political Parties: The Challenge of Governance*, ed. Joel L. Fleishman. Englewood Cliffs, N.J.: Prentice Hall.

Asher, Herbert B. 1974. "Committees and the Norm of Specialization." *Annals* 411:63-74.

————. 1975. "The Changing Status of the Freshman Representative." *Congress in Change: Evolution and Reform*, ed. Norman J. Ornstein. New York: Praeger.

Baker v. Carr. 1962. 369 U.S. 186.

Barber, James. 1965. *The Lawmakers*. New Haven: Yale University Press.

Barrilleaux, C. J. 1986. "A Dynamic Model of Partisan Competition in the American States." *American Journal of Political Science* 30:822-40.

Barrone, Michael, ed. 1988. *The Almanac of American Politics*. Washington, D.C.: The National Journal.

Basehart, Hubert H. 1980. "The Effect of Membership Stability on Continuity and Experience in U.S. State Legislative Committees." *Legislative Studies Quarterly* 5:55-68.

Bazar, Beth. 1987. *State Legislators' Occupations: A Decade of Change*. Denver: National Conference of State Legislatures.

Bean, L. 1948. *How to Predict Elections*. New York: Knopf.

Bell, Charles G., and Charles M. Price. 1984. *California Government Today: The Politics of Reform*, 2d ed. Homewood, Ill.: Dorsey.

Bernick, E. Lee, and Charles W. Wiggins. 1978. "Legislative Reform and Legislative

Turnover." In *Legislative Reform: The Policy Impact*, ed. Leroy N. Rieselbach. Lexington, Mass.: Lexington.

Beth, Loren P., and William C. Havard. 1961. "Committee Stacking and Political Power in Florida." *Journal of Politics* 23:57–83.

Beyle, Thad L. 1989. "Political Change in North Carolina: A Legislative Coup D'Etat." *Comparative State Politics Newsletter* 10:3–15.

Bibby, John F. 1979. "Political Parties and Federalism: The Republican National Committee Involvement in Gubernatorial and Legislative Elections." *Publius* 9:229–36.

———. 1983. "Patterns in Midterm Gubernatorial and State Legislative Elections." *Public Opinion*, February/March, 41–46.

Bibby, John F., Cornelius P. Cotter, James L. Gibson, and Robert J. Huckshorn. 1983. "Parties in State Politics." In *Politics in the American States*, 4th ed., ed. V. Gray, H. Jacob, and K. N. Vines. Boston, Mass.: Little, Brown.

———. 1990. "Parties in State Politics." In *Politics in the American States*, 5th ed., ed. V. Gray, H. Jacob, and R. B. Albritton. Boston, Mass.: Scott Foresman/Little, Brown.

Black Elected Officials: A National Roster. Washington, D.C.: Joint Center for Political Studies. Various years.

Blair, Diane Kincaid, and Ann Henry. 1981. "The Family Factor in State Legislative Turnover." *Legislative Studies Quarterly* 6:55–68.

Block, A. G. 1987. "Demure Tom Hannigan: Policy Man Fills Political Role." *California Journal* 18:144–50.

Born, Richard. 1979. "Generational Replacement and the Growth of Incumbent Re-election Margins in the U.S. House." *American Political Science Review* 73:811–17.

Boyd, William. 1982. "Campaign Finance and Electoral Outcomes in Wisconsin and Georgia House Races." Paper presented at the annual meeting of the Midwest Political Science Association, Chicago, Ill., April.

Brace, Kimball, Bernard Grofman, and Lisa Handley. 1987. "Does Redistricting Aimed to Help Blacks Necessarily Help Republicans?" *Journal of Politics* 49:169–85.

Brace, Kimball, Bernard Grofman, Lisa Handley, and Richard Niemi. 1985. "The 65 Percent Rule in Legislative Districting for Racial Minorities: The Mathematics of Minority Voting Equality." Paper presented at the annual meeting of the Midwest Political Science Association, Chicago, Ill., April 10–12.

Brace, Paul, and Daniel Ward. 1989. "The Transformation of the American Statehouse: A Study of Legislative Institutionalization." Paper delivered at the 1989 annual meeting of the Midwest Political Science Association, Chicago, Ill., April.

Browning, Robert X. 1989. "Indiana Elects Democratic Governor and Equally Divided House." *Comparative State Politics Newsletter* 10:1–2.

Bullock, Charles S., III. 1970. "Apprenticeship and Committee Assignments in the House of Representatives." *Journal of Politics* 32:717–20.

———. 1972. "Freshman Committee Assignments and Re-election in the United

States House of Representatives." *American Political Science Review* 66:996–1007.

———. 1973. "Committee Transfers in the United States House of Representatives." *Journal of Politics* 35:85–120.

———. 1976. "Motivations for U.S. Congressional Committee Preferences: Freshmen of the 92nd Congress." *Legislative Studies Quarterly* 1:201—12.

———. 1984a. "Racial Crossover Voting and the Election of Black Officials." *Journal of Politics* 46:238–51.

———. 1984b. "Racial Voting Patterns and Electoral Outcomes in Fort Lauderdale Elections." Athens, Ga.: University of Georgia. Typescript.

———. 1985. "U.S. Senate Committee Assignments: References, Motivations, and Success." *American Journal of Political Science* 29:789–808.

———. 1987. "Redistricting and Changes in the Partisan and Racial Composition of Southern Legislatures." *State and Local Government Review* 19:62–67.

Bullock, Charles S., III, and Susan A. MacManus. 1987. "Structural Features of Municipal Elections and Black Descriptive Representation." Paper presented at the annual meeting of the Southern Political Science Association, Charlotte, N.C., November 5–7.

———. 1989. "Structural Features of Municipalities and the Incidence of Hispanic Council Members." Paper presented at the annual meeting of the Southwestern Political Science Association, Little Rock, Ark., March 29–April 1.

Burnham, Walter Dean. 1975. "Insulation and Responsiveness in Congressional Elections." *Political Science Quarterly* 90:411–35.

Button, James W. 1989. *Blacks and Social Change: The Impact of the Civil Rights Movement in Southern Communities*. Princeton: Princeton University Press.

Cain, Bruce E. 1984. *The Reapportionment Puzzle*. Berkeley, Calif.: University of California.

Caldeira, Gregory A., and Samuel C. Patterson. 1982. "Bringing Home the Votes: Electoral Outcomes in State Legislative Races." *Political Behavior* 4:33–67.

California Commission on Campaign Financing. 1985. *The New Gold Rush: Financing California Legislative Campaigns*. Los Angeles, Calif.: Center for Responsive Government.

Calvert, Jerry. 1979. "Revolving Doors: Volunteerism in State Legislatures." *State Government* 52:174–81.

Campbell, Ballard C. 1980. *Representative Democracy*. Cambridge: Harvard University Press.

Carmines, E. 1974. "The Mediating Influence of State Legislatures on the Linkage between Interparty Competition and Welfare Policies." *American Political Science Review* 68:1118–24.

Carroll, Kathleen. 1982. "The Age Difference between Men and Women Politicians." *Social Science Quarterly* 63:332–39.

Center for the American Woman and Politics. 1976. *Women in Public Office*. New Brunswick, N.J.: Eagleton Institute of Politics, Rutgers University.

———. 1982. *Women State Legislators: Report from a Conference*. New Brunswick, N.J.: Eagleton Institute of Politics, Rutgers University.

Center for the Study of Democratic Institutions. 1984. "The Failure of State Legislative Reform: A Dialogue." *Center Magazine* 17:3–13.

Chaffey, Douglas C., and Malcolm E. Jewell. 1972. "Selection and Tenure of State Legislative Party Leaders: A Comparative Analysis." *Journal of Politics* 34:1278–86.

Christensen, Rob. 1989. "Growing Republican Ranks Help Topple Speaker in North Carolina." *State Legislatures* 15:16–19.

Chubb, John E. 1988. "Institutions, the Economy, and the Dynamics of State Elections." *American Political Science Review* 82:133–54.

Citizen's Conference on State Legislatures. 1971. *Report on the Evaluation of the 50 State Legislatures*. Denver, Colo.: Citizen's Conference on State Legislatures.

Clapp, Charles L. 1963. *The Congressman: His Work As He Sees It*. Washington, D.C.: The Brookings Institution.

Cnudde, C. F. and D. J. McCrone. 1969. "Party Competition and Welfare Policies in the American States." *American Political Science Review* 63:858–66.

Collie, Melissa. 1981. "Incumbency, Electoral Safety, and Turnover in the House of Representatives." *American Political Science Review* 75:119–31.

Constantinia, Edmond, and Kenneth Craik. 1977. "Women as Politicians: The Social Background, Personality, and Political Careers of Female Party Leaders." In *A Portrait of Marginality*, ed. Marianne Githens and Jewell Prestage. New York: McKay.

Cooper, Joseph. 1977. "Congress in Organizational Perspective." In *Congress Reconsidered*, ed. L.C. Dodd and B. Oppenheimer. New York: Praeger.

Cooper, Joseph, and David W. Brady. 1981. "Toward a Diachronic Analysis of Congress." *American Political Science Review*. 75:988–1006.

Copeland, Gary, and John Rausch, Jr. 1991. "The End of Professionalism? The Dynamics of Term Limitations." Paper presented at the annual meeting of the Southwestern Political Science Association, San Antonio, Tex., March 27–30.

Cotter, Cornelious P., and John F. Bibby. 1980. "Institutional Development and the Thesis of Party Decline." *Political Science Quarterly* 95:1–27.

Cotter, Patrick. 1986. "Legislatures and Public Opinion." *State Government* 59:46–51.

Council of State Governments. 1984. *Book of the States: 1984–85 Edition*. Lexington, Ky.: Council of State Governments.

———. 1986. *Book of the States: 1986–87 Edition*. Lexington, Ky.: Council of State Governments.

Cover, Albert. 1977. "One Good Term Deserves Another: The Advantage of Incumbency in Congressional Elections." *American Journal of Political Science* 21:523–41.

Cover, Albert, and David R. Mayhew. 1981. "Congressional Dynamics and the Decline of Competitive Congressional Elections." In *Congress Reconsidered*, 2d ed., ed. L. C. Dodd and B. Oppenheimer. Washington, D.C.: Congressional Quarterly Press.

Crane, Wilder, and A. Clark Hagensick. 1981. *Wisconsin Government and Politics*. Milwaukee, Wis.: Department of Governmental Affairs, University of Wisconsin.

Crittenden, J. 1967. "Dimensions of Modernization in the American States." *American Political Science Review* 61:989–1001.

Darcy, Robert, Susan Welch, and Janet Clark. 1985. "Women Candidates in Single and Multi-Member Districts: American State Legislative Races." *Social Science Quarterly* 66:945–53.

———. 1987. *Women, Elections, and Representation.* New York: Longmann.

Dauer, Manning J. 1984. "Florida's Legislature." In *Florida's Politics and Government,* 2d ed., ed. Manning J. Dauer. Gainesville: University Presses of Florida.

Davidson, Roger H. 1981. "Subcommittee Government: New Channels for Policy Making." In *The New Congress,* ed. Thomas E. Mann and Norman J. Ornstein. Washington, D.C.: American Enterprise Institute.

Davidson, Roger H., and W. Oleszek. 1976. "Adaptation and Consolidation: Structural Innovation in the U.S. House of Representatives." *Legislative Studies Quarterly* 1:37–66.

Dawson, R. E., and J. A. Robinson. 1963. "Inter-party Competition, Economic Variables, and Welfare Policies in the American States." *Journal of Politics* 25:265–89.

Diamond, Irene. 1977. *Sex Roles in the Statehouse.* New Haven: Yale University Press.

Downs, A. 1957. *An Economic Theory of Democracy.* New York: Harper and Row.

Dubeck, Paula. 1976. "Women and Access to Political Office: A Comparison of Female and Male State Legislators." *Sociological Quarterly* 17:42–52.

Dye, Thomas. 1966. *Politics, Economics, and the Public.* Chicago, Ill.: Rand McNally.

———. 1981. *Politics in States and Communities.* Englewood Cliffs, N.J.: Prentice Hall.

Eisenstein, James. 1984. "Patterns of Campaign Finance in Pennsylvania's 1982 Legislative Elections." Paper presented at the annual meeting of the Pennsylvania Political Science Association.

Elazar, Daniel. 1972. *American Federalism: A View from the States.* New York: Harper and Row.

Engstrom, Richard L., and Michael D. McDonald. 1982. "The Underrepresentation of Blacks on City Councils: Comparing the Structural and Socioeconomic Explanations for South/Non-South Differences." *Journal of Politics* 44:1088–99.

Erikson, Robert. 1971. "The Advantage of Incumbency in Congressional Elections." *Polity* 3:395–405.

Eulau, Heinz. 1985. "Committee Selection." In *Handbook of Legislative Research,* ed. Gerhard Loewenberg, Samuel C. Patterson, and Malcolm E. Jewell. Cambridge, Mass.: Harvard University Press.

Eulau, Heinz, and Vera McCluggage. 1985. "Standing Committees in Legislatures." In *Handbook of Legislative Research,* ed. Gerhard Loewenberg, Samuel C. Patterson, and Malcolm E. Jewell. Cambridge, Mass.: Harvard University Press.

Fenno, Richard F. 1973. *Congressmen in Committees.* Boston, Mass.: Little, Brown.

———. 1978. *Homestyle.* Boston, Mass.: Little, Brown.

Ferejohn, John. 1977. "On the Decline of Competition in Congressional Elections." *American Political Science Review* 71:166–76.

Fiorina, Morris P. 1977. *Congress: Keystone of the Washington Establishment.* New Haven: Yale University Press.

Fowler, Linda L., Scott R. Douglas, and Wesley D. Clark, Jr. 1980. "The Electoral Effects of House Committee Assignments." *Journal of Politics* 42:307–19.

Francis, Wayne. 1985a. "Costs and Benefits of Legislative Service in the American States." *American Journal of Political Science* 29:626–42.

———. 1985b. "Leadership, Party Caucuses, and Committees in U.S. State Legislatures." *Legislative Studies Quarterly* 10:243–88.

———. 1986. "Agenda Setting and the Potential for Reciprocity in Legislatures: Measurement by Inference." Paper presented at the annual meeting of the Midwest Political Science Association, Chicago, Ill., April.

Francis, Wayne, and John Baker. 1986. "Why Do U.S. State Legislators Vacate Their Seats?" *Legislative Studies Quarterly* 11:119–26.

Francis, Wayne, and James W. Riddlesperger. 1982. "U.S. State Legislative Committees: Structure, Procedural Efficiency, and Party Control." *Legislative Studies Quarterly* 7:453–71.

Garand, James C. 1991. "Electoral Marginality in State Legislative Elections, 1968–1986." *Legislative Studies Quarterly* 16:7–28.

Garand, James C., and Donald Gross. 1984. "Change in the Vote Margins for Congressional Candidates: A Specification of Historical Trends." *American Political Science Review* 78:17–30.

Gertzog, Irwin N. 1976. "The Routinization of Committee Assignments in the U.S. House of Representatives." *American Journal of Political Science* 20:693–712.

Gibson, James L., Neal Cotter, John F. Bibby, and Robert J. Huckshorn. 1985. "Wither the Local Parties? A Cross-Sectional and Longitudinal Analysis of the Strength of Party Organizations." *American Journal of Political Science* 29:139–60.

Gierzynski, Anthony, and Malcolm E. Jewell. 1989. "Legislative Party Campaign Committee Activity: A Comparative State Analysis." Paper presented at the annual meeting of the Midwest Political Science Association, Chicago, Ill.

Giles, Michael W., and Anita Pritchard. 1985. "Campaign Expenditures and Legislative Elections in Florida." *Legislative Studies Quarterly* 10:71–88.

Gormley, William T. 1989. "Custody Battles in State Administration." In *The State of the States*, ed. Carl E. Van Horn. Washington, D.C.: CQ Press.

Grau, Craig H. 1981a. "Competition in State Legislative Primaries." *Legislative Studies Quarterly* 6:35–54.

———. 1981b. "The Neglected World of State Legislative Elections." Paper presented at the annual meeting of the Midwest Political Science Association, Chicago, Ill.

Gray, V. 1976. "A Note on Competition and Turnout in the American States." *Journal of Politics* 38:153–58.

Gross, Donald, and J. C. Garand. 1984. "The Vanishing Marginals, 1824–1980." *Journal of Politics* 46:224–37.

Hain, Paul L. 1974. "Age, Ambitions, and Political Careers: The Middle-Age Crisis." *Western Political Quarterly* 27:265–74.

———. 1985. "State Legislative Career Patterns: Selected Trend in Tennessee Since 1797." Paper presented at the annual meeting of the American Political Science Association, New Orleans, La.

Hamm, Keith E. 1987. "The Prevalence of Subgovernments: Evidence from Nebraska State Legislative Committee Decision Making." Paper presented at the annual meeting of the Midwest Political Science Association, Chicago, Ill.

Hamm, Keith E., and David M. Olson. 1987. "The Value of Incumbency in State Legislative Elections: Evidence from the 1982–1986 Elections in Five States." Paper presented at the annual meeting of the American Political Science Association, Washington, D.C.

———. 1988. "Mid-Session Vacancies in State Legislatures, 1981–1986." Paper presented at the annual meeting of the Western Political Science Association, San Francisco, Calif., March.

Hansen, Karen. 1989. "Are Coalitions Really on the Rise?" *State Legislatures* 15:11-12.

Heard, Alexander, ed. 1966. *State Legislatures in American Politics*. Englewood Cliffs, N.J.: Prentice Hall.

Hedges, Roman, and Jeffrey L. Getis. 1983. "A Standard for Constructing Minority Legislative Districts: The Issue of Effective Voting Equality." Rockefeller Institute Working Papers, no. 6.

Hedlund, Ronald. 1984. "Organizational Attributes of Legislatures: Structure, Rules, Norms, Resources." *Legislative Studies Quarterly* 9:51–122.

———. 1989. "Entering the Committee System: State Committee Assignments." *Western Political Quarterly* 42:597–625.

Hedlund, Ronald, Patricia Freeman, Keith E. Hamm, and Robert M. Stein. 1979. "The Electability of Women Candidates: The Effects of Sex Role Stereotypes." *Journal of Politics* 41:513–24.

Hedlund, Ronald, and Diane Powers. 1987. "Constancy of Committee Membership in 16 States: 1971–86." Paper presented at the annual meeting of the Midwest Political Science Association, Cincinnati, Ohio.

Herman, Robin. 1981. "Kremer Holds Key Role in Rush to Adjourn." *New York Times*, June 28.

Herrnson, Paul S. 1986. "Do the Parties Make a Difference? The Role of Party Organizations in Congressional Elections." *Journal of Politics* 48:589–615.

———. 1988. *Party Campaigning in the 1980s*. Cambridge, Mass.: Harvard University Press.

Hill, David B. 1981. "Political Culture and Female Representation." *Journal of Politics* 43:159–68.

Hinckley, Barbara. 1978. *Stability and Change in Congress*, 2d ed. New York: Harper and Row.

———. 1981. *Congressional Elections*. Washington, D.C.: Congressional Quarterly Press.

Hjelm, Victor, and Joseph Pisciotte. 1968. "Profiles and Careers of Colorado State Legislators." *Western Political Quarterly* 21:698–722.

Hofferbert, R. I. 1964. "Classification of American State Party Systems." *Journal of Politics* 26:550–67.

Hoover, Ken. 1989. "Can Pugnacious Ross Johnson Unify a Fractious Caucus?" *California Journal* 20:15–17.

Huckshorn, Robert J., and John F. Bibby. 1982. "State Parties in an Era of Political Change." In *The Future of American Political Parties: The Challenge of Governance*, ed. Joel L. Fleishman. Englewood Cliffs, N.J.: Prentice Hall.

Hyneman, Charles S. 1938. "Tenure and Turnover of Legislative Personnel." *Annals of the American Academy of Political and Social Science* 23:21–31.

Indiana State Election Board. 1986. *Reports and Receipts of Expenditures of a Political Committee*. Indianapolis, Ind.

Ingram, Helen, Nancy Laney, and John McCain. 1980. *A Policy Approach to Political Representation*. Baltimore: Johns Hopkins University Press.

Jacklin, Michele. 1989. "Conservative Democrats Are Victorious in Connecticut House." *State Legislatures* 15:13–15.

Jacobson, Gary C. 1980. *Money in Congressional Elections*. New Haven: Yale University Press.

———. 1983. *The Politics of Congressional Elections*. Boston, Mass.: Little, Brown.

———. 1985. "Party Organization and Distribution of Campaign Resources: Republicans and Democrats in 1982." *Political Science Quarterly* 4:603-25.

———. 1987. "The Marginals Never Vanished: Incumbency and Competition in Elections to the U.S. House of Representatives, 1952–1982." *American Journal of Political Science* 31:126–41.

Jacobson, Gary C., and Samuel Kernell. 1983. *Strategy and Choice in Congressional Elections*. New Haven, Conn.: Yale University Press.

James v. City of Sarasota. 1985. Case no. 79-1031-Civ-T-GC (M.D. Fla.)

Jeffe, Sherry Bebitch. 1987. "Can a Speaker Make Policy and Still Hold Power?" *California Journal* 18:243–46.

Jewell, Malcolm E. 1967. *Legislative Representation in the Contemporary South*. Durham: Duke University Press.

———. 1969. *The State Legislature: Politics and Practice*. New York: Random House.

———. 1972. "The Governor as a Legislative Leader." In *The American Governor in Behavioral Perspective*, ed. Thad L. Beyle and J. Oliver Williams. New York: Harper and Row.

———. 1980. "Survey on Selection of State Legislative Leaders." *Comparative State Politics Newsletter* 1:7–21.

———. 1981. "Editor's Introduction: The State of U.S. State Legislative Research." *Legislative Studies Quarterly* 6:1–25.

———. 1982. *Representation in State Legislatures*. Lexington: University Press of Kentucky.

———. 1986. "A Survey of Campaign Fund Raising by Legislative Parties." *Comparative State Politics Newsletter*.

———. 1987. "The Prospects for Nationalizing State Legislative Elections." *Electoral Politics*.

Jewell, Malcolm E., and David Breaux. 1988. "The Effect of Incumbency on State Legislative Elections." *Legislative Studies Quarterly* 13:495–514.

Jewell, Malcolm E., and Penny M. Miller. 1988. *The Kentucky Legislature: Two Decades of Change*. Lexington, Ky.: University Press of Kentucky.

Jewell, Malcolm E., and David M. Olson. 1982. *American State Political Parties and Elections*, rev. ed. Homewood, Ill.: Dorsey Press.

———. 1988. *Political Parties and Elections in American States*, 3d ed. Chicago, Ill.: Dorsey Press.

Jewell, Malcolm E., and Samuel C. Patterson. 1966. *The Legislative Process in the United States*. New York: Random House.

———. 1977. *The Legislative Process in the United States*, 3d ed. New York: Random House.

———. 1986. *The Legislative Process in the United States*, 4th ed. New York: Random House.

Johnson, Marilyn, and Susan Carroll. 1978. "Statistical Report: Profile of Women Holding Public Office, 1977." *Women in Public Office: A Biographical Directory and Statistical Analysis*, ed. Kathy Stanwick and Marilyn Johnson. Metuchen, N.J.: Scarecrow.

Johnson, Richard R. 1987. "Partisan Legislative Campaign Committees: New Power, New Problems." *Illinois Issues*, July, 16–18.

Jones, Ruth. 1984. "Financing State Elections." In *Money and Politics in the United States*, ed. Michael J. Malbin. Chatham, N.J.: Chatham House Publisher.

———. 1986. "State and Federal Legislative Campaigns: Same Song, Different Verse." *Election Politics* 3:8–12.

Jones, Ruth, and Thomas J. Borris. 1985. "Strategic Contributing in Legislative Campaigns: The Case of Minnesota." *Legislative Studies Quarterly* 10:89–105.

Katz, Jeffrey. 1991. "The Unchartered Realm of Term Limitation." *Governing* 3:34–39.

Keefe, William J. 1966. "The Functions and Powers of the State Legislatures." In *State Legislatures in American Politics*, ed. Alexander Heard. Englewood Cliffs, N.J.: Prentice Hall.

Keefe, William J., and Morris S. Ogul. 1985. *The American Legislative Process*, 6th ed. Englewood Cliffs, N.J.: Prentice Hall.

———. 1989. *The American Legislative Process*. Englewood Cliffs, N.J.: Prentice Hall.

Kernell, Samuel. 1976. "Toward Understanding 19th Century Congressional Careers: Ambition, Competition, and Rotation." Paper presented at the annual meeting of the Midwest Political Science Association, Chicago, Ill.

Ketchum v. Byrne. 1985. 630 F. Supp. 551 (N.D. Ill.).

Key, V. O., Jr. 1949. *Southern Politics*. New York: Knopf.

———. 1956. *American State Politics: An Introduction*. New York: Knopf.

Kirkpatrick, Jeane. 1974. *Political Women*. New York: Basic Books.

Kirkpatrick, Samuel A. 1978. *The Legislative Process in Oklahoma*. Norman: University of Oklahoma Press.

Kurtz, Karl. 1990. "The Changing State Legislature (Lobbyists Beware)." *Leveraging State Government Relations*. Washington, D.C.: Public Affairs Council.

Lee, Anne F. 1987. "Hawaii Legislature Begins New Political Era." *Comparative State Politics Newsletter* 8:7–8.

———. 1988. Personal communication to Keith E. Hamm.

LeLoup, L. 1978. "Reassessing the Mediating Impact of Legislative Capability." *American Political Science Review* 72:616–21.

Lenz, Timothy, and Anita Pritchard. 1989. "The Effects of Changing from Single-Member to Multi-Member Districts: The Case of Florida." Typescript. Boca Raton, Fla.: Florida Atlantic University.

Lockard, Duane. 1972. "The Legislature as a Personal Career." In *Strengthening the States: Essays on Legislative Reform*, ed. Donald G. Herzberg and Alan Rosenthal. Garden City, N.Y.: Doubleday.

Loomis, Burdett. 1990. "Political Careers and American State Legislatures." Paper presented at the Eagleton Institute of Politics Symposium on "The Legislature in the Twenty-first Century," Williamsburg, Va.

Lyons, William, and Robert Durant. 1980. "Assessing the Impact of Immigration on a State Political System." *Social Science Quarterly* 61:473–84.

McClure, Mary. 1987. "Leaders Among Equals." *Journal of State Government* 60:219–22.

McDaniels v. Mehfoud. 1988. CR 88r0020.R (E.D. Va., December 30).

MacManus, Susan A., and Charles S. Bullock III. 1987. "Race, Ethnicity, and Ancestry as Voting Cues in City Council Elections." Paper presented at the Conference on Ethnic and Racial Minorities in Advanced Industrial Democracies, University of Notre Dame, South Bend, Ind., December 3–5.

McNeil v. Springfield Park District. 1988. 658 F. Supp. 1015 (C.D. Ill. 1987).

Mandel, Ruth B. 1981. *In the Running: The New Women Candidates*. New Haven: Ticknor and Fields.

Masters, Nicholas A. 1961. "Committee Assignments in the U.S. House of Representatives." *American Political Science Review* 55:345–57.

Matthews, Donald. 1985. "Legislative Recruitment and Legislative Careers." In *Handbook of Legislative Research*, ed. Gerhard Loewenberg, Samuel Patterson, and Malcolm Jewell. Cambridge: Harvard University Press.

Mayhew, David R. 1974a. *Congress: The Electoral Connection*. New Haven: Yale University Press.

———. 1974b. "Congressional Elections: The Case of the Vanishing Marginals." *Polity* 6:295–317.

Miller, Larry W., and Roland E. Smith. 1978. "The Impact of Financial Considerations and 'Frustrations' on the Exit of Texas Legislators." Paper presented at the annual meeting of the Midwest Political Science Association, Chicago, Ill.

Minnesota Ethical Practices Board. 1986. *1986 Campaign Finance Summary*. St. Paul.

Moncrief, Gary. 1979. "Committee Stacking in the Texas House of Representatives." *Texas Journal of Political Studies* 2:44–57.

———. 1985. The Correlates of Adaptation in State Legislatures: A Comparative and Diachronic Application of Organization Theory." Paper presented at the annual meeting of the Western Political Science Association, Las Vegas, Nev.

———. 1988. "Dimensions of the Concept of Professionalism in State Legislatures: A Research Note." *State and Local Government Review*. 20:128–32.

Moncrief, Gary, and Malcolm E. Jewell. 1980. "Legislators' Perceptions of Reform in Three States," *American Politics Quarterly* 8:106–27.

Moncrief, Gary, and Joel A. Thompson. 1988. "The Policy Consequences of State Legislative Reform." Paper presented at the annual meeting of the Midwest Political Science Association, Chicago, Ill.

———. 1989. "Electoral District Characteristics and State Legislators' Backgrounds." Paper presented at the annual meeting of the Midwest Political Science Association, Chicago, Ill.

———. 1991. "The Term Limitation Movement: Assessing the Consequences for Female (and Other) State Legislators." Paper presented at the annual meeting of the Western Political Science Association, Seattle, Wash., March.

Moncrief, Gary, Joel A. Thompson, Michael Haddon, and Robert Hoyer. 1992. "For Whom the Bell Tolls: Term Limits and State Legislatures," *Legislative Studies Quarterly* 17:37-47.

Moody, Bradley. 1987. "Tenure and Turnover in the Alabama Legislature: 1971–1987." Paper presented at the annual meeting of the American Political Science Association, Chicago, Ill.

Muir, William K., Jr. 1982. *Legislature*. Chicago, Ill.: University of Chicago Press.

National Association of Latin Elected and Appointed Officials Education Fund. 1987. *National Roster of Hispanic Elected Officials*. Washington, D.C.

National Commission on Excellence in Education. 1983. *A Nation at Risk: The Imperative for Education Reform*. Washington, D.C.: Government Printing Office.

National Conference of State Legislatures. 1987. *State Legislators' Occupations: A Decade of Change*. Denver, Colo.

Nechemias, Carol. 1985. "Geographic Mobility and Women's Access to State Legislatures." *Western Political Quarterly* 38:119–31.

———. 1987. "Changes in the Election of Women to U.S. State Legislative Seats." *Legislative Studies Quarterly* 12:125–42.

Nelson, Candice. 1978–79. "The Effect of Incumbency on Voting in Congressional Elections, 1964–1974." *Political Science Quarterly* 93:665–78.

Niemi, Richard, and Laura Winsky. 1987. "Membership Turnover in U.S. State Legislatures: Trends and Effects of Districting." *Legislative Studies Quarterly* 12:115–23.

O'Connor, Robert. 1985. "Parties, PACs and Political Recruitment: The Freshman Class of the Pennsylvania House of Representatives." Paper presented at the annual meeting of the Midwest Political Science Association, Chicago, Ill.

Oregon Secretary of State, Elections Division. 1986. Summary Report of Campaign Contributions and Expenditures: 1986 General Election. Salem: Oregon Secretary of State.

Parker, Glenn. 1980. "The Advantage to Incumbency in House Elections." *American Politics Quarterly* 8:449–64.

Patterson, Samuel C., and G. A. Caldeira. 1984. "The Etiology of Partisan Competition." *American Political Science Review* 78:691–707.

Patterson, Samuel C., and Malcolm E. Jewell. 1984. "Elections in the American States." Paper presented at the Research Planning Conference on Comparative State Politics, Stanford University.

Peabody, Robert L. 1985. "Leadership in Legislatures: Evolution, Selection, and Functions." In *Handbook of Legislative Research*, ed. Gerhard Loewenberg,

Samuel C. Patterson, and Malcolm E. Jewell. Cambridge: Harvard University Press.

Perkins, Lynette P. 1981. "Member Recruitment to a Mixed Goal Committee: The House Judiciary Committee." *Journal of Politics* 43:348–64.

Pfeiffer, D. 1967. "The Measurement of Inter-Party Competition and Systemic Stability." *American Political Science Review* 61:457–67.

Pollard, Vic. 1980. "Will the Imperial Speakership Survive the Assault on Government?" *California Journal* 11:197–99.

Polsby, Nelson W. 1968. "The Institutionalization of the U.S. House of Representatives." *American Political Science Review* 62:144–68.

Porter, Mary, Cornelia Matasar, and Anne B. Matasar. 1974. "The Role and Status of Women in the Daley Organization." In *Women in Politics*, ed. J. Jaquette. New York: Wiley.

Pound, William. 1988. "Twenty-five Years of State Legislative Reform." Paper presented at the annual meeting of the Midwest Political Science Association, Chicago, Ill.

Price, H. Douglas. 1975. "Congress and the Evolution of Legislative Professionalism." In *Congress in Change: Evolution and Reform*, ed. Norman J. Ornstein. New York: Praeger.

Ranney, A. 1965, 1971, 1976. "Parties in State Politics." In *Politics in the American States*, three editions, ed. H. Jacob and K. N. Vines. Boston, Mass.: Little, Brown.

Ranney, A., and W. Kendall. 1954. "The American Party System." *American Political Science Review* 48:477–85.

Ray, Bruce A. 1980. "Federal Spending and the Selection of Committee Assignments in the U.S. House of Representatives." *American Journal of Political Science* 24:494–510.

Ray, David. 1974. "Membership Stability in Three State Legislatures: 1893–1969." *American Political Science Review* 68:106–12.

———. 1982. "Historical Research on American State Legislatures: A Proposed Agenda." Paper presented at the annual meeting of the Social Science History Association.

Ray, David, and J. Havick. 1981. "A Longitudinal Analysis of Party Competition in State Legislative Elections." *American Journal of Political Science* 25:119–28.

Reynolds v. Sims. 1964. 377 U.S. 533.

Robbins, Steven P. 1989. *Organization and Behavior*. Englewood Cliffs, N.J.: Prentice-Hall.

Robeck, Bruce W. 1971. "Committee Assignments in the California Senate: Seniority, Party, or Ideology?" *Western Political Quarterly* 24:527–39.

Rodgers, Harrell R., Jr., and Charles S. Bullock III. 1972. *Law and Social Change*. New York: McGraw Hill.

Rodgers, Jack, Robert Sittig, and Susan Welch. 1984. "The Legislature." In *Nebraska Government and Politics*, ed. Robert D. Miewald. Lincoln: University of Nebraska Press.

Rohde, David W., and Kenneth A. Shepsle. 1973. "Democratic Committee Assignments in the House of Representatives: Strategic Aspects of a Social Choice Process." *American Political Science Review* 67:889–905.

Rom, Mark, and Andrew Aoki. 1987. "How Big the Pig: Wisconsin Campaign Contributions, Legislative Vote Scores, and the Party in Government." Paper presented at the annual meeting of the Northeast Political Science Association.

Rose, Gary L. 1987. "Party Organization Activity in the 1986 Connecticut State Legislative Election." Paper presented at the annual meeting of the Northeast Political Science Association.

Rosenthal, Alan. 1972. "The Scope of Legislative Reform: An Introduction." In *Strengthening the States: Essays in Legislative Reform*, ed. Donald G. Herzberg and Alan Rosenthal. Garden City, N.Y.: Doubleday.

———. 1974a. *Legislative Performance in the States: Explorations of Committee Behavior*. New York: Free Press.

———. 1974b. "Turnover in State Legislatures." *American Journal of Political Science* 18:609–16.

———. 1981. *Legislative Life*. New York: Harper and Row.

———. 1986. "The Legislature." In *The Political State of New Jersey*, ed. Gerald M. Pomper. New Brunswick, N.J.: Rutgers University Press.

———. 1987. "The Legislative Institution—Transformation and/or Decline." Paper prepared for the State of the State Symposium.

———. 1989. "The Legislative Institution: Transformed and at Risk." In *The State of the States*, ed. Carl E. Van Horn. Washington, D.C.: Congressional Quarterly Press.

———. 1990. *Governors and Legislatures: Contending Powers*. Washington, D.C.: CQ Press.

Rosenthal, Alan, and Rod Forth. 1978. "The Assembly Line: Low Production in the American States." *Legislative Studies Quarterly* 3:270.

Rule, Wilma. 1981. "Why Women Don't Run: The Critical Contextual Factors in Women's Legislative Recruitment." *Western Political Quarterly* 34:60–77.

Sapiro, Virginia. 1982. "Private Costs of Public Commitments or Public Costs of Private Commitments? Family Roles Versus Political Ambition." *American Journal of Political Science* 26:265–79.

Sapiro, Virginia, and Barbara G. Farah. 1980. "New Pride and Old Prejudice: Political Ambition and Role Orientations among Female Partisan Elites." *Women and Politics* 1:13–36.

Scheidt, Bruce. 1987. "Enigmatic Barry Keene: The Senate's Foremost Duke-Basher." *California Journal* 18:145–48.

Schlesinger, Joseph A. 1955. "A Two-Dimensional Scheme for Classifying the States according to Degree of Interparty Competition." *American Political Science Review* 49:1120–28.

———. 1966. *Ambition and Politics: Political Careers in the United States*. Chicago, Ill.: Rand McNally.

———. 1984. "On the Theory of Party Organization." *Journal of Politics* 46:369–400.

———. 1985. "The New American Political Party." *American Political Science Review* 79:1152–69.

Sharkansky, I. 1968. *Spending in the American States*. Chicago, Ill.: Rand McNally.

Shepsle, Kenneth A. 1978. *The Giant Jigsaw Puzzle: Democratic Committee Assignments in the Modern House*. Chicago, Ill.: University of Chicago Press.

Shepsle, Kenneth A., and Barry Weingast. 1981. "Political Preferences for the Pork Barrel." *American Journal of Political Science* 25:96–111.

Shin, Kwang, and John Jackson. 1979. "Membership Turnover in U.S. State Legislatures: 1931–1976." *Legislative Studies Quarterly* 4:95–114.

Sigelman, Lee. 1981. "Special Elections to the U.S. House: Some Descriptive Generalizations." *Legislative Studies Quarterly* 6:577–88.

Sigelman, Lee, and Albert K. Karnig. 1976. "Black Representation in the American States." *American Politics Quarterly* 4:237–46.

Simon, Lucinda. 1987a. "The Climb to Leadership: Career Paths and Personal Choices." *Journal of State Government* 60:245–51.

————. 1987b. "When Leaders Leave." *State Legislatures* 13:16–18.

Smith, Steven S., and Christopher J. Deering. 1983. "Changing Motives for Committee Preferences of New Members of the U.S. House." *Legislative Studies Quarterly* 8:271–81.

Smith, Steven S., and Bruce A. Ray. 1983. "The Impact of Congressional Reform: House Democratic Committee Assignments." *Congress and the Presidency* 10:219–40.

Sokolow, Alvin D., and Richard W. Brandsma. 1971. "Partisanship and Seniority in Legislative Committee Assignments." *Western Political Science Quarterly* 24:740–60.

Solomon v. Liberty County. 1988. 11th CA. December 12.

Sorauf, Frank J. 1988. *Money in American Elections.* Glenview, Ill.: Scott, Foresman/Little, Brown College Division.

Squire, Peverill. 1988a. "Career Opportunities and Membership Stability in Legislatures." *Legislative Studies Quarterly* 13:65–81.

————. 1988b. "Member Career Opportunities and the Internal Organization of Legislatures." *Journal of Politics* 50:726–44.

————. 1989. "Reform and Institutionalization of the California Assembly." Paper presented at the annual meeting of the Midwest Political Science Association, Chicago, Ill., April.

Squire, Peverill, and Stanley Scott. 1984. *The Politics of California Coastal Legislation.* Berkeley: Institute of Governmental Studies.

Standing, W. H., and J. A. Robinson. 1958. "Inter-Party Competition and Primary Contesting: The Case of Indiana." *American Political Science Review*, 52:1066–77.

State of California Fair Political Practices Commission. 1987. *1986 General Election: Campaign Receipts and Expenditures, July 1, 1986 through December 31, 1986.* Sacramento.

Stonecash, Jeffrey M. 1989. "Working at the Margins: Campaign Finance and Party Strategy in New York Assembly Elections." *Legislative Studies Quarterly* 13:4.

Stonecash, Jeffrey M., and Thomas D'Agostino. 1987. "Working at the Margins: Campaign Finance and Party Strategy in New York Legislative Elections." Paper presented at the annual meeting of the Southern Political Science Association.

Stonecash, Jeffrey M., and Nina Tamrowski. 1989. "Careerism in the New York Legislature: 1850–1989." Paper presented at the annual meeting of the New York Political Science Association.

Stoper, Emily. 1977. "Wife and Politician: Role Strain among Women in Public Office." In *A Portrait of Marginality*, ed. Marianne Githens and Jewell Prestage. New York: McKay.

Sullivan, Kevin. 1989. "The Battle's Still on in Rhode Island." *State Legislatures* 15:19–21.

Sutton, C. David. 1982. "Party Competition in the South's Forgotten Region: The Case of Southern Appalachia." In *Contemporary Southern Political Attitudes and Behavior*, ed. Lawrence Moreland, Todd Baker, and Robert Steed. New York: Praeger.

Swanson, Wayne R. 1969. "Committee Assignments and the Nonconformist Legislator: Democrats in the U.S. Senate." *Midwest Journal of Political Science* 13:84–94.

———. 1984. *Lawmaking in Connecticut: The General Assembly*. New London, Conn.: Privately published, Connecticut College.

Tennessee Secretary of State, Elections Division. 1986. *Campaign Financial Disclosure Statement*. Nashville.

Thomas, Sue. 1989. "The Impact of Women in State Legislative Policies." Paper presented at the annual meeting of the American Political Science Association, Atlanta, Ga.

Thomas, Sue, and Susan Welch. 1989. "The Impact of Gender on Activities and Priorities of State Legislators." Paper presented at the annual meeting of the Midwest Political Science Association, Chicago, Ill.

Thompson, Joel A. 1986. "State Legislative Reform: Another Look, One More Time, Again." *Polity*. 19:27–41.

Thompson, Joel A., and William Cassie. 1990. "Milking the Cow: Campaign Contributions to State Legislative Candidates in North Carolina." Paper presented at the annual meeting of the North Carolina Political Science Association, Salisbury, N.C.

Thompson, Joel A., and Mark Lanier. 1987. "Measuring Economic Development: Economic Diversity as an Alternative to Standard Indicators." *Policy Studies Review*. 7:77–90.

Thornburg v. Gingles. 1986. 105 S. Ct. 2137.

Tidmarch, C. M. 1982. "Party Competition in State Legislative Elections, 1970–1978." Paper presented at the annual meeting of the American Political Science Association, Washington, D.C.

Tidmarch, C. M., E. Lonergan, and J. Sciortino. 1986. "Interparty Competition in U.S. States: Legislative Elections, 1970–1978." *Legislative Studies Quarterly* 11:353–74.

Tolchin, Susan, and Martin Tolchin. 1973. *Clout: Womanpower and Politics*. New York: Coward, McCann, and Geoghegan.

Tucker, Harvey J. 1982a. "Interparty Competition in the American States: One More Time." *American Politics Quarterly* 10:93–116.

———. 1982b. "It's about Time: The Use of Time in Cross-Sectional State Policy Research." *American Journal of Political Science* 26:176–96.

———. 1984. "The Nationalization of State Policy Revisited." *Western Political Quarterly* 37:435–42.

Tucker, Harvey J., and Ronald E. Weber. 1985. "Electoral Change in the U.S.: System versus Constituency Competition." Paper presented at the annual meeting of the American Political Science Association, New Orleans, La.

Tufte, Edward. 1973. "The Relationship between Seats and Votes in Two-Party Systems." *American Political Science Review* 67:540–54.

Uslaner, Eric M. 1974. *Congressional Committee Assignments: Alternative Models for Behavior*. Beverly Hills, Calif.: Sage Publications.

———. 1978. "Comparative State Policy Formation, Interparty Competition, and Malapportionment: A New Look at 'V.O. Key's Hypothesis'." *Journal of Politics* 40:409–32.

Van Der Slik, Jack R. 1988. "Legislative Performance: Comparing Aspirations, Styles and Achievements of Women and Men Members of the Illinois General Assembly." Paper presented at the annual meeting of the Midwest Political Science Association, Chicago, Ill.

Van Horn, Carl E. 1989. "The Entrepreneurial States." In *The State of the States*, ed. Carl E. Van Horn. Washington, D.C.: CQ Press.

Vargas, Hector P., Jr. 1988. "The Fledgling Hispanics: A Look at Cuban-Americans in the 1988 Florida Legislature." Unpublished.

Wagner, Holly. 1986. "Costly Campaigns Attract Special Interest Dollars." *State Government News* 29 (October): 19–20.

Wagner, Holly, and Kent D. Redfield. 1986. *Lawmaking in Illinois*. Springfield, Ill.: Office of Public Affairs, Sangamon State University.

Wahlke, John, Heinz Eulau, William Buchanan, and LeRoy Ferguson. 1962. *The Legislative System*. New York: Wiley.

Washington Public Disclosure Commission. 1986. *1986 Election Financing Fact Book*. Olympia, Wash.

Weber, Ronald E., and T. W. Parent. 1985. "National Versus State Effects on State and Local Elections." Paper presented at the annual meeting of the Midwest Political Science Association, Chicago, Ill.

Weber, Ronald E., Harvey J. Tucker, and P. Brace. 1991. "Vanishing Marginals in State Legislative Elections." *Legislative Studies Quarterly* 16:29–47.

Weberg, Brian. 1988. "Changes in Legislative Staff." *State Government* 61:190–97.

Weissberg, R. 1978. "Collective vs. Dyadic Representation in Congress." *American Political Science Review* 72:535–47.

Welch, Susan. 1978. "Recruitment of Women to Public Office: A Discriminant Analysis." *Western Political Quarterly* 31:372–80.

Welch, William P. 1974. "The Economics of Campaign Funds." *Public Choice* 20:84–97.

———. 1977. "The Allocation of Political Moneys: Parties, Ideological Groups, and Economic Interest Groups." Working paper no. 72, Department of Economics, University of Pittsburgh.

Werner, Emmy E. 1968. "Women in the State Legislature." *Western Political Quarterly* 11:40–50.

Westefield, Louis P. 1974. "Majority Party Leadership and the Committee System in the House of Representatives." *American Political Science Review* 60:1503–1604.

Wiggins, C. W., and J. Petty. 1979. "Cumulative Voting and Election Competition: The Illinois House." *American Politics Quarterly* 7:345–65.

Williams, Christine. 1988. "Women, Law, and Politics: Recruitment Patterns in the Fifty States." Paper presented at the annual meeting of the Midwest Political Science Association, Chicago, Ill.

Williams, Steven D. 1985. "Tennessee Senate Creates Speaker Pro Tem Position." *Comparative State Politics Newsletter* 6:12.

Wisconsin State Board of Elections. 1987. *Biennial Report of Wisconsin State Elections Board*, vol. 2. Statistical report. September. Madison, Wis.

Women's Research and Education Institute. 1988. *The American Woman 1988–89*. New York: W. W. Norton and Company.

Wunnicke, Pat, and Sharon Randall. 1986. "Leadership 1980s Style." *State Legislatures* 12:26–29.

Zimmerman, Joseph F. 1981. *The Government and Politics of New York State*. New York: New York University Press.

Contributors

David Breaux is Assistant Professor of Political Science at Mississippi State University. His research appears in such journals as *Legislative Studies Quarterly* and *American Politics Quarterly*.

Charles S. Bullock III is Richard B. Russell Professor of Political Science at the University of Georgia. His research interests include legislative politics, civil rights, and public policy. He is the coauthor of *Public Policy and Politics in America* and numerous articles in professional journals.

Patricia Freeman is Associate Professor of Political Science at the University of Tennessee, Knoxville. Her research interests are in the area of state politics. She has published in *Western Politics*, *Journal of Politics*, and *Legislative Studies Quarterly*.

Anthony Gierzynski completed his Ph.D. at the University of Kentucky (1989) and served as a research associate at the Social Science Research Institute at Northern Illinois University. He is presently an assistant professor at the University of Vermont. He is author of *Legislative Party Campaign Committees in the American States* and coauthor of two articles appearing in *Legislative Studies Quarterly*.

Keith Hamm is Professor of Political Science at Rice University. He has published numerous articles on various aspects of state politics in such journals as *Legislative Studies Quarterly*, *Journal of Politics*, and *Social Science Quarterly*.

Ronald Hedlund is Vice Provost for Research at the University of Rhode Island. He is the recipient of three National Science Foundation research grants and the coauthor of *Representatives and Represented*. He has published numerous articles in professional journals.

Malcolm Jewell is Professor of Political Science at the University of Kentucky. He is the author or coauthor of many books and articles on state politics and legislatures, and he is a founding coeditor of *Legislative Studies Quarterly*.

William Lyons is Professor of Political Science at the University of Tennessee, Knoxville. He has written in the areas of urban politics and public policy, state politics, and research methodology. His articles have appeared in *Social Science Quarterly*, *American Journal of Political Science*, *Political Methodology*, and *Journal of Politics*.

Gary F. Moncrief is Professor of Political Science at Boise State University. His research has been published in *Legislative Studies Quarterly*, *Western Political Quarterly*, *American Politics Quarterly*, and *Journal of Politics*.

229

David M. Olson is Professor of Political Science at the University of North Carolina at Greensboro. He is the author or coauthor of several books, including *Political Parties and Elections in American States* (with Malcolm Jewell).

William Pound is Executive Director of the National Conference of State Legislatures and a frequent contributor to *State Legislatures* and *Book of the States*.

Peverill Squire is Associate Professor of Political Science at the University of Iowa. He is the editor of *The Iowa Caucuses and the Presidential Nominating Process*, and his articles on various aspects of American politics have appeared in *American Political Science Review*, *Journal of Politics*, *Public Opinion Quarterly*, *Legislative Studies Quarterly*, and other journals.

Joel A. Thompson is Professor and Chair of Political Science at Appalachian State University. His research has appeared in such journals as *Journal of Politics*, *Legislative Studies Quarterly*, *Polity*, and *Western Political Quarterly*. He is coeditor of *American Jails: Public Policy Issues*.

Harvey J. Tucker is Professor of Political Science and Associate Director of Graduate Studies at Texas A & M University. His research interest is comparative state politics, and his research has been published in *American Journal of Political Science*, *Journal of Politics*, and *Western Political Quarterly*.

Ronald E. Weber is the Wilder Crane Professor of Political Science at the University of Wisconsin, Milwaukee. He has published numerous articles on state and local politics and electoral systems. Professor Weber is currently coeditor of the *Journal of Politics*.

Index